FIGHTING FOR A FOOTHOLD

Fighting for a Foothold

HOW GOVERNMENT AND MARKETS UNDERMINE BLACK MIDDLE-CLASS SUBURBIA

Angela Simms

Russell Sage Foundation   NEW YORK

ROR: https://ror.org/02yh9se80
DOI: https://doi.org/10.7758/bwmi8829

Library of Congress Cataloging in Publication Control Number: 2025037620
ISBN 9780871548252 (paperback) / ISBN 9781610449182 (ebook)

Text design by Linda Secondari. Front matter DOI: https://doi.org/10.7758/bwmi8829.7665

RUSSELL SAGE FOUNDATION
112 East 64th Street, New York, New York 10065
10 9 8 7 6 5 4 3 2 1

To Mom, Dad, and Josh . . . and to pressing toward a world overflowing with love and light

CONTENTS

viii   Contents

ILLUSTRATIONS

Figures

Tables

ABOUT THE AUTHOR

ANGELA SIMMS is assistant professor of sociology and urban studies at Barnard College–Columbia University.

I'M A DAUGHTER of the "DMV"—the metropolitan area of Washington, DC, Maryland, and Virginia. My mom and dad raised my brother and me in Prince William County, Virginia, a suburban jurisdiction about twenty miles south of DC. Prince William is approximately fifteen miles southwest of Prince George's County, Maryland, another DC-area suburban jurisdiction—and the county at the heart of this book. I came of age in the 1980s and '90s, when Prince William was mostly White (it has since become more ethno-racially diverse). Prince George's County became majority-Black and middle-class in the 1990s.

My parents, Everitt and Joan, and my maternal grandparents, Joshua and Helen, were deeply shaped by the social and economic patterns of the DC region. (My paternal grandparents and my dad were Jamaican-born; my dad immigrated to the United States at eighteen.) Before Mom was in a position to pursue white-collar work in the federal government in the 1970s, Helen, my grandmother—who told her grandchildren to call her "Mum Mum" because "Grandma" was too old-fashioned—and my grandfather, Joshua, who died before I was born, decided to leave Henrico County, Virginia, in the 1940s. They sought greater economic and social opportunities in DC. Or as Mom tells it, Mum Mum told Granddad that she was leaving "the country"—Henrico County is a rural area outside of Richmond—for DC and he was welcome to join her, but she was going either way.

When we would visit Henrico County with Mum Mum, or take other long road trips, she would pack a feast in a wicker picnic basket—fried chicken, potato salad, green beans, baked beans, corn bread, yellow cake, and ginger ale. I realized as an adult that she brought those foods not just because she always preferred home-cooked meals over restaurants. Rather, having grown up in Virginia, she knew that anytime Black motorists stopped, they could be harassed by White people, and even lose their lives.

As a young married couple, Joshua and Helen settled in northeast Washington, DC, in a neighborhood called Brentwood, on Thirteenth Place. They arrived with ambition, hope, and persevering spirits, but not extensive formal education. Both attended all-Black, under-resourced high schools, as was typical of schools for Black youth in the Jim Crow South. My grandmother attended high school through her sophomore year. My grandfather graduated with his high school diploma. In DC, Joshua received on-the-job training to become an autobody mechanic, a well-paid trade. Granddad's earnings were sufficient for supporting the family, including paying the mortgage on the family's home. The mortgage obtained through Riggs Bank had standard terms—even monthly payments at a fixed interest rate. This was a blessing at a time when Black Americans often were forced to use alternative financial arrangements for buying properties that led to paying exorbitant amounts of interest.

Joshua and Helen raised their three children—Joan (my mom), the oldest, and Carolyn and Garry—in a three-bedroom, all-brick row house. They were members of Bethesda Baptist Church and enjoyed their neighborhood of working-class/lower-middle-class families. Thirteenth Place was racially mixed when my grandparents arrived in the 1950s, but it became all-Black in the ensuing years. Mum Mum often talked about how the "last White man on Thirteenth Place lived next door."

When I visited my grandmother in the 1980s and '90s, her street was all-Black. I recall the smell of trash on hot summer days as I rode my bike up and down Thirteenth Place. The smell came from a waste transfer station that opened in 1988 about a quarter-mile from Mum Mum's home. In 2018, the DC council initiated an eminent domain process to close this station. The council's action came in the context of significant new private investment in the area, particularly near the Rhode Island Avenue Metro (subway) station, and as White residents moved into Brentwood.[1]

With financial stability through my grandfather's occupation, my grandmother was able to decide the extent to which she did paid work outside of the home. She supplemented the family's income by, in her words, "sometimes doing White folks' laundry and cleaning White folks' houses." Her reputation for ironing kept her services in high demand—I often heard my older relatives say, "No one can starch and iron a shirt like Helen!" My grandmother also handled the family's finances, and she was adamant about "setting something aside."

All three of Joshua and Helen's children graduated from college. And each of them attained white-collar professional work and homes in suburbia. Their ability to realize their potential stemmed in part from laws enacted during the modern civil rights movement, notably, the Civil Rights Act of 1964, which prohibited racial discrimination in education and employment, and the Fair Housing Act of 1968, which prohibited racial discrimination in the rental and sale of homes.

My maternal grandparents' agency in pursuing economic opportunity and a stable place to live with dignity laid the foundation for the entry of my mom, aunt, and uncle into the Black middle class, and eventually my entry and my brother's entry as well: I'm a university professor, and my brother is a nurse anesthetist. My Black American grandparents, Joshua and Helen, born in the 1920s in the Jim Crow South, beat the odds within their own lifetimes and had children and grandchildren who exceeded their socioeconomic status.

Mom graduated from Howard University, the Historically Black College in Washington, DC. While in college, she had a paid internship with the Atomic Energy Commission, a federal agency that was seeking to racially diversify its workforce. That position enabled her to gain experience and skills for work as an analyst, first at the US Census Bureau, then at the Internal Revenue Service. She retired after forty years of government service. As a little girl, I remember her saying to me in March and April, "Please don't tell people where I work during tax season, Sweetcake."

Dad immigrated to the United States at eighteen and worked his way through college. He did a variety of jobs, from agricultural labor to bartending. He first attended the University of Maryland Eastern Shore, a Historically Black College. Once Maryland's colleges racially desegregated, he transferred to the University of Maryland (UMD) in College Park, the state's flagship campus. After Dad graduated from UMD, he earned a graduate degree in psychology from George Washington University in DC. He initially worked at the Census Bureau (where he and my mother met when she was selling Girl Scout cookies).

But Dad spent most of his career as a psychologist in medium- and maximum-security prisons. Indeed, part of what drew my parents to Prince William County was its proximity to Lorton Correctional Facility in southern

Fairfax County, where my dad worked for twenty years. Lorton is no longer in operation, but in the 1980s and '90s it was the primary prison for people convicted of crimes in DC. Dad served during the heart of the crack cocaine epidemic and the violence that ensued in the 1980s and 1990s in the District of Columbia. Thus, he, an upwardly mobile Black man with a middle-class profession and income, regularly interacted with Black men who had not had his educational and employment opportunities.

Soon after marrying, my parents bought the house I grew up in. The home was in a section of eastern Prince William County called Woodbridge. Joan and Everitt were the only Black couple in Sleaford Court, a cul-de-sac. Mom recounted to me that within days of moving in the next-door neighbor's daughter came over to introduce herself, and as the girl ran back home, Mom heard her exclaim, "You're wrong, Mom, they [my mom and dad] do have furniture!" Our house was a single-family split-level home—upon walking in, you went either up or down stairs. It was white, with brick accents and emerald green shutters. Stately magnolia and maple trees stood in the front yard, and dozens of twenty-foot-tall oak trees grew in our back-yard. (I always schemed to avoid raking leaves in the fall!)

While we were the only Black family in Sleaford Court, there were a couple of Black families on the street just beyond our cul-de-sac. My brother Joshua and I played with other children in the neighborhood, most of whom were White, but we were rarely the only Black kids in our play group. We raced on our bikes and played roller-blade hockey in the street and basketball on the hoop my parents bought for us—it stood at the end of our driveway. In the neighborhood and at school, Josh and I did not regularly experience overt racialized incidents, though a White kid once called Josh the N-word in the heat of an argument. Racial distinctions usually came up in passing, in ways that simply reminded Josh and me that we were different and that our difference stood out. The first year Josh and I were on the swim team, our White teammates inquired about why the water sat on the surface of our Afros.

When my family and I lived in Prince William County, my mater-nal aunt and uncle lived in Prince George's. They resided in Mitchellville, an upper-middle-class portion of the county. Most neighborhoods in Mitchellville then and now feature spacious single-family homes centered on luscious green lawns. During my childhood, I took many trips from Woodbridge to Mitchellville. My family and I would drive in our sky-blue

Ford Taurus station wagon, which from the time I was eight years old always smelled mildly of the curry goat that had spilled in it one summer as we prepared for the family reunion on my father's side. Our trips along Interstate 95 and the Capital Beltway took forty-five minutes to over an hour, depending on traffic. When we encountered slowdowns—and we often did—I remember my mom shrugging, sighing, and saying, "You just can't predict the 95 corridor."

On what felt like excruciatingly long journeys, I would pepper my parents with questions. I recall asking them during one of my inquiry sessions why there were so many more Black people in Prince George's than in Prince William. I also asked why we lived so far from my aunt and uncle. They dodged the first question but responded to the second by saying that Prince William was closer to my dad's job at Lorton Correctional Facility. They also said the schools were "better" in Prince William, the implication being that Prince William, home to more White residents, offered enhanced educational opportunities for Josh and me. My parents' decision about what county to call home in the DC region and my experiences in this metropolitan area—first as a child, then as an adult working as a federal government civil servant, and most recently while conducting the research for this book—reflect the economic, political, and other social processes taking shape not just in this region but across the United States.

During my childhood, and later as an adult, I traversed the DC region regularly. As a girl, I often visited relatives—aunts, uncles, cousins, and Mum Mum. Later, as an adult, I took in cultural opportunities across the region and continued to enjoy time with my family, who have lived in various DC region jurisdictions, including DC, Prince George's, Montgomery, and Howard Counties. I have lived in all three parts of the DMV—DC, Maryland, and Virginia. I grew up in Virginia, then lived in DC for seven years after accepting a position in the federal government following graduate school. And I lived in Maryland for two years as I conducted research for this book.

The DMV Revisited

In 2006, after completing a master's in public policy at the University of Texas at Austin, I moved to DC. I had been selected as a Presidential Management Fellow and served as a legislative analyst at the US Office of Management and Budget (OMB) for seven years. My tenure at OMB spanned the George W. Bush and Barack Obama administrations. Through that role, I gained new perspectives that started to answer Little Angie's inquiries about what led to the racial segregation patterns across DC-area jurisdictions.

Serving during a Republican administration, then a Democratic one, I came to appreciate that certain postures of government are foundational to American governing processes, not political party–dependent. My responsibilities in both administrations involved ensuring that the testimony of executive branch political appointees before Congress and legislation signed into law reflected overall administration policy goals to the fullest extent possible. I did this by facilitating the editing process for political official testimony and executive communications to Congress regarding pending legislation.

Required by my role to engage regularly with high-level elected officials and political appointees in both the Republican and Democratic Parties, I gained an insider view of both parties' policy priorities. The documents that crossed my desk and the deliberative processes I was embedded in demonstrated that government policies were not closing racial disparities. I often wondered: What prevents our country from achieving racial equity? What is government's role in achieving that goal? After seven years of government service, these questions led me to pursue a doctorate in sociology. I sought knowledge and skills for doing research to answer these questions.

The questions Little Angie asked at eight years old looked at the world from the *inside out*—from my family of origin, a middle-class Black household navigating the DC metropolitan area's economic and social opportunities and constraints. Now, as a sociologist with federal government experience, I look from the *outside in*. I conduct research to expand our understanding of the mechanisms creating and reinforcing race and class inequities. Little Angie's intuitive questions on display in the Ford Taurus station wagon decades ago have evolved into questions about the political and economic systems shaping our social world and the ways in which some people benefit at others' expense. My hope is that my book equips us to build social systems designed for *all* people to thrive.

ACKNOWLEDGMENTS

WRITING THIS BOOK has been a collective experience. And I have been blessed by beautifully robust communities—professionally and personally. I'm grateful for the training and support I received during my PhD program at the University of Pennsylvania. Chenoa Flippen, Dorothy Roberts, Karyn Lacy, and Daniel Gillion offered me superb guidance on research processes, data analysis, and writing and editing. Chenoa, my primary adviser, was especially available to answer big and small questions at each step of my doctoral journey. I thank Kathy Edin and Stefanie DeLuca for inviting me to be a part of the research team for their "How Parents House Kids" project, which enabled me to sharpen my skills in conducting ethnographic research. Chenoa Flippen, Camille Charles, and Kathy Edin equipped and encouraged me as I prepared for my comprehensive exams and wrote my master's thesis.

I'm also grateful to Audra Rodgers, UPenn Sociology's graduate coordinator. Her warmth and sound advice about how to navigate the social and professional challenges of graduate school were invaluable. I also lift up the 2013 cohort of sociology PhD students at UPenn. Through them, I found community for studying and for fun adventures in Philly. In particular, I am grateful for my cohort member and friend Sarah Adeyinka-Skold. On too many days to count, we camped out at the McNeil Building all day to study and write, often walking home together after 9:00 PM. And I thank the University of Pennsylvania for my initial five-year funding package and for an additional year of funding.

The largest portion of data in this book are ethnographic—fieldwork observations and interviews I conducted in Prince George's County, Maryland. I could not have done this research—and thus written this book—without the people of Prince George's. I remember sitting toward the back of a nearly empty room and, after the hearing ended, seeing a council member wave his hand and ask me to come up and introduce myself. It was not common for someone unknown to council members to attend midday meetings several days in a row. From that point until I completed my last interview, I was welcomed by Prince George's officials. Many ethnographers struggle to build trust in the field. That was not the case for me. I would not have been able to interview all county council members, most of the school board, federal government officials, and senior civil service staff across all levels of government without the leaders of Prince George's. I also appreciate the Prince George's residents who took time to speak with me. They are private people, not public figures, and they trusted me with their stories, without receiving compensation for their time.

In 2019, I was blessed with a tenure-track position in sociology at Barnard College-Columbia University, with teaching responsibility in sociology and urban studies. Mignon Moore was chair when I joined the Barnard Sociology Department, and she took me under her wing. During my six years at Barnard, I have benefited tremendously from her unwavering mentorship, whether through formal evaluations, during impromptu conversations in her office, or in emails identifying resources. She also generously sponsored my book workshop when I was a fellow at the Russell Sage Foundation. I also appreciate the support I have received from the current Barnard Sociology chair, Debra Minkoff, from resources to check-ins over coffee.

Additionally, urban studies directors Gergo Baics and Aaron Passell have been steadfast supporters of my scholarship, as well as other urban studies faculty, and I thank them for their feedback on my work and for their encouragement. Adam Reich, in the Columbia Sociology Department, has also championed my work and offered helpful feedback. I appreciate, too, Mary Rocco, an urban studies faculty member who has become one of my closest friends. Upon my arrival, she helped me adjust to Barnard and to life in New York City more broadly, and she has offered many insights as I've worked through book manuscript drafts. Amy Zhou, a Barnard Sociology colleague who started her tenure at Barnard the same year I did, has also been a great friend and supporter of my scholarship.

Barnard College, as an institution, has offered me research funding and granted me a year of pre-tenure leave, and the college approved a second year of pre-tenure leave when I was awarded an external fellowship. Taken together, my colleagues in the Barnard and Columbia Sociology Departments and the urban studies program have given me community and the resources I have needed to excel as a scholar and teacher.

Prior to my PhD program at UPenn, I received excellent undergraduate and master's instruction at William & Mary and the University of Texas at Austin, respectively. I thank William & Mary for naming me a William and Mary Scholar, and UT for awarding me the Barbara Jordan Fellowship; these covered my tuition and fees at the two institutions. I am especially grateful for mentorship from W&M professors, particularly Simon Stow, Christopher Howard, Ronald Rapoport, and Melvin Ely, who saw my potential and went above and beyond to open doors for me. After earning a master's at UT, I worked as a legislative analyst in the federal government, at the Office of Management and Budget.

I thank my OMB colleagues, especially Richard Green and Jim Jukes, for teaching me about governance processes and policy analysis. When I was discerning whether to leave OMB for a PhD, Xav Briggs, then an OMB political appointee, offered helpful guidance on how to transition to academia and what to focus on once there. I do not take my professional trajectory for granted. As a Black scholar and policy professional, I know many Black people who have not received the resources and social support they have needed to thrive. I have—and for that I am immensely grateful.

I also thank the Russell Sage Foundation, which selected me to be a Visiting Scholar during the academic year 2023–2024. While at RSF, I crafted the first draft of my book manuscript. The seventeen members of my cohort contributed to strengthening my manuscript through my formal presentation, lunch meetings, pop-up conversations in the hall, and after-work meetups. In particular, Carolyn Barnes, Andrew Cherlin, Tracey Meares, Leslie McCall, Abigail Saguy, and Julie Suk offered detailed feedback on drafts. And I'm grateful for the delicious meals, and equally delicious conversations, that Chef Jackie and Sous-chef Junior offered during my year at RSF.

While at the Russell Sage Foundation, I held a book workshop before submitting my manuscript for peer review. Those I selected to read chapters— Adam Reich, Karyn Lacy, Kimberley Johnson, L'Heureux Lewis-McCoy, and Richard Ocejo—and others in attendance, offered detailed comments that supported me in leveraging the full potential of my data and in seeing the range of literatures with which I am in conversation. L'Heureux, both before and after the book workshop, has been a kind and wise mentor.

I appreciate too the careful, thorough feedback of my three anonymous book manuscript reviewers. After the peer review was completed, Nicole Trujillo-Pagan read chapters and offered great insight as I polished my manuscript. I also thank colleagues who provided feedback on early drafts of the book manuscript, including Anna Rhodes, Kathy Edin, and colleagues within the Association of Black Sociologists, the American Sociological Association, and the Eastern Sociological Society. Barbara Combs supported my scholarship and encouraged me after I participated in a conference she hosted while I was a PhD candidate. I have also benefited greatly from the mentorship of Ruth Lopez-Turley through a Veritas program designed to support Christian scholars, as well as the mentorship of Brian Foster through an Association of Black Sociologists program.

During my first year of pre-tenure leave, I worked with a developmental editor, Jane Jones, and her team as I drafted chapter components. I participated in two programs under Jane's leadership: "Elevate" (now called "Book Brilliance") and "Refine and Revise." These programs taught me how to break the book project into manageable chunks and provided early feedback on my burgeoning ideas. Elevate, and Refine and Revise also helped me to structure my days and gave me a cohort of other book writers to work alongside.

Before my second year of leave as a Russell Sage Scholar, I attained an advanced contract for my book manuscript with the Russell Sage Foundation Press. RSF's director of publications, Suzanne Nichols, has helped me immensely. She has been a sage and a shepherd, guiding my manuscript through the proposal, first draft, book workshop, peer review, and publication phases. I am grateful that she believed in the promise of my work and has remained committed to the project's completion.

Beyond my professional world, my community consists of nurturing family and friends. Some, like my parents, Joan and Everitt Simms, have known me from birth. In the preface, you see that I speak of my younger self as Little Angie. My parents empowered Little Angie to be bold and to dream big. Mom and Dad ensured that I had every opportunity to explore the world and to excel, and I thank them for their love and support. My dad instilled in me a love for scholarly inquiry and encouraged my passion for social justice by telling me to "keep the fire in my belly." My mom was very hands-on, whether making my Halloween costumes from scratch, serving as my Girl Scout troop leader for eight years, or sitting with me at the kitchen table to help me with homework. I also thank my younger brother, Joshua Simms, for his friendship and encouragement throughout my life. We are both athletic and competitive and always have each other's back, whether racing each other down the street or lending an empathetic ear as we've navigated life's myriad challenges.

Beyond my immediate family, I would not be who I am without my "Jackson Family." Jackson is my mother's maiden name. My maternal grandparents—Helen and Joshua, my primary family, Mom's younger siblings, Aunt Carolyn and Uncle Garry, and their families make up the Jacksons. As I was growing up, my grandmother hosted family gatherings at her home in Washington, DC, to celebrate holidays, birthdays, and just because. We are a gregarious family—"lots of strong personalities," as my mom likes to say. My "big" personality and sense of possibility emerged from within my boisterous family.

I'm also blessed by deep friendships. My friend Angel Preston, whom I have known for just under twenty years, is one of my oldest and dearest friends. Throughout this book-writing journey, she helped me stay grounded in my Christian faith and reminded me to have fun and to talk about something other than my book. My friends Tolu Wise, Martha St. Jean, Ashley Vaughn, Soohee Kang, and Hafeeza Anchrum are also dear friends and women of God who propel me forward. I have much appreciation too for the "Barrett Girls." (Barrett was the name of our freshman-year dormitory at William & Mary.) We have known each other for over twenty years. Courtney Salaway and Taylor Libby have remained especially close. It is an honor and delight to do life with all of these incredible women. I also thank my building doorman, Reggie Thomas, who listened patiently and laughed with me when I came home from a long day of writing.

My Christian faith and the churches I have belonged to kept me spiritually fortified throughout my book-writing journey. While living in Philly, I was a member of Mother Bethel African Methodist Episcopal Church, where Dr. Diane Faust was particularly supportive. I was also blessed by rich Christian fellowship at Epiphany Fellowship Church and Antioch Christian Fellowship. While I was conducting my fieldwork in

Prince George's, I attended Reid Temple African Methodist Episcopal Church. Since moving to New York City in 2019, I have been a member of Renaissance Church, where I am blessed beyond words to grow alongside people as we seek to love each other as Christ loves us. Through this community, I'm continually reminded that I am a child of God before anything else—God's daughter, not what I do (yes, even writing books!).

As I said at the outset, writing this book has been communal. And the final and most important person I must thank is God, who exists in relationship—the Father, Son, and Holy Spirit—and who has communed with me profoundly throughout this book-writing journey. I'm humbled that the Divine Imagination that created me has also empowered me to co-create with Him through this book. My friend Soohee said to me just before this book's publication: "Isn't it incredible that Jesus, the Word Made Flesh, and who left us His Word so that we can know him, has partnered with you to speak life into the world?!" I am in awe of all that God has done in and through me—and I expect that exceeding abundance will continue, for life overflowing is God's nature. I love you, Jesus, and I pray that your will would be done through this book, and that this book will play a part in bringing as much heaven to earth as possible.

The Suburban Black Middle Class in Sociohistorical and Geographic Context

THIS BOOK EXAMINES the suburban Black middle class in the United States. More specifically, it focuses on the capacity of local majority-Black jurisdictions to provide high-quality public goods and services—from clean drinking water to K-12 schools. I focus on public goods and services because they are the material foundation for a high quality of life for most Americans and because local jurisdictions with high-quality public goods and services offer the conditions for household and neighborhood income and wealth accumulation that reinforce both families' and local governments' financial standing, and hence their material well-being.

"Race" refers to ascribing inherent social significance to physical features, or phenotypes, most notably skin color, even as human genetic variation does not map to racial categories. In the United States, "race" designates a person's *political status*. Racial categories are political in that they: (1) are established through government policies, (2) institutionalize racial groups' access to government-conferred rights and privileges and racial groups' relationships with each other, and (3) shape the terms of racial groups' incorporation into market, government, and other social systems.[1] Since the US colonial period, elite European men have asserted that "White"/European people are at the top of the racial hierarchy and that "Black"/African people are at the bottom. Throughout this book, I use "Black" and "African American" interchangeably, and the same applies to "White" and "European American."

https://doi.org/10.7758/bwmi8829.4251

I view White domination (White supremacy) and anti-Blackness as a tethered relation, two parts of a whole, each one side of the same coin.[2] I prefer the term "White domination" over "White supremacy" because I believe "dominance" calls attention to the violence and other forms of force that elite White people, and the institutions they control, have used to achieve their interests at Black people's expense. Given the racialized social landscape that I explain throughout this book, it is critical to identify contemporary mechanisms through which White dominance rests upon anti-Blackness. Otherwise, we might interpret current racial and class variation in life chances and life outcomes as stemming from personal short-comings, not differences in access to material and social resources. To be clear, whether Black or White, rich or poor, people can be more or less hard-working or talented. But *group-level* differences in outcomes at the scale we see today cannot be explained by such behaviors and abilities unless we are seeking to have a eugenics conversation by another name.

My research reveals the extent to which the class- and geography-advantaged portion of the Black population realizes the same returns to its status as similarly situated White Americans. I also show how social processes connected to social status differences—namely, race and class, polit-ical boundaries, and geographic location within metropolitan areas—shape tax revenue generation in local jurisdictions, and thus local governments' ability to maintain high-quality public goods and services. Altogether, this book has two main subjects: the conditions shaping Black middle-class quality of life in suburbia and the role of local jurisdictions in mediating that quality of life.

In seeking to explain the racial gap in life chances between Black and White Americans, scholars have largely focused on individual, household, and neighborhood-level factors separately, not in tandem. The term "life chances" denotes disparities in experiences consequential for life outcomes across social groups. Researchers have investigated life chances in terms of families' income and wealth; racial residential segregation; access to high-performing K-12 public schools and postsecondary education; qualification for and proximity to stable, high-paying jobs; neighborhood location within regions; neighborhoods' public and private amenities; and levels of violence in communities.[3]

My research investigates how levels of social organization—individual and household, neighborhood, local jurisdiction—and their material advantages and disadvantages shape the financial capacities of the other levels. I also highlight how these interconnected relationships are themselves embedded within metropolitan area and state government and market arrangements that leverage historical, and extend contemporary, White domination and anti-Blackness.

Furthermore, this book focuses on *suburban* jurisdictions, whereas most prior research has focused on cities. It is important to examine suburban jurisdictions because, from an economic perspective, they offer different commercial and residential opportunities and limitations given that, generally speaking, cities tend to be commercial centers while suburbs have some commercial activity but are primarily residential areas. And from geography, zoning, and planning perspectives, suburbs, by design, tend to be less dense, another factor shaping residential and commercial patterns. Residential and commercial activity have significant implications for tax bases and thus local jurisdictions' capacity to generate local tax revenue.

Finally, social scientists have focused too little attention on the fact that local jurisdictions' material advantages and disadvantages are a function of federal, state, and local tax policies. Tax structures have long been, and continue to be, mechanisms of enacting White domination and anti-Blackness.[4] Such systems are less overt than lynching, but as this book explains, they are no less effective at squeezing the life out of Black people and the local jurisdictions that serve them. National, state, and local policies converge within counties and other local political units, compounding the positive effects for majority-White jurisdictions and the negative effects for majority-Black jurisdictions, given the history of White domination and anti-Blackness from the slavery era to the Jim Crow period to the present. Yet all too often local governments that provide lower-quality public goods and services are blamed for failing their residents. To assess local governments fairly, we must fully account for their fiscal, or financial, opportunities and constraints, many of which are beyond their direct control.

This book contends that racial status differences are at the heart of the unequal distribution of material resources in the United States. My core argument is that the suburban Black middle class receives fewer returns to its class status than the suburban White middle class. Not only that, I argue that the suburban Black middle class *subsidizes* the wealth accumulation of the White middle class. *Fighting for a Foothold* lays out how majority-Black jurisdictions, given their embeddedness in racialized regional political economy relationships, endure unique constraints stemming from historical and contemporary anti-Black policies. In this book, "political economy" refers to inter-relationships between government policies and actions and market institutions and actors.

Overview of the Social Processes Shaping Black Suburbia

Local governments are, in a sense, constellations of opportunity structures—including, among others, education, employment, and neighborhoods. Opportunity structures are the institutions through which people pursue the material and social resources underpinning their lives. This book centers local jurisdictions, counties, as the primary unit of analysis to show how Americans access, activate, and attain yields from opportunity structures, particularly those funded by local government tax revenue, such as K-12 public schools. The yields to US residents from opportunity structures within the local jurisdictions they call home lead, in turn, to varying life chances for Black and White Americans.

College degrees and white-collar work, in particular, are core indicators of middle-class status in the United States.[5] And living in a single-family home in suburbia is another staple of middle-class life. The proportion of African Americans with middle-class status living in suburbia expanded significantly in the wake of laws prohibiting racial discrimination in education, employment, and housing. These laws were enacted during the modern civil rights movement of the 1950s and '60s.[6] Growth in the share of Black people attaining middle-class status seemingly portended a decline in the relevance of racial status for Americans' life chances.[7]

But while the size of the Black middle class has expanded over the past sixty years, Black Americans, irrespective of class, continue to fare worse than White Americans in most social domains—from the likelihood of living in a neighborhood contaminated by pollutants to access to effective and affordable health care, to the chances of being involved in the criminal-legal system, to the likelihood of their homes appreciating in market value, to their chances of working in a high-paying white-collar job with promotion potential.[8]

In 2024, the gross domestic product (GDP) of the United States was about $30 trillion. United States GDP is the "market value of the goods and services produced by labor and property located in the United States."[9]

This measure, arguably more than any other, shows the scale of material wealth in the United States. Therefore, the question is not *whether* there are enough resources for all Americans to prosper materially, but rather, how *equitable* is the distribution of resources across the population? And to the extent that there is inequity, what mechanisms shape it, whose interests are served by it, and at whose expense does inequity exist? I use "equity" to refer to the fairness of material resource distributions. Indicators of fairness include, among others, just returns for one's effort, skill, and contribution to shared societal interests, such as maintaining the integrity of governing and economic institutions.

My focus on a suburban Black middle-class local jurisdiction enables us to gain sound analytical traction for disentangling how race and class operate simultaneously and mutually inform each other, yet remain distinct, as they shape the foundations of material resource distributions in the United States. Analyzing the outcomes of the most resource-advantaged subgroup within a racial group experiencing legacy and continuing racial discrimination helps us specify the pathways through which racial inequity is maintained and the degree to which, and how, class status shapes racial status and racial status shapes class status. We also see that the concentrations of Black and White people in geographic areas that are bounded by political borders enable White Americans to keep, compound, and further leverage the dividends attendant to their racial status that they have accrued over the course of US history.

This book continues the line of research showing that from the Civil War Reconstruction period forward, class-advantaged Black people have experienced "privilege and peril," to use terms from sociologist Mary Pattillo's canonical book *Black Picket Fences*.[10] Middle-class African Americans are "privileged" when compared to Black Americans who are poor, but they are in "peril" relative to their White middle-class counterparts. While arguing in *Black Picket Fences* that racial residential segregation facilitates White Americans' disproportionate access to material resources, Pattillo also points out that desegregation in and of itself does not address the fundamental drivers of racial inequity entrenched in US economic, political, and other social processes:

> The problems confronting middle-class African Americans are not solved by simply moving away from a low-income Black family and next door to

a middle-class white family. The fact that a neighborhood's racial makeup is frequently a proxy for the things that really count for one's quality of life in the United States—well-resourced schools, economic stability, appreciation in property values, political clout, and availability of desirable amenities—attests to the ways in which larger processes of discrimination penalize Black Americans at the neighborhood level. Racial inequalities perpetuate the higher poverty rate among African Americans and ensure that segregated Black communities will bear nearly the full burden of such inequality.[11]

Political scientist Valerie Johnson, author of *Black Power in the Suburbs*, conducted research in Prince George's County in the late 1990s and early 2000s to learn the extent to which Black political authority led to marked gains in Black Americans' material conditions in the county. She concluded that "the incorporation of Black officials into suburban governance structures, while representing important progress, has not fundamentally altered the economic arrangements that reproduce racial inequality. Fiscal constraints, limited tax bases, and regional economic structures continue to constrain Black political power."[12]

Finally, two books published in the late 1990s and early 2000s—Dalton Conley's *Being Black, Living in the Red*, and Melvin Oliver and Thomas Shapiro's *Black Wealth/White Wealth*—called attention to the significant wealth gap between Black and White Americans.[13] These scholars highlighted the significance of a person's wealth—their savings and assets less their debts—over and above their income. Wealth buffers hardship and enables people to make investments in education and businesses, among other things.

In many respects, I pick up where Pattillo, Johnson, Conley, and Oliver and Shapiro left off regarding the structural dimensions of Black people's incorporation into US society, and I combine their insights with those of social scientists who focus on the fiscal capacity of local jurisdictions.[14] Local governments' fiscal capacity—their ability to garner sufficient tax revenue for maintaining high-quality public goods and services—is tethered to the wealth and market value that has accumulated within their political boundaries.

To be sure, local jurisdictions' revenue raising is directly determined by what their states allow them to tax. But there are many *indirect* factors outside of local officials' influence that also shape conditions for raising sufficient revenue to maintain high-quality public goods and services. Majority- and plurality-White jurisdictions, on average, benefit from the clustering, or concentration, of White households' income and wealth and from the fact that more White households than Black households are *upper*-middle-class.[15]

According to the Federal Reserve's Survey of Consumer Finances, in 2022 median White household wealth was about $285,000, while Black median household wealth was about $45,000.[16] That is, the median White family has about $240,000 more in wealth than the median Black family, a disparity ratio of six to one.[17] For most Americans, their incomes consist of wages and salaries. The US Census Bureau breaks down the income of US residents into fifths, or quintiles. Given this framework, what I refer to as the "core middle class" is the third quintile. I call the fourth quintile "upper-middle class," and the fifth quintile "wealthy" or "elite." The second quintile is the "working class," and the first quintile is "low-income" or "economically distressed" households. In 2021, the overall median household income for all US residents was $70,784.[18] The median for White non-Hispanic households was $77,999, and for Black households it was $48,297.[19] Thus, the White-Black household income gap is about $30,000.[20]

White Americans' higher incomes and wealth accumulation reflect the cumulative effects of White domination and anti-Blackness—first through chattel slavery for the first 240 years of American history, then through Jim Crow segregation for another 100 years, and now through contemporary policies that reinforce racial difference through non-race-explicit means. During the slavery era, White elite men forced the majority of people of African descent to work without any compensation.

This period of chattel slavery created two core axes of economic and political power for White Americans generally, even as they did not all benefit from it equally: disproportionate wealth accumulation, and government and market processes based on the exclusion of Black people from opportunity structures, while also extracting from Black people and communities. Certainly, the degree to which individual White Americans have and continue to benefit from their racial status depends on their position in other social status hierarchies, most notably, class and gender. But as I explain later in this chapter, racial status is still *the* primary axis determining material and social resource distribution in the United States.

One of the main tools for enacting exclusion and extraction practices after chattel slavery ended in 1865 has been forcing Black people
to live in all-Black neighborhoods. Social scientists refer to this pattern of
racial groups clustering in certain neighborhoods as "racial residential segregation."[21] Today, even after 1965 immigration reform led to a significant
increase in the number of non-White Americans—most immigrants
after 1965 have come from Latin American, Asian, African, and Caribbean
countries, not Europe—Black Americans remain the most segregated racial
group.[22] Even more telling, while the second generation of immigrants from
African and Caribbean countries is retaining some of the class and ethnic
group advantages of their first-generation parents, they experience anti-
Black discrimination akin to the experience of African Americans who were
born in the United States and have native-born parents. That is, the life
chances of immigrants who are racialized as Black show that White domination and anti-Blackness continue to shape access to opportunity structures,
and therefore Americans' life chances generally.[23]

The geographic separation of racial groups is not maintained through
benign processes. Until the Fair Housing Act of 1968, neighborhood boundaries were established and policed by violent White mobs and myriad
White-dominant institutions' policies and practices, among them: Federal
Housing Administration (FHA) mortgage insurance terms, which only
insured mortgages in White neighborhoods; racial discrimination enacted
by banks and other lenders when letting mortgages; realtors "steering" Black
and White homebuyers to different neighborhoods; appraisers assessing
higher market values for homes in White neighborhoods than for those
in Black neighborhoods, regardless of other factors; and local government
zoning boards setting the terms for the placement of residential, commercial,
and industrial units, and determining the kinds of units that can be built,
in ways that advantage White people and communities.[24]

Laws enacted during the modern civil rights era that prohibited racial
discrimination in employment and education (Civil Rights Act of 1964),
the rental and sale of housing (Fair Housing Act of 1968), and participation in political elections and elected offices (Voting Rights Act of 1965)
facilitated Black upward socioeconomic mobility and enabled African
Americans to participate in electoral politics as voters and officeholders.
But these laws only forbade racial discrimination *going forward*. They did

not correct for the exclusion and extraction principles still embedded in education, employment, housing, and other opportunity structures, thus leaving scarring effects unhealed, while creating new wounds for Black Americans.

Furthermore, antidiscrimination laws have largely failed to monitor for racial discrimination, and they have not enforced meaningful penalties for violating these laws' provisions.[25] Civil rights laws enacted in the 1960s have had limited impact on closing racial outcome gaps because they did not offer recompense for past harm, placed the onus on the people experiencing harm to seek redress through the courts, and did not design economic and political systems that purposefully pursued racial equity. In fact, the very people in need of government support to confront rights violations have been forced to use their time, money, and energy to seek remedies. And courts have retreated from a full-throated antiracist stance by ruling that the "disparate impact" of laws across racial groups is usually not sufficient to prove racial discrimination.[26] Discrimination must be explicit and intentional, raising the bar for racial and ethnic groups reaching for government interventions to be made whole.

In light of the persistent gap in life chances between Black and White Americans, it is critical to identify contemporary mechanisms underpinning racial disparities. The suburban Black middle class is arguably best positioned to overcome anti-Black racism. This subgroup of African Americans ostensibly "plays by the rules" for achieving a stable and high quality of life in the United States: attaining a college education or equivalent postsecondary training; earning a median or higher income; and buying a home in the suburbs, which are generally the fastest-growing parts of metropolitan areas.

Furthermore, majority- and plurality-Black local jurisdictions are where most African Americans live their daily lives.[27] As of the 2010 census, all racial groups' majorities were in suburbia.[28] Additionally, in majority-Black counties, Black Americans usually have political control. Therefore, they have the potential to enact policies aligned with Black Americans' interests, even as there are varying policy priorities among African Americans.

In the next section, I describe my research site and why I selected it. In the succeeding section, I elaborate on the political and economic significance of suburban jurisdictions and local government public goods and services provision.

Prince George's County, Maryland: A "Best-Case Scenario" of Black Economic and Political Empowerment

When I considered potential research sites, I sought to examine a local jurisdiction that had the greatest chance of "winning" despite White domination and anti-Black racism. The two criteria I used to determine whether a location had ideal conditions for Black residents were: (1) a majority-Black and middle-class population, as measured by median income and college degree attainment, and (2) Black-led government for at least ten years. The two metropolitan areas in the United States with the longest tenure of high concentrations of middle-class African Americans are Atlanta and Washington, DC.[29]

I chose the DC region over Atlanta because it has the local jurisdiction with the largest concentration of Black middle-class people in a single jurisdiction, Prince George's County, Maryland. And Prince George's has held this position for over twenty years.[30] In the Atlanta region, the Black middle-class population is more dispersed across the city and its surrounding suburban jurisdictions, such as DeKalb and Cobb Counties.[31] Since the 1990s, Prince George's has also had Black leaders in the highest elected offices, including the county executive and the state's attorney as well as members of the county council and the school board. Therefore, Black leaders in Prince George's have had time to develop and evaluate political agendas and to realize returns from policymaking.

Data and Analytical Strategy

My findings are based on a nearly two-year (twenty-three-month) ethnography of Prince George's County.[32] I conducted my research from September 2016 to July 2018. During that period, I observed the development of the fiscal year 2018 budget. I attended most of the county council's full council and committee hearings related to funding authorization and revenue appropriations to agencies, as well as hearings regarding government agency oversight. Beyond formal policy development meetings, I went to community forums, such as town hall convenings sponsored by council members and the county executive. Additionally, I observed neighborhood association meetings, church festivals, and other resident-organized gatherings.

Additionally, I conducted fifty-eight interviews: thirty with county leaders and twenty-eight with county residents.[33] All residents were African American, and most were middle-class based on their income and education levels. I interviewed all county council members, most of the school board members, former and current Maryland state officials, and former and current US congressional representatives. I also spoke to county government agency administrators and senior civil servants, as well as union, business, church, and nonprofit organization leaders. (See appendix 2 for resident and leader demographics and more information about methods.)

I recruited respondents through purposive sampling at gatherings, such as the community meetings I attended. I sought class, age, gender, geographic location, and family status variation. Some residents voluntarily identified as immigrants, but I did not ask about their immigration status. There was no pattern of difference in experiences in the county between native-Black Americans and Black immigrants, or in what they sought from residence in Prince George's.

This combination of direct observation and interviews allowed me to assess how policy decisions were made and to inquire about the intentions behind leaders' and residents' actions, in addition to the meanings they gave them. I paired my ethnographic data with budget and other government documents and newspaper and other media reports regarding Prince George's County's fiscal capacity. Lastly, I compare Prince George's County spending per resident (per capita) and per student (per pupil) to that of two neighboring counties with smaller Black and larger White populations: Montgomery County, Maryland, and Fairfax County, Virginia. I use publicly available budget data from Prince George's, Fairfax, and Montgomery Counties to make this comparison.

Altogether, more than two years of immersion in Prince George's County, the wide range of my interviews with county leaders and residents, and the public availability of budget data for my analysis equipped me to conduct a rigorous ethnographic study. This study meets widely accepted standards for qualitative studies, which are characterized by cognitive empathy, or my ability to understand my respondents' worldviews and how they positioned themselves in it; heterogeneity, or sufficient exposure to the range and subtleties of my field of study; palpability, that is, concrete examples to show how I developed my conceptualizations and theories; and self-awareness, or my ability to appreciate how my embodiment and social identities shaped how respondents perceived and received me.[34]

I spent about ten hours a week at the Prince George's County municipal office when the council was in session. These regular observations allowed me to build rapport with my respondents, especially county council members. Most of my observations were made in the municipal building meeting rooms as council committees and the full council deliberated policy. By intentionally waiting until six months into my fieldwork to start my interviews with council members, I was able to understand how the Prince George's government operated both officially and unofficially. Between sessions, I often chatted with council members' staffs, and through these civil servants I learned policy and budget development process nuances that I would not have gleaned otherwise.

Many of these staff members were longtime residents of the county and thus had experienced the county's transition from majority-White to majority-Black. They shared with me what it felt like to have a "Black middle-class Mecca," as they often called it, a place of their own. As a Black middle-class woman myself, I felt at ease with them and they seemed at ease with me. We could as readily talk about family and pop culture as we could about policy. Moreover, we had similar class and educational backgrounds. And it did not hurt that I am a "hometown girl," from the DMV (I grew up in Woodbridge, Virginia).

With both staff and council members, I sensed that they took pride in me as a Black woman conducting research at an Ivy League university. The length of my tenure in the field also allowed me to become familiar with individual council members' interests and perspectives. And my regular presence enabled them to observe me as a consistent, careful researcher invested in understanding the county thoroughly—its residents, county leaders, and other stakeholders, and their needs, interests, opportunities, and constraints. Council members also introduced me to other county, state, and federal leaders whom I might not have been able to speak to without their vote of confidence.

Most council members agreed to speak to me for an hour, but gave me one and a half to two hours of their time for interviews, often pushing back other meetings on their schedule to accommodate the extra time with me.

My sociology training and public policy background (seven years working in the federal government) alongside my field observations of Prince George's County equipped me to ask questions core to social science regarding the mechanisms leading to social inequity and to do so in terms that my respondents were already using themselves. For example, many council members said, "We have to tell our story." I often kicked off interviews with council members using this question: "What is the story of Prince George's County?" It was an open-ended way to understand their perspective on what they believed were the factors shaping the county's capacity to provide a high quality of life to residents through public goods and services and other resources. Since leaving the field in 2018, I have presented my research to the full county council and at a council member's town hall meeting.

When discussing quality of life in Prince George's County, council members and residents alike described conditions within the jurisdiction itself by comparing what Prince George's offered to the two suburban jurisdictions bordered by Prince George's—Montgomery and Fairfax Counties. This perspective was in large part due to how regularly Prince Georgians traversed the region, crossing county lines daily or weekly as they worked, worshiped, shopped, pursued recreational activities, and entertained themselves. My respondents often noted that these two counties had the quality of life they want. Nevertheless, my decision to compare Prince George's budget only to those of Montgomery and Fairfax was motivated by more than Prince Georgians' familiarity with those counties.

Prince George's and the Significance of Its Nearest Neighbors

I limit my comparison to the two counties neighboring Prince George's—Montgomery and Fairfax Counties—because all three counties are contiguous with Washington, DC, and because both Montgomery and Fairfax border Prince George's. The geographic nesting of these suburban jurisdictions, particularly their proximity to each other and to DC, gives residents and commercial enterprises comparable access to the principal city, DC, the region's main economic driver. Counties nestled next to DC also offer physical and social infrastructure connectivity. The people and capital flowing into, within, and between these jurisdictions share features in common.

For instance, prospective residents and commercial enterprises have similar travel times by car into DC, and the Metro transit system of subway and bus lines enables seamless movement between DC and these three suburban jurisdictions. Many people live in one jurisdiction while maintaining significant family and other social ties in neighboring jurisdictions. At the church I attended during my fieldwork, dozens of cars had DC tags, indicating that they belonged to DC residents who drove out to Prince George's for church services.

To be sure, other DC region counties also contribute to the metropolitan area's political economy dynamics. But it is challenging to make direct comparisons between these jurisdictions and Prince George's County, given that further flung counties offer significantly different cultural, mobility, and cost-of-living opportunities. In the next section, I broadly describe the geography of the DC region, with an emphasis on the three suburban counties at the heart of my research.

The DC Metropolitan Area in Geographic Context

The map in figure I.1 depicts the DC region's county-level jurisdictions, as well as its interstate highways—95, 270, 66—and the Capital Beltway, which encircles the District. Also shown are the major bodies of water in the region, the Potomac River and the Chesapeake Bay. Prince George's County sits between Montgomery and Fairfax Counties, and because all three jurisdictions share a border with Washington, DC, they offer residents and businesses roughly equivalent access to the city, the core site of economic activity in the metropolitan area.

I depict other counties in the DC region to display the geographic relationships between the core counties encircling DC and more peripheral counties, such as Prince William County in Virginia, where I grew up. Figure I.2 captures the District of Columbia, the three counties contiguous with DC—Prince George's, Montgomery, and Fairfax—and the subway transit system, Metro, which is operated by Washington Metropolitan Area Transit Authority.

Having described Prince George's County's geographic context, I turn in the next section to why counties, particularly those in suburbia, are important units of analysis when examining Americans' access to material resources.

Figure I.1 The Washington, DC, Metropolitan Area

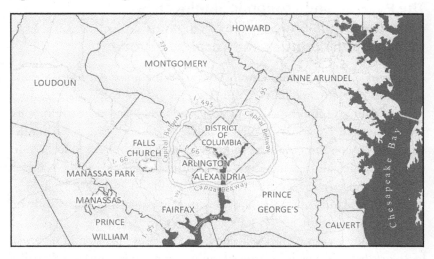

Source: Map by Dr. Dirk Kinsey. I was connected to Dirk Kinsey through the Columbia Population Research Center at Columbia University and am grateful to him for producing all of the maps in this book.

Figure I.2 Washington, DC, Metropolitan Area with Transit Lines

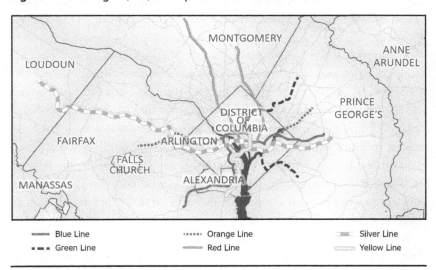

Source: Map by Dr. Dirk Kinsey.

The Political and Economic Significance of Public Goods and Services Provision by Suburban Counties and Local Government

Americans experience their citizenship through county governments and other local governance units. Counties embody the confluence of three levels of political authority—federal, state, and local—and these institutions' protections and provisions, including public goods and services.[35] Counties are the most common political subunit across US states; other local units include municipalities, cities, and school districts, among others. What all of these local governance bodies have in common is authority derived from state constitutions. The US Constitution confers authority only on the national government and state governments.

Specifically focusing on public goods and services provision in *suburban* local jurisdictions is vital for understanding variation in Americans' quality of life. As noted, since 2010, most Americans, including majorities of all four US racial groups (Black, White, Asian, and Native/Indigenous) and Latinos of any race, live in suburbia, not in cities. That is, most Americans live in metropolitan areas but on city peripheries, not in cities themselves.[36] Yet our social science knowledge about the range of suburban experiences across racial and class statuses lags our understanding of experiences within cities.[37]

Furthermore, the United States has 387 metropolitan areas. There are 3,144 counties and about 19,000 cities and municipalities.[38] Given the scale of local jurisdictions across the country, it is critical to understand the axes of differentiation in local jurisdictions in a context of significant political fragmentation, and thus diffusion of political power. It is also crucial to know how local jurisdictions' fiscal experiences are shaped by their embeddedness within metropolitan areas, given that people traverse local jurisdiction boundaries at will, but local jurisdictions' financial capacities are shaped by who chooses to live and establish businesses within their borders.

All Americans rely on public goods and services to maintain their daily lives. Yet their access to them and the quality of what they receive vary demonstrably based on the local jurisdiction they call home. The unevenness of the quality of public goods and services reflects local governments' ability to garner sufficient revenue to invest in public goods and services, both what they generate through their own tax authority and what is transferred to them by state and federal governments. State governments are the primary cost-sharing partner with local jurisdictions, but the federal government provides critical support too, from funding for major infrastructure projects, like the construction and maintenance of interstate highways, to funding for medical care through Medicaid, Medicare, and public health programs.

I argue that local jurisdictions' fiscal capacity is fundamentally interconnected with the fiscal capacity of its neighboring jurisdictions. According to the Prince George's County council chair, Prince George's is "the poorest of the rich." That is, compared to other local jurisdictions across the United States, Prince George's is a wealthy county. But compared to the counties it borders—Montgomery and Fairfax—and other counties with smaller Black and larger White populations, Prince George's is much less financially robust. The council chair's assessment highlights the importance of analyzing counties' financial standing, and consequently their ability to invest in their public goods and services, by using two metrics simultaneously: (1) the amount of revenue they generate in a given fiscal year, and (2) the revenue they collect, relative to other jurisdictions in their metropolitan area, especially those they border.

A community meeting I attended in March 2018 exemplifies the ongoing struggle in Prince George's County, even as a majority middle-class jurisdiction, to provide high-quality public goods and services consistently. On a temperate March evening, about fifty people gathered in the multipurpose room of a recreation center in Hillcrest Heights for the monthly civic association meeting. Hillcrest Heights is an inner-ring neighborhood in Prince George's consisting mostly of modest two-story, single-family brick homes. Everyone in attendance was Black, the average age appeared to be in the late fifties and early sixties, and there were about equal numbers of men and women. People sat in brown folding chairs, facing a podium. At a little past 7:00 PM, the civic association president called the meeting to order.

One of the items on the agenda was litter and illegal dumping in the community. A Black woman in her mid-thirties, representing Prince George's

Department of the Environment (DoE), spoke about how the county planned to address the various types of refuse that residents sought to have removed. The DoE representative had the following exchange with residents:

> DoE Representative: As a community, we have to take back our community. We can pick up the litter that's getting on our nerves— help me with that. If you've called County Click and your issue was not addressed, it's time for you to act.
>
> Resident (*Black woman, late fifties*): What about cleanup of illegal dumping of furniture and mattresses in the neighborhood?
>
> DoE Representative: That sounds like a comprehensive community cleanup. There's a four-year wait-list—it's really popular. I'll connect you with my colleague.

In this conversation, the county budget for trash collection is not mentioned. But it is the proverbial elephant in the room. The DoE representative began her remarks by seeking to persuade a room of mostly older adults, many of them senior citizens, to pick up the litter in their neighborhood ("it's time for you to act"). She stated that they probably called the county to activate the public service of litter cleanup ("If you've called County Click . . . ") but did not receive the response they desired. Rather than state that Prince George's did not have the staff and material resources to meet residents' requests, the representative shifted the responsibility for refuse removal back to residents. She said that there was a "four-year wait-list" for the collection of large items, like mattresses, meaning, in practical terms, that the service was nonexistent. She even noted in passing that bulk trash cleanups were "really popular," indicating that many Prince George's communities had this need but did without. Prince George's challenges in meeting residents' sanitation needs reflect how it navigates its budget constraints: by reducing or eliminating public goods and services or reducing agency staffing.

What led to Prince George's financial constraints? What are the consequences for the quality of public goods and services delivery in the county? Later in this chapter, I explain the theories I use to conceptualize the factors shaping Prince George's fiscal capacity. But before I do that, I need to describe how race and class status hierarchies and racial capitalism shape Americans' access to material and social resources.

In the next section, I explain the political and economic significance of race and class categories and how racial capitalism, as enacted by White elite men, leverages those statuses to enable White wealth accumulation. I describe how government policies and market practices throughout US history—from the slavery era onward—have perpetuated this political economy system. I make the case that while other social statuses, including class and gender, contribute to variation in Americans' life chances, racial status hierarchy, with "Whiteness" dominant and "Blackness" subordinated, has been, and continues to be, the primary social axis creating inequitable distributions in material and social resources across Americans.

Understanding the centrality of racial capitalism in US society equips us to study how even a majority–middle-class Black jurisdiction like Prince George's County fails to attain the conditions for providing consistent high-quality public goods and services. Readers who are less invested in lines of inquiry related to the significance of social status differences and racial capitalism may wish to skip ahead to the following section, "My Theoretical Framework," where I explain the concepts I develop based on my research.

Racial Capitalism and Material and Social Resource Distribution in the United States

The paradox of freedom for some grounded in unfreedom for others is nowhere better exemplified than in the construction of the most iconic buildings of American democracy—the US Capitol Building, where the Senate and the House of Representatives convene to deliberate American laws; and the White House, the office of the president, who executes those laws. Both the White House and the Capitol were built by enslaved people who did not count in the "we" of the "we the people" named in US founding documents.[39] Not only could enslaved people not consent to be governed, they could not even consent to uses of their bodies.

The freedom-unfreedom paradox is baked into the bedrock of American society. And I contend that racial capitalism underpins US political economy relationships and social processes at all scales of social organization—household, neighborhood, local government, metropolitan areas, states, and the nation as a whole. In this section, I connect the dots across levels of social organization, time (the slavery era, the Jim Crow period, and the present), and core US market and government institutions and related social processes. I show that Americans have differential access to US opportunity structures owing to the inheritances accompanying their racial status and the current ways in which Americans experience the US institutions mediating their life chances. This sociohistorical background reveals many of the mechanisms shaping fiscal capacity variation across local jurisdictions in US metropolitan areas. Resource accumulations at each level of social organization shape the capacities of the other scales.

In *Capital*, political economy theorist Karl Marx identifies the primary social relationship cleavage as that between people who control "the means of production"—those who own factories or other profit-generating entities—and people who work for a wage.[40] While Marx acknowledges that colonization, slavery, and racial difference contributed to the original material accumulations of Europeans who settled in the Americas, his theory of capital does not include racial differentiation as *essential* to capitalist formations.

In contrast, racial capitalism contends that the economic systems that were initiated in the US colonial project and have evolved to the present are anchored in profit-making and resource accumulation based on racial hierarchies that White elite men have used to determine who is worthy of full human regard and thus has the right not to be extracted from. One of these foundational extractive processes has been settler colonialism and dispossession, whereby European men forcibly removed Indigenous peoples from land and engaged in forms of genocide. The other was chattel slavery, whereby European men forced African people to work without compensation.[41] Philosopher Charles Mills argues that elite White men embedded a "racial contract" within US governing and market institutions.[42]

In the introduction to their edited volume *Histories of Racial Capitalism*, Destin Jenkins and Justin Leroy highlight the superior-subordinate relationships that racial capitalism creates and its reliance on racial hierarchy. They argue that racial capitalism is "the process by which key dynamics of capitalism—accumulation/dispossession, credit/debit, production/surplus, capitalist/worker, developed/underdeveloped, contract/coercion, and others—become articulated through race." Jenkins and Leroy posit that racial inequality has two purposes: "First, the violent dispossessions inherent to capital accumulation operate by leveraging, intensifying, and creating racial distinctions. Second, race serves as a tool for naturalizing the inequalities produced by capitalism."[43] The second purpose, naturalization, highlights decision-makers' efforts to convince Americans to accept racial hierarchy as a biologically inherent form of human difference rather than reveal the truth that racial difference is violently imposed.

Other scholars contend that class status is broadly mediated by nonclass "social differences," not just by racial status.[44] Relevant social categories other than race include, among others, gender, religion, and sexuality. Consistent with scholars who argue that "social difference" should be the focus of capitalist formations, not race exclusively, political scientist Adolph Reed cautions against racial reductionism. He emphasizes that only a subset of White Americans accrue significant wealth from American capitalist formations. Reed also notes that some Black elites, even the Black middle class, have pursued forms of capitalism, both in the Jim Crow and post-Crow periods, that do not evince political solidarity with Black people across the socioeconomic spectrum, on which the Black poor are the most marginalized by both White and Black people.[45]

This complexity is important to account for, as it attenuates how people who embody multiple social statuses experience the benefits and burdens of racial capitalism. But we need to see both the forest—racial capitalism—and the trees—how other social statuses mediate the extent to which and how the profits of racial capitalism are distributed among White Americans. That is, Reed and other scholars' attention to the importance of other social categories does not diminish the unique role of racial distinctions in US society.

Racial hierarchy has led to the greatest *scale* of resource differences across Americans. Let us start with the magnitude and centrality of chattel slavery in US political economy structures. According to historian Edward Baptist, author of *The Half Has Never Been Told*, "The idea that the commodification and suffering and forced labor of African Americans is what made the United States powerful and rich is not an idea that people necessarily are happy to hear. Yet it is the truth." Baptist substantiates his claim with startling facts, among them: "The 3.2 million people enslaved in the United States had a market value of $1.3 billion in 1850—one-fifth of the nation's wealth and almost equal to the entire gross national product."[46] And this figure is just the monetary value of Africans' bodies; it does not account for the broader economic contributions of these people to the

US economy through their uncompensated skill and labor across industries' production chains.

During the nineteenth century, cotton was one of the primary commodities traded in futures markets, akin to the oil market today. And enslaved Black labor underpinned cotton's cultivation. Interstate trade in enslaved people and the cotton trade fueled industrial development—from railroad systems, which efficiently transported cotton to markets, to state bonds backed by Black people's market value, to insurance on Black people to hedge against the lost productivity of "human property." Mortgages in the United States were not first created for homebuying but to facilitate the slave trade. In other words, the United States as a world power during the nineteenth century was built by Black people's backs—and skills and genius. For instance, the rice that would become "Carolina Gold" in South Carolina's "Lowcountry" reflects the engineering and rice cultivation skill and basket sewing knowledge of the Gullah Geechee people who come from ethnic groups in present-day West African countries, including Sierra Leone, Liberia, and Côte d'Ivoire. West Africans mastered rice farming before the Transatlantic Slave Trade began.[47]

When the Thirteenth Amendment to the US Constitution, which ended chattel slavery, was enacted, four million Africans were emancipated. They constituted about 13 percent of the US population of about 31 million.[48] The other Civil War–era constitutional amendments were the Fourteenth Amendment, which granted formerly enslaved people citizenship and the "equal protection of the laws," and the Fifteenth Amendment, which granted Black men the right to vote.[49]

Although chattel slavery ended in 1865 and Black Americans ostensibly became equal citizens, the political economy logics of slavery—institutionalized relationships and exchanges and the incentives and disincentives they produced, which are anchored in exploitation of Black labor and Black people's exclusion from US opportunity structures—continued. And this happened despite the deployment of over two hundred thousand Black soldiers to fight for the Union—a critical contribution to the Union victory over the Confederate States of America—and despite what sociologist W.E.B. Du Bois calls the "General Strike," which occurred when millions of enslaved people stopped working in forced labor camps ("plantations") and shifted their efforts to supporting the Union cause.[50] This en masse work stoppage, in a sense, was a larger-scale and more coordinated act of resistance than self-manumitting ("running away"); "everyday acts of resistance," such as breaking tools and work slowdowns; and revolts in specific locations.[51]

The twelve years of post—Civil War Reconstruction shone a ray of light in the darkness of White domination and anti-Blackness. During this period, Black men were elected to federal, state, and local offices across Southern states. These elected officials increased state and local taxes on property and goods, displaying African Americans' commitment to expanding public goods and services to Black and White residents—from sanitation infrastructure to public schools—despite the fierce opposition from Whites aroused by such tax levies, including lynching.[52] Black people also established colleges and universities—known today as HBCUs (Historically Black Colleges and Universities)—as well as churches and businesses, and they bought land and farmed. From 1861 to 1900, over ninety HBCUs were established.[53] In other words, they created a life for themselves that reflected the dignity and expansiveness of their humanity.

But after Reconstruction ended in 1877, White elite men at the helms of government and market institutions ushered darkness back in when they established the Jim Crow racial regime. This new "racial project" enabled White Americans to keep the material resources they had unjustly acquired during the slavery era.[54] Jim Crow segregation also empowered White Americans to parlay their material resource advantages into new means for controlling Black people, while benefiting from them. Du Bois, in *Black Reconstruction*, and more recently Mehrsa Baradaran, in *The Color of Money*, show that during Reconstruction the Freedmen's Savings Bank for emancipated people was established in lieu of reparations for slavery.[55]

That is, once Special Field Order 15, which for a short period redistributed land to Black people, was rescinded, there was no other meaningful attempt by the US government to compensate Black Americans for enslavement or to offer immediately available assets that would lead to African Americans' economic stability outside of laboring for White people. Through the Freedmen's Savings Bank, African Americans were encouraged to deposit their wages, with the hope of later having enough money to buy land, start a business, or invest otherwise. But the White men who ran the bank did not steward Black Americans' deposits responsibly. Rather, bank executives used African Americans' money (the modern equivalent of around $1.5 billion) for speculation in things like high-risk railroad projects and real estate and made loans to friends. Eventually, the bank failed, and Black Americans were forced to forfeit half of what they had deposited.

White elites in Southern states forced the majority of African Americans into debt peonage farming, commonly known as sharecropping, and other forms of low-compensation labor. It is worth noting, however, that—despite considerable headwinds—at the peak of Black land ownership in the early 1900s, African Americans owned about fifteen million acres of land.[56] Many Southern states also used "convict leasing" to secure Black labor for corporations. Under convict leasing, Black people could be arrested for "vagrancy" when they refused to work for White land owners, and if they could not pay the fine, they were leased to businesses that paid it.[57] As the Black Great Migration unfolded from the late 1800s through the mid-1900s, during which about six million Black people "voted with their feet," White people enforced severe racial residential segregation in Northern and Western cities and created a segmented labor market that limited Black people's life chances and socioeconomic upward mobility.[58]

Furthermore, when Black Americans "beat the odds," such as by purchasing land and establishing businesses, and achieved other forms of economic independence from White Americans, they faced violent hostility from Whites. The Equal Justice Initiative (EJI) finds that 4,084 Black people experienced "racial terror" lynching between the years 1877 (the year Civil War Reconstruction ended) and 1950.[59] White Americans' motivations for these acts of brutality revolved around fears of interracial sex between Black men and White women, Black people's "transgressions" in performing racial deference toward White people, allegations of violent crime, and public spectacle as a means of disciplining Black people who sought social, economic, and political standing that was "out of place" (that is, not sufficiently subordinated to White people).[60]

White violence against Black towns and neighborhoods was also prevalent during this period, whether carried out by hastily organized White mobs or organized White terror groups, such as the Ku Klux Klan. During the summer of 1919 alone (often referred to as "Red Summer"), over thirty anti-Black race riots occurred in Southern, Northern, and Western states.[61] Black soldiers returning from World War I assumed that "closing ranks" with White soldiers during the war would lead to their experiencing equal citizenship when they returned home.[62] During World War II, this same sentiment was captured in "Double-V"—victory over authoritarianism both abroad and at home. But after both wars, Black servicemen and women were met with open violence from White people who insisted on resubordinating all Black people to "their place."[63]

Under Jim Crow racial regimes, which were in effect across the United States until the 1960s—by law in Southern states and by custom in Northern states—Black people still contributed to US society through their ingenuity, labor, culture—and taxes. Yet African Americans did not realize the full rights and privileges of US citizenship through their tax payments, given that the public goods and services they received were of lower quality than those White Americans enjoyed.[64]

Another way to see the centrality of racial hierarchy in the United States is to compare the effects of racial status to other sociopolitical status distinctions. During the slavery era, White women had limited property rights. While White women could neither vote in most states nor own most forms of property, they were not ineligible to benefit materially and socially from US society to the same degree as Black Americans during the seventeenth through nineteenth centuries. For instance, many states made exceptions to their property laws to enable White women to own and sell enslaved people.[65] And after slavery ended in 1865, White women's dependence on Black women to perform domestic labor in their households, across class groups, enabled them to enjoy a higher quality of life and more autonomy, on average, than did Black men and women.[66]

White women have also benefited from White men's disproportionate wealth accumulation because material resources, and the benefits accrued and conferred, are shared among White household members. Finally, when "affirmative action" policies—measures designed to enforce the Civil Rights of 1964, which prohibited discrimination on the basis of race, color, religion, sex, or national origin—were in effect to ensure that the named protected groups could apply and interview for jobs, be hired for them, and promoted in them, White women experienced the greatest rates of hiring, promotion, and other forms of advancement.[67]

Regarding class, low-income and working-class White people have and continue to benefit from opportunities from which Black people, across the class spectrum, have been excluded. During the colonial period, many White working-class and poor people were indentured servants upon arrival: they worked for a period of time for the person who paid for their passage from Europe to the then-British colonies. But indentured servants were not enslaved for life, nor were their children deemed by law to be enslaved for life. And many indentured servants later helped to maintain the slave regime, such as by working as overseers in forced labor camps ("plantations") or as patrols who caught self-manumitting people ("runaway slaves").[68]

In the mid-1800s, the Homestead Acts enabled working-class White Americans to gain land at no cost in states west of the Mississippi River, and these White Americans violently opposed Black people having the opportunity to do the same.[69] For instance, Oregon enacted laws to exclude Black people from the state. And locales throughout the United States were "sundown towns," meaning that Black people could be beaten or killed if they were in the municipality after dark, unless they had permission to be there from White people.[70]

White Americans across the class spectrum also benefited from earlier access to social safety net programs. For instance, the Social Security Act, as initially enacted in 1935, did not cover agricultural and domestic work, the sectors where most Black Americans labored.[71] Similarly, more White Americans experienced worker safety and minimum wage protections through the Fair Labor Standards Act of 1938 because they were more likely to work in industrial sectors covered by the law.[72] European Americans also had earlier and greater access to high-paying unionized jobs, given that, with the exception of the Congress of Industrial Organizations (CIO), unions largely excluded Black people altogether or admitted them only on second-class terms.[73] Since World War II, as I explain in the next section, White working-class and poor people have continued to be able to activate ladders of upward socioeconomic mobility.

Economically constrained Whites and women have never faced persistent existential threat to their very lives. They were not lynched or harmed by other Americans in the thousands, with no one being held accountable.[74] Nor have White women and working-class and low-income Whites experienced the violently enforced residential hyper-segregation that has separated Black people from other Americans and from access to core American economic and political opportunity structures.

Finally, perhaps most telling of all, when people with significant political authority or other influential figures seek to close the chasm between White and Black Americans' life chances, they are killed, whether through mob or vigilante violence or by federal, state, or local government.[75] Here, we can think of key individuals, like President Abraham Lincoln, whose death in 1865 led to the sharp curtailing of Black inclusion processes he had begun to implement, such as land redistribution in the South through Special Field Order 15.[76] We can also think of Rev. Dr. Martin Luther King Jr., who, when assassinated in 1968, was organizing the Poor People's Campaign, an intentionally interracial effort highlighting economic inequality in the United States. Participants in the campaign from across the country were planning to camp on the National Mall in Washington, DC, as a form of protest.[77]

In the late 1800s and early 1900s, during what is known as the Gilded Age, when industrialization was taking shape in cities and rural America, interracial agrarian movements were also aggressively quelled by White elites. Known as populists, these farmers sought to unionize and otherwise organize collective practices that would enable them to grow and sell crops and maintain access to markets and a decent standard of life in a context of rapidly growing economic inequality.[78]

In the 1970s, the US Federal Bureau of Investigation (FBI) actively sought to break up the Black Panther Party for Self-Defense, which was also seeking cross-racial solidarity regarding shared economic interests.[79] When Chicago police killed Black Panther Party leader Fred Hampton, he was spearheading such a campaign. It is not individuals per se but the social movements and consciousness-raising they galvanize that threaten the White dominance, anti-Blackness social regime.

Historian and public affairs scholar Manning Marable argues in his book *How Capitalism Underdeveloped Black America* that US government and market institutions, at all levels, have systematically under-invested in Black communities and extracted labor from Black people.[80] And philosopher Nancy Fraser draws a distinction between "exploited" and "expropriated" people in capitalist societies, identifying differences in experience between Black and White laborers in the United States. She argues that, in the United States, White people, as citizen-workers, have experienced exploitation and Black people, as formerly enslaved people–cum–(technical) citizen-workers, have experienced expropriation. Fraser contends that "'Race' emerges, accordingly, as the mark that distinguishes *free subjects of exploitation* from *dependent subjects of expropriation*."[81] She also argues that "far from being sporadic . . . expropriation has always been part and parcel of capitalism's history, as has the racial oppression with which it is linked."[82]

As my research shows, those who endure the most expropriation, namely, Black Americans, do not have state protection from predation by capitalists and other dominant market actors, nor do they have recourse with the state after they have experienced harm. Expropriated groups serve a crucial function for capitalists. Fraser contends that, "by definition, a system devoted to the limitless expansion and private appropriation of surplus value gives the owners of capital a deep-seated interest in acquiring labor and means of production below cost. . . . Expropriation lowers capitalists' costs of production."[83]

Fraser and Marable elucidate contradictions at the heart of capitalism—most notably, profit made at the expense of people's well-being—and how those contradictions are reconciled through racial difference. Moreover, they show that racial distinctions enable White Americans to generate profits and to accumulate material resources, with elite White Americans benefiting the most. For European Americans, the American Dream of homeownership and other forms of wealth attainment rest on the nightmare of African Americans' material resource deprivation. As I lay out in the next section, where I explain my theory contributions, Black people and Black spaces have served, and continue to serve, as repositories from which White people make withdrawals to build wealth.

American capitalism is embedded in global capitalist formations and historical processes. And these worldwide economic systems are increasingly complex, with one of the primary characteristics greater and greater financialization. That is, capitalism is shifting from a focus on providing tangible goods and services to an emphasis on financial markets, where money is directed more toward investments in stocks, bonds, and complex financial instruments.[84] Financialized capital relies heavily on debt. Lender-debtor relationships reflect the material resource deprivations and accumulations that people have inherited and have access to now.

In the United States today, common tools used to create and reinforce cycles of indebtedness for individuals and households include, among others, subprime mortgages, high-interest and variable-rate payday, and other personal and business loans, many of which are traded in global markets.[85] Another tool fomenting indebtedness among individuals and households, albeit less direct than loans, is the racially segmented labor market: African American workers are systemically under-employed and underpaid, irrespective of their skill and experience, and are less likely to be promoted and more likely to be fired.[86] These employment experiences reduce Black Americans' economic means, leading to African Americans' need for stop-gap measures like loans. At the local government level, indebtedness cycles occur as majority-Black jurisdictions let bonds. Black jurisdictions are often more likely to receive less favorable terms from municipal bond markets as they seek to build infrastructure, from schools to roads.[87] Furthermore, African American individuals and households and majority-Black jurisdictions have a greater propensity to need loans in the first place because they historically have had, and continue to have, the fewest opportunities to attain money through intergenerationally transferred wealth.

W. E. B. Du Bois, while an American scholar, called attention to the central role of race in capitalism *globally*, as well as to how Western countries create exploitative economic relationships between themselves and non-Western countries.[88] He argued that these unjust international relationships, as well as competition between Western countries, led to wars. In the essay "The African Roots of the War," written in 1915, a year after World War I began, Du Bois highlights how Western countries specifically target the African continent.[89] He focuses on Africa because of the vastness of its earthen minerals and other materials Western countries use in their production processes. Du Bois contends that though Western-led slave trading officially ended in the mid-nineteenth century, Western countries engaged in new forms of expropriation from Africa and other parts of the world.

Scholars and activists throughout the twentieth and twenty-first centuries have echoed Du Bois's conclusions about what motivates Western countries' desire to control African, as well as Asian, Caribbean, and Central and South American, countries.[90] Presently, Western exploitation of non-Western countries usually occurs through multinational corporations, trade agreements, and international financial institutions, like the International Monetary Fund, World Bank, and World Trade Organization. International financial institutions ostensibly exist to support the economic development of formerly colonized countries, many of which officially became independent from Western countries after World War II. But these global financial institutions generally promote neo-liberal, or market-focused, economic projects, including privatization of the public sector, trade liberalization, and deregulation of industries, all of which largely benefit Western stakeholders and a small elite within developing countries.[91]

Du Bois's 1915 essay stressed that the world would remain at war, or on the brink of war, true peace elusive, until there is economic and political equity attained through democratic rule within and between countries, and where no country or business has undue influence on the world order.[92] Indeed, the invention of "color," or "race," as a meaningful distinction between people, Du Bois argues, was a strategy for justifying the violence and cruelty Western countries unleashed in pursuit of their economic goals: "'Color' became in the world's thought synonymous with inferiority, 'Negro' lost its capitalization, and Africa was another name for bestiality and barbarism. Thus, the world began to invest in color prejudice. The 'Color Line' began to pay dividends."[93]

Thus, akin to Marable and Fraser, Du Bois argues that Western countries enacted and maintain a "color line" as a pretext for expropriation. Furthermore, by pursuing resources and labor overseas, Western elites can extend a higher quality of life to broader segments of Western populations while still continuing to hoard resources for themselves. Western elites' desire to keep the fruit of their ill-gotten gains, while maintaining social stability in their countries, leads them to seek resources overseas. Using material goods and labor from non-Western countries lowers production costs, thereby enabling higher levels of consumption among people with modest incomes in Western countries. And rising consumption levels expand the global economy and hence the profits of capitalists.

This global perspective on Western countries' internal relationships, relationships between Western countries, and Western countries' relationships with non-Western countries is related to Black jurisdictions' capacity to garner sufficient tax revenue for public goods and services because economic and political positioning *across* countries has consequences for material resource distribution *within* countries. Grossly uneven material resource distributions and access to capital within and across countries shape the conditions that underpin the rewards and penalties US individuals, households, and local jurisdictions experience as they participate in markets.[94]

Today, Black jurisdictions, whose populations largely consist of the descendants of Africans who were forced to come to the United States by Europeans, endure myriad economic constraints that stem from the evolution of US and worldwide economic and political processes. Middle-class Black Americans in suburbia are not exempt from economic and political arrangements embedded within stark asymmetries in economic and political power. And White Americans—albeit to varying degrees, given their class, gender, and other social statuses—continue to benefit from contemporary political economy arrangements, such as tax systems.

Ultimately, African Americans are distinct among US social groups in terms of the scale, forms, and duration of their economic and political marginalization. Though gender and class have reinforced social inequity, and continue to do so, they have never had the same totalizing intergenerational effects of racial status. Furthermore, the policies and other tools used to increase gender and class equity have been more effective than those ostensibly designed to end White domination and anti-Black racism. To be sure, over time the floor of life conditions has been lifted for most Americans across social statuses.

Yet throughout US history, "Whiteness" has attenuated the experience of other marginalized social categories. The persistence and pervasiveness of racial hierarchy across social domains indicates that racial status is *the* fundamental social fulcrum, the central pivot point, in US capitalist formations and political systems. Therefore, echoing W. E. B. Du Bois, who argued in *The Souls of Black Folk* that the "problem of the twentieth century is the problem of the color line," I declare that the problem of the twenty-first century is *still* the problem of the color line.[95]

My perspective on the role of White domination and anti-Black racism in American political economy structures is what some scholars call a "strong" racial capitalism stance, in contrast to the perspective of scholars who view race as historically contingent and/or as one of several significant social statuses driving the relationships and exchanges embedded in capitalist processes.[96] In framing racial capitalism this way, I am not *only* referring to the versions of Marxism and neo-Marxism arguing that racial distinctions (White, Black, Asian, and Native American in the US context) are a tool used by White capitalist elites to differentiate and degrade (cheapen) certain workers to maintain lower wages for all workers.[97] I also am not *only* emphasizing the distinct material base undergirding racial categories— that is, White elite men's enrichment through slavery-based production.[98] Although I believe that both of these perspectives contain partial truths, they leave yet more political economy terrain to explain, including: (1) how all levels of social organization mutually inform and reinforce each other; and (2) how governance structures mediate and amplify the effects of racial difference, thus enabling racial capitalism's legitimation and continued profitability for all White Americans, albeit to varying degrees, at Black Americans' expense.

Scholar Cedric Robinson writes in his book *Black Marxism* that racial capitalism is in many ways an outgrowth of European feudalist regimes of the 1400s.[99] According to Robinson, in the American colonial political project, White male elites invented "race" and racial hierarchy using the components of social difference established in the European feudal period of the ninth through fifteenth centuries. Robinson argues that Europeans transferred supposed inherited and essential social role differences to physical characteristics, most notably, skin tone.

Robinson emphasizes the historical evolution of economic processes and how governments inherit logics from prior regimes, as well as how ruling groups assert exclusive rights and resource access for themselves at others' expense. My definition of "racial capitalism," which I explain in the next section, like Robinson's discussion of the relationships between race and class, focuses on race and class being distinct terms yet close cousins that continually shape and reshape each other's political, economic, and other facets of social significance. Also akin to Robinson, I highlight the evolution of political economy arrangements over time through the adoption of prior material resource distribution logics.

By focusing on how racial capitalism, as conceived in the American colonial project, has evolved, while retaining the core logics of the initial project—exclusion and extraction—we see that racial capitalism is contested by subordinated groups. Indeed, rearticulations of racial capitalism show that White elite men's power is not absolute; if it were, it would go unchanged. At the same time, the immense power that White elite men wield through violence and monopoly control of material resources and political power equips them to erect new forms of White domination even when social unrest forces them to make reforms.

My Theoretical Framework: A Macro-Meso Explanation of the Racial and Fiscal Subordination of Majority-Black Jurisdictions

Taken together, my theories show how racial and financial subordination are connected at the national, regional, and local government levels. First, I describe figure I.3's components, then I explain the theories in the figure. Figure I.3 is funnel-shaped. At the top of the framework you see arrows

Figure I.3 A Macro-Meso Theory of Racial and Fiscal Subordination

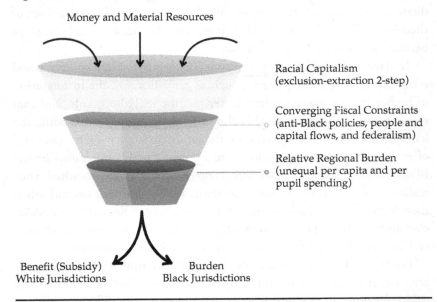

Money and Material Resources

Racial Capitalism
(exclusion-extraction 2-step)

Converging Fiscal Constraints
(anti-Black policies, people and
capital flows, and federalism)

Relative Regional Burden
(unequal per capita and per
pupil spending)

Benefit (Subsidy)   Burden
White Jurisdictions   Black Jurisdictions

Source: Figure by Fatima Koli. I was connected to Fatima Koli through the Empirical Reasoning Center at Barnard College-Columbia University. I am grateful to her for creating this diagram.

indicating that "money and material resources" flow through US society. Money and material resources, at the macro social process level, the highest rung on the funnel, are mediated by racial capitalism, what I call the "exclusion-extraction 2-step" (EE2S). The next level below EE2S is the meso theory explaining how the political economy processes of metropolitan areas create unique financial constraints for Black jurisdictions, what I call "converging fiscal constraints" (CFC). CFC has three parts: (1) the cumulative weight of anti-Black policies, (2) raced and classed flows of people and capital into local jurisdictions, and (3) federalism, shared authority across levels of government.

The next rung below CFC is "relative regional burden" (RRB), which is both a theory showing the consequences of CFC for Black jurisdictions and a specific measure of the degree to which a local jurisdiction is burdened by or benefits from its metropolitan area's political economy arrangements.[100] I measure RRB in terms of per capita/per person and per pupil/per student spending. As the diverging arrows at the bottom of the figure indicate,

I argue that RRB creates a benefit, or subsidy, for majority-White juris-dictions and a burden for majority-Black jurisdictions. This nested set of theories—EE2S, CFC, and RRB—illuminates financial interrelationships between levels of social organization.

To date, political economy research has largely focused on city-based economic development patterns, such as gentrification, the in-migration of higher-income residents into lower-income neighborhoods, and that research usually analyzes neighborhood-level change.[101] In this book, the local jurisdiction—more specifically, the suburban county—is the core unit of analysis. My research contributes to a growing body of literature on the Black middle class and Black elites regarding the extent to which they realize the same returns to their class status as White Americans and, when they do not, the mechanisms that mediate inequity.[102] Research on middle-class and elite Black people calls attention to both the improved life chances of a portion of the Black population and to racism's persistence.

Furthermore, my theories show that local government political bound-aries become mechanisms for White Americans' material resource and wealth *hoarding*. In a context where racial groups have significantly different amounts of material resources (recall that the White-Black wealth gap is about six to one), political borders facilitate, reinforce, and amplify racial stratification because they enable racial group clustering in particular places to have significant consequences for material resource access.

I specify how racial capitalism is enacted through the concept of exclusion-extraction 2-step. Exclusion entails *creating racial boundaries* and the primary racial boundary in the United States is between those categorized as "White" and those categorized as "Black." Under this racial regime, White people systematically have greater access to core material (food, clothing, shelter) and social resources (autonomy and freedom of choice), on average. The social boundaries related to race and racism have a geographic correlate, racial residential segregation, which spatially instantiates the racial hierarchy. This geographic component renders the enactment of racism more effi-cient, and it concentrates negative fallout among Black Americans, while shielding White Americans from the most devastating consequences of racism, as they benefit from it.

Take the criminal-legal system as an example: Policing practices in White and Black neighborhoods are usually quite different, with Black com-munities more likely to experience the aggressive policing practices, like "stop and frisk," used by police seeking to find evidence of wrongdoing. White Americans are less likely to experience aggressive policing strategies and therefore tend to think of the police as a nonhostile presence that promotes safety. In 2010, Michelle Alexander's book *The New Jim Crow* brought the incarceration crisis to the attention of millions of White Americans. Most Black Americans already knew well what police, and the broader criminal-legal system, were capable of because they lived it daily.[103]

Extraction refers to *stealing from or expropriating from people*. Processes enabling extraction occur through bald violence, such as slavery and settler colonialism; through legislation and other formal action, such as laws that place more polluting industries in or near Black people's neighborhoods; and through everyday customs and behavior, such as the expectation of many White people that they should be deferred to and comfortable in all social situations with Black people and their ostracization of African Americans who do not meet that expectation.[104] Many forms of extraction use multiple means. For example, slavery entailed both violent force and slave codes that defined "race" and the implications for the rights of people of African descendant (they had none).[105] Taken together, we might call violence, laws, and customs forms of coercion that facilitate extraction. Coercion is necessary because those who are subordinated resist their social status and must be compelled to participate in society on unjust terms.

The EE2S has two core components that evolved from slavery to the Jim Crow era, and from the Jim Crow period to the present. First, the EE2S established who is human and/or whose humanity matters most and whose interests will be pursued, protected, and privileged. Second, the EE2S established forms of coercion as a means of social control for Black Americans.

Another key dimension of EE2S is that it has two speeds. As the Texas two-step dance has a rate that shifts between fast-fast and slow-slow, so the pace of exclusion and extraction processes varies. The fast component consists of market activity and government policies that take resources over a matter of months or a few years. A recent example is the home foreclosure crisis connected to the Great Recession of 2009–2011. In the several years prior to 2009, mortgage lenders blanketed Black neighborhoods with subprime and other less-than-optimal home mortgage and refinancing options, irrespective of individual homebuyers' credit history and other indicators of financial stability. As noted, racial residential segregation is the spatial component of exclusion and facilitates efficient, targeted race-based extraction. In this case, segregation enabled mortgage lenders to quickly and at scale originate thousands of subprime mortgages in Black communities. The history of government policy and market practices that disproportionately invested in White people and White spaces had led to pent-up demand for home-buying in Black neighborhoods and less familiarity with, or belief that they would have access to, mainstream mortgages.[106]

The slow component of the EE2S consists of processes akin to the erosion of soil—weathering that is scarcely detectable but that has long-term cumulative effects. An example is school funding levels across local jurisdictions in the DC region. In chapter 4, which focuses on Prince George's County Public Schools, I note that Prince George's does not spend demonstrably less per pupil than neighboring Whiter, wealthier counties. Weathering occurs through Prince George's serving twice the number of students who qualify for free- and reduced-priced meals (about 60 percent in Prince George's and about 30 percent in Montgomery and Fairfax Counties), indicating these students come from economically distressed households. Students who face financial limitations at home tend to need more funding to support their learning. This increased investment per student that Prince George's makes means the county trades off spending elsewhere in the school system. Downstream implications of weathering in the school system include, among other things, difficulty retaining the most experienced teachers, who can earn more in neighboring counties, and difficulty maintaining schools and building new ones, which requires hundreds of millions of dollars in new revenue.

Additionally, the two speeds of the EE2S exacerbate each other's effects. Slow forms of extraction diminish Black households' income and the quality of Black neighborhoods' infrastructure, thus allowing fast forms of extraction to have a quicker, more detrimental impact. We can see how chronic exclusion and extraction practices make acute practices worse through a health analogy: a person with a chronic condition, such as heart disease, is likely to endure a more serious case of acute illnesses that affect the cardiovascular system, like the flu, and likely take longer to recover. Today the EE2S plays out in less overt ways than during the slave and Jim Crow periods, given that explicit anti-Black racism is illegal. Most laws and other official government and market activity do not mention race outright. Instead, White-dominant institutions and actors leverage mechanisms or proxies that are connected to racial groups. For instance, given that White Americans have more material resources than Black Americans, on average, policies that seek to protect household and neighborhood wealth accumulation generally offer more benefits to White Americans than to Black Americans.

EE2S captures the contours of national political economy systems. For the next level below the national, metropolitan areas, I have developed a theory identifying the factors that contribute to the fiscal subordination of majority-Black local jurisdictions. I call this theory converging fiscal constraints (CFC). Certainly, each region has a unique history of how the political, economic, and other social processes have evolved. (I discuss the history of the DC region in the next chapter.) But I believe the relationships I identify in the DC region are likely to be present in other metropolitan areas with large concentrations of Black middle-class people, such as the Atlanta, Houston, and Charlotte regions, because the core principles of racial capitalism are endemic to the United States.

Using the case of the jurisdiction with the highest concentration of middle-class Black people (Prince George's County), which is nestled between two Whiter and wealthier jurisdictions (Montgomery and Fairfax Counties), I develop a theory to show that racial subordination, through EE2S, leads to the Black county's persistent fiscal subordination due to multiple social forces uniquely bearing down on Black jurisdictions, irrespective of their class composition. These forces yield burdens for the Black jurisdiction and benefits for the White jurisdictions.

CFC has three currents. Together, these streams are meso-level mechanisms facilitating White Americans' hoarding of material resources because they create distinct harms for majority-Black jurisdictions that yield dividends for majority-White jurisdictions. The first stream of CFC is *the concentration of the consequences of anti-Black policies in Black jurisdictions.* Downstream economic, political, and other social effects from the slave era to the Jim Crow period to the present moment have enabled White people and spaces—neighborhoods and local jurisdictions—to derive, on average, more benefit from these policies and Black people and spaces to experience more burden.

The second stream of CFC is *the sorting of people and capital into local jurisdictions.* The proportions of racial and class groups in a local jurisdiction shape its tax base, and therefore its revenue-generating potential, as well as residents' demand on the budget for public goods and services. Demand on the budgets of wealthy jurisdictions, most of which are majority- or plurality-White, are reduced because they garner more tax revenue and have less responsibility for moderate- and low-income households. Property taxes, in particular, are garnered through tax rates levied on the value of residential and commercial units. Given the White-Black wealth gap, White Americans and the local governments serving them irrespective of their effort today inherit advantage while Black Americans and the local governments serving them inherit disadvantage.

The third and final stream of CFC is *federalism*, which refers to the governance structure of the United States: shared political power between national and state institutions. Local jurisdictions, as already noted, derive authority from their state constitutions. Counties' political boundaries concentrate material resource advantages and disadvantages, creating a mechanism through which White Americans hoard material resources.

CFC parallels the term "intersectionality," which developed in legal scholarship during the 1970s to highlight the illegibility of Black women's experiences of discrimination because they were women and Black simultaneously.[107] When legal scholar Kimberle Crenshaw coined the term, she imagined a four-way traffic intersection—the common point where roads come together and traffic flow is managed with traffic lights. A car with a green light allowing it to move through the intersection assumes that other cars have red lights and will stop or yield appropriately so that it can proceed safely.[108]

In converging fiscal constraints, the Black jurisdiction is the moving car. When it moves through the intersection to generate revenue for public goods and services provision, it assumes that cars on the other streets will stop, in the case of anti-Black racism, or yield fairly, in the case of the flows of people and capital. With federalism, the assumption is that all jurisdictions have an equitable capacity to generate sufficient tax revenue for public goods and services. Yet Black people have never been made whole from past discrimination and continue to face new forms of anti-Black racism. Black jurisdictions receive and retain disproportionately fewer upper-middle-class residents and disproportionately more moderate- and low-income residents, leading to tepidly expanding tax bases and greater pressure on their budgets as they seek to meet the needs of financially constrained households.

Moreover, in our federalist system, shared authority between levels of government forces Black jurisdictions to use the same tools that White jurisdictions deploy to generate revenue—most notably, property taxes—but these tools are less effective for Black jurisdictions because the tools are tethered to racial capitalism, a political economy arrangement designed, since the slave era, to exclude and extract from Black Americans. In this scenario, the answer is not to create more precisely timed or otherwise improved traffic lights. The appropriate remedy is new avenues for meeting the economic, political, and social needs of Americans. In the book's conclusion, I discuss policy recommendations along these lines.

CFC helps us to see that Americans' quality of life varies based on the local jurisdiction in which they live. In a political economy context where European Americans are generally more financially advantaged than African Americans, European Americans have a financial incentive to maintain majority-White neighborhoods and local jurisdictions. White Americans benefit even more when they can keep what they earn in their White-majority locales, while also benefiting from close—but not too close—geographic proximity to Black neighborhoods. The political economy and geographic factors salient in this scenario mean that European Americans can keep revenue generated in White-majority jurisdictions, while gaining access to the lower-paid workers who live in neighboring less-wealthy jurisdictions. For the DC area, that looks like people earning their living as nannies and cooks in Montgomery and Fairfax County homes and restaurants, while living in and sending their children to school in Prince George's County.

To capture the direct and indirect effects of jurisdictions' financial interdependence due to their embeddedness within metropolitan areas, I have coined the term "relative regional burden." The fiscal fitness of a jurisdiction is not just a measure of its ability to generate revenue but also a reflection of the fiscal capacity of neighboring jurisdictions. Again centering Prince George's County—the jurisdiction with the highest concentration of middle-class Black Americans and thus the majority-Black local jurisdiction best positioned to overcome the exclusion-extraction 2-step—we see that this local jurisdiction subsidizes the fiscal capacity of the two bordering counties, which both have smaller Black and larger White populations. I measure this subsidy by examining the per capita/per person spending in Prince George's County compared to per person spending in

Montgomery and Fairfax Counties. Per capita spending is calculated by dividing the total budget by the total number of residents. Similarly, per pupil spending is calculated by dividing the total budget for K-12 public schools by the number of students in the school system.

CFC and RRB indicate that the relationships between counties in metropolitan areas are not just *stratified*, a term that does not fully account for interdependency, but are better characterized as *symbiosis*. Counties with the greatest per capita and per pupil spending are ranked highest and experience relative regional benefit, and those ranked lowest experience relative regional burden. With Prince George's County taking on more responsibility for moderate- and low-income residents in the DC region, neighboring jurisdictions have more revenue to invest in the middle- and upper-middle-class interests of their residents. That is, higher-ranked counties, like Montgomery and Fairfax, enjoy conditions for generating sufficient tax revenue not only because they have a greater proportion of the DC region's upper-middle-class residents and the commercial enterprises serving them (which also generate revenue), but also because they benefit from a nearby county's absorption of harder-to-serve populations.

My theories of converging fiscal constraints and relative regional burden explain the fundamental social processes shaping what Josh Pacewicz and John Robinson call the "racialization of municipal opportunity" in their 2021 article "Pocketbook Policing." Pacewicz and Robinson seek to explain the puzzle of higher fines and fees in majority-Black jurisdictions than in majority-White jurisdictions, even Black jurisdictions that are majority-middle-class, suburban, and Black-led. The term "racialization of municipal opportunity" highlights that "the production of racial disparities in the municipal capacity to generate desirable revenue" is fundamentally embedded within "the distinctive regime of growth politics."[109] They also note that "racism is baked into the fiscal mechanics of local government, even when residents are fairly affluent and nonwhite officials are at the helm."[110]

"Racialization of municipal opportunity" is also a term that draws attention to three interconnected social processes shaping local jurisdictions' ability to garner sufficient tax revenue for maintaining high-quality public goods and services: (1) growth politics, which emphasizes attracting and retaining lucrative commercial development (for example, convention and business centers catering to upper-income people); (2) the historical legacies of policies, or the downstream effects of laws that are no longer in effect or have been amended but that nonetheless continue to shape Americans' access to material resources in ways that reinforce or extend racial disparities; and (3) contemporary policies—the federal, state, and local laws in place now (for example, reliance on property taxes as a primary source of locally generated tax revenue).

Some scholars of gentrification processes have also drawn attention to the inherent interconnection of race and class in determining which neighborhoods will experience market and/or government investment that leads to higher-income people moving into relatively lower-income neighborhoods. Zawadi Rucks-Ahidiana, in her article "Theorizing Gentrification as a Process of Racial Capitalism," defines "gentrification" as a "racialized process of class change" and argues that "gentrification inherently occurs in racialized spaces as all neighborhoods are defined by their racial demographics," even as "not all gentrifying neighborhoods experience racial *change* [emphases in the original]."[111]

Like Pacewicz and Robinson, Rucks-Ahidiana highlights how Black-majority spaces' lower levels of financial capacity and histories of under-investment by public and private institutions render them vulnerable as contemporary political economy processes unfold. Private investors, with profit maximization as their goal, inject capital strategically, often through speculation. They infuse resources where public and/or private investment has begun or is imminent, thus increasing the probability of increased "rent" in the near future.[112]

Gentrification scholars like Rucks-Ahidiana focus on whether Black residents can afford to live in their neighborhoods after market and government investment in Black neighborhoods and after White residents become a greater share of neighborhoods' populations. Certain locations are more susceptible to gentrification than others. The most apt to gentrify are Black neighborhoods proximate to already high market value spaces, or to spaces expected to be increasingly valuable because of new or improved public and private amenities. This dynamic is especially strong in areas with tight housing markets, such as Washington, DC.[113] My theories of CFC and RRB show that the "racialization of municipal opportunity" and government and market investment patterns are downstream consequences of the racialized political economy relationships in metropolitan areas formed within and between cities and suburbs, and within and between suburbs.

Gentrification scholars tend to focus on cities, but growth politics, as Pacewicz and Robinson show, inheres in city and suburban jurisdictions alike.

Ultimately, this book brings racial capitalism from the periphery to the center of explanations for why local jurisdictions vary in fiscal capacity and trajectories. I argue that racial capitalism, underpinned by the exclusion-extraction 2-step, has fast and slow speeds in how quickly profits are attained through the predation of Black people and Black spaces. I have also identified social processes within the EE2S that shape the fiscal capacity of local jurisdictions. The first process is converging fiscal constraints—the cumulative effects of anti-Black policies, raced and classed flows of people and capital into local jurisdictions, and federalism. The second process is relative regional burden, a measure that captures the extent to which a local jurisdiction is burdened by or benefits from economic processes within its metropolitan area.

Because racial difference is at the core of American political economy arrangements, to not account for this inheritance when developing government policy amounts to what I call "color callous racism." Current laws and those we propose lie on a spectrum: at one end they reinforce and extend racialized power and resource asymmetries, and at the other end they promote racial equity (for example, through programs providing reparations for Black Americans and neighborhoods). Color callous racism has three meanings. First, it refers to heinous (callous) disregard for Black people's lives, in the sense that Black life is not valued, protected, and invested in to the same extent as White people's lives are. Federal, state, and local government policies have largely either failed to intervene in instances of anti-Black racism, such as when White mobs lynched Black people and no one was held accountable, or promoted racial harm, such as through policies transferring wealth to White Americans and disparate enforcement of drug laws that leads to greater incarceration rates for Black Americans. Such government failure, particularly at the federal level, violates Black Americans' right to the "equal protection of laws," as articulated in the Fourteenth Amendment.[114]

The second dimension of "color callous racism" evokes the layers of skin formed by friction and pressure, like the callous that develops on a middle finger from writing with a pen. Those layers of skin signal the body's recognition that it needs to toughen an area experiencing greater friction and pressure than other areas of the body. "Color blindness"—what I have relabeled "color callous"—is an attempt by political and economic elites to insulate themselves from social friction and pressure, as well as from responsibility for redistributing the disproportionate material resources attained by White Americans.

Contestation over economic and other social injustices resulting from race and class hierarchies have been endemic to US society from the slavery era to the present.[115] To some extent, class status differences map to education, skill, and experience-level distinctions. But non-merit-based factors, among them, racial discrimination and White Americans' greater access to social networks conferring advantage, also influence who attains jobs, loans, and other means for building wealth.[116]

While Americans may not visibly protest society's terms of existence daily, we should be careful not to conflate compliance with agreement that the terms of US society are fair. Social friction connected to social hierarchies has sometimes led to levels of social upheaval that we characterize as mass social movements, such as the modern civil rights movement of the 1950s and '60s and, more recently, the protests associated with the Occupy Wall Street and Black Lives Matter movements.[117] All of these movements seek redress for race and class injustices. White elites' insistence that resource variation is "color-blind" is a tool for short-circuiting any meaningful reckoning with entrenched and long-standing injustices.

With the third and final dimension of "callous," we see that, just as a finger develops more layers of skin over time when there is persistent friction and pressure on the finger, making it better able to withstand stronger and varying forms of such challenges to its equilibrium, so too have American governance regimes developed multiple means for deflecting full deliberation on distortions to Americans' life chances wrought by legacy and ongoing forms of anti-Black racism. After centuries of anti-Black policies, White-dominant institutions are adept at deploying strategies that co-opt or otherwise absorb, diffuse, and rearticulate Black Americans' calls for redress.

During my fieldwork, I experienced an example of the color callousness of assertions of "color-blindness" when Prince George's officials regularly told me and others to use the county's full name, "Prince George's County," rather than the jurisdiction's initials, "PG." People across racial and class groups in the DC metropolitan area use the initials, usually as an easy shorthand or even as an affectionate diminutive, but it is also true that Prince George's County is the only majority-Black suburban jurisdiction in the

DC region that is regularly referred to by its abbreviation. Prince George's officials who sought to have people exclusively use the county's full name were reinforcing the county's status as a full peer of neighboring jurisdictions.

During the slave and Jim Crow eras, White people often called Black adults by their first names (never Mr., Ms., or Mrs.) to remind Black people of "their place"—their inherent and permanent subordination to White people. To be called by others the name one has selected for oneself— exercising one's agency—indicates respect and affirms one's humanity. At a hearing regarding the county's economic development strategies, a council member exemplified this sentiment: "There are people who say 'PG' and say it in a disparaging way. They ought not to let that come out of their mouths." The question of how to refer to Prince George's County encapsulates Black people's fight for footholds in multiple domains at once.

Philosopher Hannah Arendt penned *Eichmann in Jerusalem: A Report on the Banality of Evil* in the aftermath of World War II, during which the Nazis regime in Germany killed millions of Jews and other people it deemed unworthy of life.[118] As the title suggests, evil often occurs in plain sight, such as through pedestrian bureaucratic processes carried out by people who have outsourced their moral responsibility to government authority. Arendt argues that failure to think critically about one's complicity in evil leads us to absolve ourselves too easily of culpability for enabling evil to metastasize at astonishing scale. Throughout US history, White Americans in power have had a posture of banal evil toward Black people.

Sociologist Eduardo Bonilla Silva, in his book *Racism Without Racists*, articulates four frames of "color-blind" ideology.[119] This ideology is a means for reconciling the belief that the United States is generally a fair country, and thus devoid of social evil, with the reality of how Black people have been incorporated into US political, economic, and other social systems: (1) *abstract liberalism*, which prioritizes meritocracy without considering the impact of sociohistorical processes on racial groups' access to the inputs enabling fair competition; (2) the *naturalization* of differences between racial groups that suggest innate variation in racial groups' capacities and interests; (3) *cultural* explanations of racial groups' behaviors as morally superior or inferior; and (4) *minimization* of racism by highlighting "bad actors" rather than systemic racism. Bonilla-Silva's frames show that White-dominant institutions effectively say to Black Americans: "You do not have as much as White people because something is *broken* about Black people."

To state what might be obvious but is nevertheless worth saying outright: human frailty and folly occurs across racial groups, whether corrupt politicians, people who do not work hard, or wounded people who lash out at others. After all, race is a political category, not a biologically based axis of human differentiation. By definition, there cannot be anything *inherently* wrong with Black people that cannot be traced to economic, political, and other social systems.

Social scientists focus on structure and agency, noting that institutions and social processes shape the choice-set available to individuals and social groups as they navigate their lives. Variation in choice-set arises because some people receive more returns for the same effort and have different options in the first place, owing to social statuses that confer undue advantages. Among the most common nonstructural explanations for Black people's lower socioeconomic outcomes are their lower marriage rates, when compared to White people, and that more Black children than White children grow up in single-parent households. Sociologists, such as Regina Baker and Christina Cross, find that Black children who are raised in a two-parent home have access to more income and experience more parental involvement. But Black children in two-parent homes still fare worse than their White peers who grow up with married parents, indicating that racial groups experience US opportunity structures in inequitable ways, leading to differences in life chances and outcomes.[120]

This book highlights relationships between individual, household, neighborhood, and local jurisdictions' material well-being. More specifically, it reveals the social processes through which the fiscal choice-set for local jurisdictions is racialized, such that when majority-Black jurisdictions use the same tools used by majority-White jurisdictions, they receive less for the same inputs. In this context, it is impossible to enact "race-neutral" policies.[121] Therefore, policies should be evaluated based on the degree to which they reinforce the exclusion-extraction 2-step or offer more just and inclusive mechanisms for material resource distribution. In the next section, I lay out the constitutional provisions and federal policies that most contribute to the EE2S and to converging fiscal constraints. We cannot understand the capacity of Prince George's County to invest in public goods and services without appreciating the county's choice-set and the shaping of that choice-set by legacy and contemporary government policies and market practices.

The Impact of Racial Capitalism on the Distribution of People and Resources Within US Metropolitan Areas: Implications for Local Jurisdictions

To understand the fiscal fortunes of majority-Black and majority-White local jurisdictions, we must first consider their position within the governance frameworks of the United States. The US political system of federalism is a type of representative democracy. According to the Constitution, "the powers not delegated to the United States by the Constitution, nor prohibited by it to the States, are reserved to the States respectively, or to the people." This clause means that, by design, states—and by implication, local governments, the units to which states delegate authority—have significant power to shape Americans' life chances. While the Constitution states that federal laws supersede state laws, it limits the breadth of this national authority.[122]

States delegate authority to their local jurisdictions—counties, cities, municipalities, utility and school districts, and so on. In this political context, local jurisdictions have fixed responsibilities and authorities. But local governments' financial capacity to meet the demand for public goods and services—that is, to execute one of their core responsibilities— is variable. States support the fiscal capacity of their local political units by conferring tax revenue generation authority on them and by transferring state-generated revenue to them. States do not guarantee equal public services provision across local jurisdictions, nor do they guarantee that all local governments will have an equal capacity to generate sufficient revenue.

Disparities in financial standing between Black households and majority-Black jurisdictions and White households and majority-White jurisdictions are the downstream of policies that targeted resources at White Americans, and that continue to yield dividends to this day. Post–World War II national trends in the development of US regions reflect the opportunities and constraints created by government policies and court cases. Housing policies have been the most consequential.

From enactment of the Federal Housing Act of 1949 until enactment of the Fair Housing Act of 1968, the federal government insured home mortgages on a racially discriminatory basis. During this period, only "low-risk" neighborhoods and buyers were eligible for loans backed by the Federal Housing Administration. And Black neighborhoods and buyers were deemed inherently "high-risk."[123] Not only did FHA-backed loans absolve banks of default risk, but this federal guarantee also made mortgage terms more accessible to a broader swath of Americans, including lower-middle-class and working-class White Americans. The favorable terms included mortgages spanning up to thirty years, with consistent payments over the life of the mortgage at low and fixed interest rates.[124] Black Americans, excluded from what became the mainstream mortgage market, usually were forced to buy homes "on contract" and thus were often subject to nonstandardized lending terms set by private individuals offering loans at higher and varying interest rates.[125]

Another major federal investment in White Americans in the post–World War II period was the Servicemen's Readjustment Act (1944), commonly known as the GI Bill.[126] Under the GI Bill, veterans were eligible for home-buying support, such as down payment grants, and other benefits that made mortgages more feasible and enabled them to qualify for higher-value homes in well-resourced neighborhoods. And this benefit amplified the effectiveness of FHA mortgage policies for White veterans. The GI Bill also offered education and employment benefits to veterans, such as tuition payment and hiring preferences. But as with home mortgages, Black veterans were severely limited as they sought to activate their education and employment benefits in Jim Crow America. The GI Bill itself did not mention race. But by requiring service members to use the benefits it offered in contexts shaped by anti-Black racism and racial capitalism, the law became a vehicle for White upward socioeconomic mobility and had a limited impact on improving Black veterans' life chances.

Federal and state governments also built high-speed, multi-lane interstate highways. Nationwide highway construction began in earnest through the Federal-Aid Highway Act of 1956.[127] These highways, alongside FHA-insured mortgages and GI Bill benefits, enabled "White flight" en masse to suburbs. Again, prior to the Fair Housing Act of 1968, Black people largely were unable to secure mortgages in most suburban neighborhoods. To build these highways authorities demolished city neighborhoods, a disproportionate share of which were majority-Black communities. This large-scale destruction of Black neighborhoods undermined Black people's social ties and material well-being as they were displaced to other city neighborhoods.[128]

Without highways facilitating car travel to and from cities, White Americans could not have lived in suburbia and commuted to cities for work as easily as they did. And as suburban development intensified, more and more economic activity within metropolitan areas took place in suburbia itself, reducing the need to go to the city for work. Increasing economic growth in suburbs created a spatial mismatch between where the majority of the Black population lived—in cities—and the location of well-paying jobs.[129]

The racial wealth gap and concentrations of racial groups in certain parts of metropolitan areas reveal the on-ramps to opportunity created for White Americans by federal policies and the ensuing concentrations of wealth and material resources in certain geographic spaces. Local jurisdictions with political authority in geographic spaces with concentrations of wealth have more of the conditions necessary for an expanding tax base and therefore revenue to invest in public goods and services.

The Fair Housing Act of 1968 has been insufficient for achieving racial equity in the rental and sale of housing, and one of the key reasons for the law's ineffectiveness is that White Americans' household wealth rests upon maintenance of the exclusion-extraction 2-step. White neighborhoods, particularly those farthest removed from Black neighborhoods, have the highest market value.[130] White homeowners, banks, and realtors benefit financially from majority-White spaces. And until the last three decades of the twentieth century, when racial discrimination in housing was outlawed, most metropolitan areas had "chocolate cities" and "vanilla suburbs."[131]

In addition to increasing numbers of native-born Black Americans in suburbia, most newly arriving immigrants now go to suburbs' ethnic enclaves upon arrival, not to enclaves in cities.[132] Most of these immigrants come from Latin American, Asian, African, and Caribbean countries. Racial and class groups' length of tenure in suburbs matters because the longer groups are present in these locations, and the greater the size of their population there, the higher the likelihood that they can pursue their interests through local and state political processes, or that local governments will respond to their needs indirectly, even when non-Whites' interests diverge from those of longtime White residents.[133]

Another key axis of difference today is variation in quality of life *across* suburban jurisdictions, not just between cities and suburbs.[134] At the same time, because White Americans' wealth is portable, they tend to live in better-resourced neighborhoods whether they live in cities or suburbs. The significance of White people's wealth, irrespective of geographic location, is starkly evident in the DC region as the share of DC's population that is White and wealthy has increased at the same time that the affluent White population has also expanded in DC's far-flung suburbs.[135]

As racial and class groups sort into local jurisdictions in metropolitan areas, Black jurisdictions, even those that are majority-middle-class, like Prince George's, are more likely to attract and retain a greater share of the region's moderate- and low-income households because they are more affordable places to live than wealthier White suburbs. This is especially the case where rapid nearby gentrification has displaced less economically advantaged people. Many of those who are priced out of DC move to Prince George's County, not only because it is affordable, but also because it is contiguous with the District and connected to the Metro, the region's subway and bus transit system.

When the churn settles, on average, most White people in most regions across the United States are more likely than Black people, irrespective of class status, to attain a "package deal": a home appreciating in value and neighborhoods with high-quality public goods and services, particularly high-performing schools.[136]

Summary of the Chapters

In chapter 1, I lay out the sociohistorical context that has created unique fiscal constraints for Prince George's County, given that majority-Black locales, even those that are majority-middle-class, endure historical and ongoing forms of racial capitalism and anti-Black racism. I highlight how both government and market structures, since the founding of the United States, have been designed for White Americans' wealth accumulation. I also discuss the evolution of these institutions and social processes over time and how they reinforce and extend White Americans' wealth and other material resource advantages in their households, neighborhoods, and local jurisdictions.

In chapter 2, I show how my theories of converging fiscal constraints and relative regional burden capture the social forces and social processes that create different financial conditions for majority-Black versus majority-White jurisdictions. Per capita and per pupil spending disparities between Prince George's and two neighboring counties—Montgomery County, Maryland, and Fairfax County, Virginia, both of which have smaller

Black populations—elucidate the economic and political context of Prince George's County.

Chapter 3 explains the implications of a county's insufficient tax revenue for the provision of public goods and services. I show the trade-offs that Prince George's County officials made between levels of funding for core public goods and services during the fiscal year 2018 budget development processes. Such trade-offs have reduced quality of life in the county and demonstrate that Black Americans with middle-class status do not attain the same material conditions as their White middle-class peers.

In chapter 4, I show that, faced with budget limitations, public education systems struggle to educate all children well across ethno-racial and class statuses and neighborhoods. I devote a chapter to this public good in particular because it is important in itself as a core institution supporting young people's intellectual and emotional growth, and because schools are connected to other axes of inequity. Affluent residents move to locales with the best school reputations, and they use school performance as a proxy for the quality of life in jurisdictions more broadly. In addition, schools are Prince George's largest budget expenditure, as is the case in most local jurisdictions.

Chapter 5 explains Prince George's County efforts to overcome its fiscal constraints. I discuss county leaders' search for a sound financial footing by using the same strategies most local governments deploy: recruitment and retention of affluent residents and pursuit of high-end retail and recreation spaces, as well as businesses in growing industrial sectors, such as technology and health care. The county focuses on "smart growth" opportunities near transit hubs that promote walkable communities with mixes of residential, commercial, and cultural opportunities. Prince George's has had many development "wins" in recent years, but the county still struggles with "retail redlining" and other forms of racial discrimination in investment patterns that have made private development a less effective tool for Prince George's than for majority-White counties.

Finally, in chapter 6 I offer specific policy recommendations for racial and regional justice. The policy recommendations include short- and long-term solutions. I contend that the exclusion-extraction 2-step at the heart of the political economy arrangements of US metropolitan areas should be replaced with economic and political systems designed to support all Americans to thrive.

CHAPTER 1

Racial and Fiscal Subordination and Public Goods and Services Provision in Prince George's County

Even though we call ourselves living in Prince George's, we really weren't living in Prince George's, we were living in an economic commercial racial circle. A circumference. And it's called DC, and it's called Virginia, and it's called Prince George's, but when you look at the dynamics of resources and housing structures and banking and finance, it's where you live in that circle that matters.

—From author interview with former Maryland
appointed official, education activist, and retired professor

THIS CHAPTER LAYS out the national, state, and metropolitan-area political and economic processes shaping the fiscal fortunes of Prince George's County beyond the factors described in the introduction. The sociohistorical and political context provided in this chapter shows that many of the factors constraining Prince George's revenue-generating potential are beyond the control of local elected officials. Through this lens, we are equipped to interpret the empirical findings I offer in the next three chapters. Prince George's, as the epigraph states, is embedded within an "economic commercial racial circle." The social processes animating this circle create both opportunities and constraints as the county seeks to generate sufficient tax revenue for maintaining high-quality public goods and services.

https://doi.org/10.7758/bwmi8829.9422

The authority conferred on Prince George's County by the state of Maryland and in the voter referenda enacted by county residents has shaped what county officials can tax as well as the terms of those taxes, including tax rates and the amount by which taxes can be increased over time. Although state and local tax policies are stipulated in law at a particular point in time, they reflect historical and ongoing contestation between county, state, and metropolitan-area stakeholders. As we will see in the following sections, both changes in state and local laws and a lack of change reveal that stakeholders—from residents varying in race and class statuses to elected and non-elected leaders, to businesses, to developers and financial institutions, among others—have sought to realize their interests in Prince George's County. Moreover, constituencies' interests stem from their economic and political capacities and goals.

I start by explaining how Black middle-class households' financial precarity relative to White Americans—such as their limited wealth accumulation and higher rates of unemployment and under-employment—leads to the county's lower tax revenues; at the same time, it must support a population with greater needs than are found in White middle-class counties. Next, I discuss property valuation by market institutions and actors—from mortgage lenders to appraisers—that systematically undervalues and preys upon Black spaces, thus limiting the rate of increase in the market value of homes and businesses in majority-Black jurisdictions. As a result, majority-Black spaces yield less tax revenue, on average, than majority-White spaces. Then I explain why the historical support for "small government" in the United States is constitutive of a strategy for limiting Black Americans' economic options.

After addressing national processes shaping Prince George's fiscal context, the scale of analysis goes down a level, to that of the DC metropolitan area. I describe the development of local jurisdictions in the DC region after the Civil War, paying particular attention to the migration of Black populations into and within the DC region, including Prince George's County's transition from majority-White and working-class to majority-Black and middle-class in the 1990s. Next, I explain the impact of constituent-imposed limits on tax generation in Prince George's on the county's fiscal health. I then turn to financial constraints on the county imposed by the credit-worthiness assessments by bond-rating agencies, interest payments on debt, and county employee pension plan cost-sharing with Maryland, among other external factors. I conclude the chapter by discussing how Prince George's and Montgomery Counties, by jointly contributing to and benefiting from a bi-county system to provide two public goods and services—water, and parks and recreation—demonstrate that "all boats rise" when counties cooperate, rather than compete, with each other to maintain high-quality public goods and services.

Chronic Fiscal Precarity in Majority-Black Local Jurisdictions

Access to consistent, high-quality public goods and services requires investment from all levels of government—federal, state, and local—given the scale of tax revenue needed to sustain them and the significant variation in tax yields over time caused by economic cycles. Tax revenue is tethered to economic output, such as individuals' wages and corporations' incomes, and market valuation, such as the market-assessed value of people's homes. When governments take in less tax revenue owing to economic recessions or other widespread economic shocks, households also experience financial hardship, and some of these individuals and families seek support through public goods and services. Public goods and services demand often increases at the same time that governments are generating less tax revenue for funding them.

Local governments must balance their budgets each year, unlike the federal government, which routinely issues bonds, enabling the national government to carry trillions of dollars in debt. When locales garner less tax revenue than expected, they must reduce public goods and services or lay off agency staff. Majority-Black jurisdictions are more likely to experience gaps between tax revenue intake and resident demand for public goods and services, even during economic booms.[1] Government and market institutional arrangements and the political economy of metropolitan areas reflect racial capitalism logics, leading to different financial capacities for local political units. The greater fiscal vulnerability of majority-Black local jurisdictions, compared to majority-White, is evidence of what I call converging fiscal constraints. Chronic fiscal fragility in majority-Black jurisdictions increases their need for state and federal support of their public goods and services provision, compared to majority-White counties.

One way to see that Black local governments have a greater need for funding from higher levels of government is to consider how unemployment affects the financial capacity of both households and local jurisdictions simultaneously. When people lose their job, unemployment insurance (UI) helps many of them make ends meet. This income replacement mechanism is jointly paid for by the federal government and state governments.[2] To activate such assistance, people must qualify. Importantly, UI does not cover income earned through the informal economy, such as personal care services, like barbering. Black people, even those who earn middle-class incomes, are more likely to receive at least some of their income through informal "off the books" work.[3] The Black-White racial difference in income sources stems, in part, from Black people's attempts to avoid employer discrimination, which remains pervasive across industrial sectors.[4] Such discrimination gives African Americans an incentive to leave workplaces where they are not respected and/or do not attain mentoring, networking, and promotion opportunities—assuming they were hired in the first place.

Even when the economy is robust, Black Americans' unemployment rate is usually double that of White Americans, indicating the endemic challenges faced by Black Americans in the job market.[5] African Americans' strategies for meeting their material needs while also maintaining their dignity leaves them especially vulnerable during economic recessions because informal work does not give them access to the safety net of unemployment insurance. When Black households' breadwinners lose their sources of income, their local jurisdictions are likely to lose as well, twice over: First, local governments with authority from their state to collect such taxes (Prince George's County has that authority from Maryland) lose income tax revenue; and second, demand for public goods and services from households seeking to replace lost income increases.

Still, regardless of the state of the economy, local jurisdictions serving majority-Black populations usually garner less revenue than majority-White ones. As just described, Black households generally have more precarious economic positions in US employment sectors. Additionally, as discussed in the introduction, because Black families have less wealth than White families on average, they have less money saved and fewer fungible assets, such as stocks and bonds, to convert to income as they seek to weather personal hardships and economic declines. Finally, properties in majority-Black communities are undervalued by White-dominant institutions, such as appraisers and mortgage lenders.

Property Valuation in Majority-Black Versus Majority-White Jurisdictions and Implications for the Tax Yields of Local Jurisdictions

Homeownership is the primary wealth-building asset for most Americans.[6] But such wealth accumulation varies by Americans' racial status. White Americans are more likely to own a home than Black Americans. About 70 percent of White Americans are homeowners or buyers, compared to about 40 percent of Black Americans.[7] And homes owned by African Americans do not appreciate in market value as quickly as those owned by European Americans. Studies have found that even in Black neighborhoods with public goods and services and private amenities equivalent to White neighborhoods, market actors assess African Americans' homes as having lower market value than European Americans' homes.[8]

Racialized property valuation is yet another way in which Black jurisdictions lack a substrate from which to raise tax revenue comparable to those in White jurisdictions. When banks, appraisers, real estate agents, and other White-dominant institutions undervalue Black properties, majority-Black locales' tax bases are not as large as those of majority-White locales. Property tax yields are a major source of tax revenue for local jurisdictions, including Prince George's County. In this political economy context, either Black jurisdictions levy taxes at rates similar to those of majority-White jurisdictions and receive less tax revenue than their White counterparts, or they levy taxes at higher rates and thus effectively penalize the victims of racial discrimination by making them pay more for public goods and services. On top of that, public goods and services in majority-Black jurisdictions are often of lower quality than those of White-majority jurisdictions owing to constraints on Black local government investment and the history of White-dominant government and market actors underinvesting in majority-Black places.[9]

After the Fair Housing Act of 1968 was enacted, the US Department of Housing and Urban Development's scrutiny of the practices of banks and mortgage lenders increased. In recent years, government officials, Black home sellers, and other interested parties have been paying more attention to the appraisal industry. Among the cases capturing the most attention are those in which a Black family's home is assessed a certain value by one appraiser, the amount is below what the family expects, and so the family removes all indications that the home is owned by Black people, such as family photos. When the family seeks a new appraisal, the second appraisal is higher.[10]

Appraisers' valuations are based in part on comparable nearby home sales. In many instances of discrimination, appraisers compare homes of Blacks who live in majority-White neighborhoods to homes in Black neighborhoods in making their valuation.[11] Thus, there are two injustices: appraisers' use of different criteria when determining the value of African Americans' homes, irrespective of the racial composition of the neighborhood, and homes in Black neighborhoods systematically being given lower valuations than those in White neighborhoods.

Taken together, because taxes are tethered to economic productivity and property valuation processes embedded within the exclusion-extraction 2-step—whereby Black people are segregated and then expropriated from for White Americans' gain—both Black families and the local governments serving them regularly face unique financial challenges, which are exacerbated during economic downturns. Federal and state government revenue transfers to local governments equip local jurisdictions to maintain and improve public goods and services in a context where their capacity to invest in public goods and services is conditioned by locales' race and class compositions.

The consequences of racialized political economies across US metropolitan areas have worsened over the past several decades. Since the 1970s, the scale of federal and state government investment in physical and social infrastructure—roads, recreation centers, schools, health and social services—has risen at lower rates than federal and state investment in the military, police, other law enforcement agencies, and jails and prisons.[12] Yet state laws still require local governments to provide the same public goods and services. Some states also have "maintenance of effort" provisions for certain public goods and services, meaning that local governments must spend the same amount or more from one fiscal year to the next, adjusting for inflation. Such provisions are often in place for public schools. K-12 education systems are the largest expenditure for most local governments, and thus this requirement has a significant impact on their budgets. Maryland has a "maintenance of effort" requirement for its counties, which are also school districts. Funding for schools accounted for about 60 percent of Prince George's County's budget in fiscal year 2018.

In a fiscal context of increasingly insufficient and uneven funding levels over time, local governments either devise ways to generate additional revenue within their tax authority or shift responsibility for public goods and services provision to for-profit and nonprofit institutions or to households.[13] Local jurisdictions experiencing organic economic growth—stemming from the increasing market value of residential and commercial properties and from new development projects—are best positioned to weather economic vicissitudes. And White and wealthy local jurisdictions are the most likely to have these conditions. Thus, while many local governments, irrespective of their class and race composition, experience some pressure to increase tax revenue through their own tax generation authority, majority-Black jurisdictions are especially constrained because they also manage the historical and ongoing effects of racial capitalism and anti-Black racism.

Racialized Public and Private Investment in People, Neighborhoods, and Local Jurisdictions

From the 1930s to the 1960s, first under the Franklin Roosevelt administration and then under the Lyndon Johnson administration, the federal government expanded social insurance (for example, unemployment insurance and Social Security pension benefits) and social safety net programs (for example, food stamps and health care for people with low incomes). Expanded investment in Americans' health and social services indirectly supported state and local governments' financial stability because more of their residents had access to material resources, even when they lost their jobs or when regional, national, or global economic recessions took hold.[14]

Federal support for health and social services dissipated markedly during the Republican administrations of Richard Nixon and Ronald Reagan in the 1970s and 1980s. Today, federal spending levels on human and social services remain below 1960s levels.[15] Democratic presidents Roosevelt and Johnson enacted policies consistent with the theories of economist John Maynard Keynes, who contended that the federal government should invest to create broadly shared prosperity by providing public goods and services and maintaining steady employment levels.[16] He argued that federal investment was particularly crucial during economic recessions. Such "countercyclical" investment would enable the federal government, which could borrow from private industry and individuals through US Treasury bonds, to serve as a ballast in the choppy waters of economic churn.

Nixon's and Reagan's policies reflect the theories of another economist, Milton Friedman, who countered Keynes by arguing that government should not play a prominent role in the economy.[17] Friedman posited that deregulation of industry and private provision of goods and services created the greatest potential for economic growth because it increased the efficiency of business activity by allowing industry leaders to invest with minimal government restraint, a perspective often called "laissez-faire."

Importantly, while the schools of thought Keynes and Friedman represent seek to have government play different roles, neither entirely removes government. They disagree about the extent to which and how government should engage markets, and on whose behalf government should intervene. Keynes champions government taking an active role in fomenting broadly shared well-being through its policies, whereas Friedman seeks to limit government action, under the assumption that maximum economic efficiency necessarily yields material well-being for all people through the private provision of goods and services.

Nixon and Reagan largely adopted Friedman's perspective, and since the late 1970s income inequality—the gap between the richest and poorest Americans—has increased demonstrably.[18] These presidents were not opposed to government spending per se, just to spending on human and social services—the policies with the greatest potential for distributing material and social resources across the US population. Both Reagan and Nixon increased spending on forcible social control, such as prisons, as well as the military. Reductions in federally supported social service programs have left more people vulnerable when they lose household income. And at the same time, demand for public goods and services, which are provided by local governments, has increased.

Political scientist Jamila Michener, in her book *Fragmented Democracy*, describes the differences in federalist structure over the course of US history and highlights the significance of national and state government collaboration in meeting Americans' material needs:

> Before the 1930s, the American political system was characterized by "dual federalism," an arrangement by which the national government had a relatively distinct and limited role, while states and localities did most of the governing.

The 1930s ushered in an era of cooperative federalism. During this time, the role of the national government expanded significantly, but relations between the federal government and states remained largely collaborative. As the 1970s came around, the grand national policies of cooperative federalism that were aimed at building the Great Society, waging the War on Poverty, and providing civil rights protections gave way to a "new" more "coercive" or "regulated" federalism marked by heightened anxieties over "big government," deepening tensions between national and subnational sovereigns, reduced federal funding for states and localities, and the beginning of historic devolution in social welfare policies.[19]

As federal and state support of local governments retrenched in the 1970s, local jurisdictions became more reliant on high-income residents and private investment to generate sufficient tax revenue for maintaining consistent, high-quality public goods and services.[20] And historian Andrew Kahrl argues in *The Black Tax* that in local jurisdictions "competition for the people and businesses who grew tax bases became, in Reagan's America, something to celebrate, even as the winners and losers were easy to predict."[21]

President Reagan also enacted federal government tax cuts that largely benefited wealthy individual taxpayers and corporations.[22] And many state and local governments followed suit. Federal, state, and local government inability and/or unwillingness to generate adequate revenue for non-carceral public goods and services has contributed to growing income and wealth inequality and deteriorating neighborhood conditions, particularly in majority-Black communities, which have less capacity to attract and retain the upper-middle-class residents and industries most likely to fuel economic growth.[23]

"Small government," by way of tax cuts, has been one of the strategies for undermining the legislative breakthroughs of the modern civil rights movement designed to end racial discrimination.[24] Actively stripping government of authority and resources except for the military, police, and prisons amounts to "racialized anti-statism," to use political scientist Lisa Miller's term, and the "anti-state state," to use geographer Ruth Wilson Gilmore's term.[25] Constrained state investment in education, social services, housing, and other material and social goods that promote a high quality of life for the majority of Americans, alongside increased investment in the carceral state to manage the social instability stemming from increasing socioeconomic inequality, further entrenches centuries-long racial and class inequities.[26]

Still, most of the Roosevelt and Johnson administration programs, such as Social Security old-age pensions, Medicaid health insurance for low-income Americans, and Medicare health insurance for elders, remain in place. In fact, under Barack Obama's administration, Medicaid coverage expanded with enactment of the Affordable Care Act of 2010. President Donald Trump, however, has continued the conservative campaign to shred the social safety net. He sought and achieved Medicaid coverage reductions and tax cuts for wealthy Americans through the One Big Beautiful Bill Act of 2025.

Today moderate- and low-income Americans face increasing costs of living and wages that have not kept pace with households' material needs. The cost of living has risen significantly across most major US metropolitan areas over the past ten years.[27] And certain regions along the East and West Coasts, such as the Washington, DC, area, have seen the sharpest cost-of-living increases. Housing costs, for renters and buyers alike, drive much of the increased cost of living.[28]

Outside of housing for low-income Americans—whether through government vouchers or government-sponsored housing developments—most government support for housing goes to homeowners through tax code provisions, most notably, the home mortgage interest deduction and other deductions and credits related to home maintenance and improvement.[29] The mortgage interest deduction offers disproportionate financial benefits to White middle- and upper-middle-class people because White Americans are more likely than Black Americans to own homes and to experience rapidly appreciating home values.

However, the public goods and services investment trends initiated in the 1970s are just the most recent period of government retrenchment in US history. A perennial theme of American governance since the country's founding has been a tilt toward "small government." In 1788, when the US Constitution was ratified, Americans, then as now, did not agree on the roles and responsibilities of federal and state governments, nor on how those roles and responsibilities should be executed. The Federalist Papers, written by Alexander Hamilton, James Madison, and John Jay in 1787 and 1788 as states deliberated on whether to ratify the Constitution, reveal some of their consternation over the interpretation and significance of the Constitution's provisions.[30]

It was not until 1913, when the Sixteenth Amendment was ratified, that the federal government had authority to tax individual and corporate income.[31] Prior to 1913, the primary sources of national-level income were excise taxes on specific goods and tariffs. The Sixteenth Amendment significantly increased the federal government's fiscal capacity to fund a broader range of programs and enabled the national government to play a more prominent role in the US economy. This amendment set the stage for the expansion of the welfare state under President Franklin D. Roosevelt in the 1930s. Americans have always wrestled with how to enact "self-governance" through our representative democracy—from the extent of government's control over individuals' behaviors, to the regulation of commerce and the money supply, to the relative balance of power between national and state governments, to the roles of and relationships between legislative, executive, and judicial branches, among other topics.

"Small government," then, should be construed as one of many positions one can take regarding the role, size, and structure of government as it promotes the general welfare of all Americans, both as individuals and as a collective. At the same time, given that race, class, and gender have been the primary axes of social difference determining access to material and social resources, "small government" and "states' rights" have generally been tools for creating and reinforcing elite White men's interests.[32] By definition, limited government authority and capacity requires that people find a substitute for what government is not providing.

Other institutional options for meeting material needs include families, businesses, and religious and other civil society groups. Those who hold significant power outside of government due to their money and capital, land holdings, social status, and ability and willingness to use violence generally benefit more when government does not redistribute or otherwise regulate material, political, and other resources in ways that facilitate broadly shared prosperity. Elite White men have controlled the levers of both government power and the other major institutions shaping American society. This pattern is consistent with my theory of the exclusion-extraction 2-step, which posits that White dominant institutions have multiple, mutually reinforcing means for maintaining and extending their control of the social processes mediating people's life chances at all levels of social organization.

As just discussed, it was not until the early twentieth century that the US government established a substantial government-based social safety net for citizens and legal residents. These measures came in the wake of the Great Depression of 1929, a time when millions of Americans struggled to feed and house themselves because of mass unemployment. The social, economic, and political upheaval of the Great Depression and the brewing conflicts in Europe presaging World War II created conditions for Roosevelt and his allies to press for using a more expansive political imagination to meet Americans' core material needs. Before the 1930s, the US social safety net was largely provided through a patchwork of churches, settlement houses, and other charitable organizations.[33] But as noted in the introduction, when the federal government extended the social safety net in the 1930s, White domination and anti-Black racism limited its reach.[34]

Federal policymakers in the early and mid-twentieth century, nearly all of them elite White men, contended that White men, as "heads of household," "deserved" public investment, but other Americans did not, or at least not to the same degree.[35] Racialized public investment was compounded by labor union racial discrimination patterns.[36] And pre–World War II social cleavages were widened by post–World War II policies, such as Federal Housing Administration home-buying support and the GI Bill.

America's racialized playing field ensures that the rules of racialism capitalism are designed for White Americans to win. Consequently, European Americans have, on average, amassed more material resources than Black Americans and as such are equipped to continue to win. Moreover, local jurisdictions serving majority-White populations win more robust tax bases. These national trends have shaped the political economy patterns of the DC metropolitan area and continue to do so. Let us now consider the specific sociohistorical context of the DC region through the lens of development in Prince George's County.

Prince George's County in Its Regional Sociohistorical Context

While all US metropolitan areas have racial and class disparities in material resource access, the specific factors that have shaped each region are distinct. Here I explain the political, economic, and social evolution of Prince George's County in the context of the political economy arrangements of the Washington, DC, metropolitan area.

The Pre–Civil War Period in Prince George's County

Prince George's County was established in 1696. It is one of twenty-four counties (including Baltimore City) in the state of Maryland.[37] Prince George's has always had a substantial Black population, even though the county was majority-White until the 1990s. To this day, many current Prince George's residents are the descendants of enslaved Africans who cultivated crops such as tobacco, wheat, and corn.[38] Though Maryland did not secede from the United States during the Civil War, chattel slavery was legal in the state until the war ended.

Free Black communities in the county prior to the Civil War included, among others, Rossville, Valley Lane, and Oxon Hill. As footholds for Black self-determination before chattel slavery ended, they offered spaces where African Americans could establish and nurture churches, businesses, schools, social clubs, and other economic and social infrastructure and capacities that supported Black people's lives.

Prince George's County in the Reconstruction and Jim Crow Periods

After the Civil War, the Black population in Prince George's County dropped as many African Americans moved to find work in cities, such as Baltimore.[39] The Democratic Party was the primary political party in Maryland, just as it was in other former slave-holding states. White leaders imposed Jim Crow segregation laws that limited Black residents' educational, employment, and political opportunities. Most Black Prince Georgians during the Jim Crow period farmed land they owned or worked as sharecroppers or as laborers.[40] Despite racial segregation and anti-Black violence, Black Prince Georgians exercised economic, political, and social agency by building businesses, churches, mutual aid societies, fraternal orders, and other institutions organizing Black life, thus expanding the range of Black community life created prior to the Civil War.

Outside of informal measures to promote literacy and skills acquisition, Black Prince George's residents worked with the Freedmen's Bureau to gain funding for education immediately after the Civil War. In 1872, the county assumed the role of building schools, and Maryland began earmarking tax revenue for racially segregated schools. Racial segregation in schools officially became state law in 1924.[41]

In the first few decades of the twentieth century, however, most county schools were built through agreements between Black Prince Georgians and the Rosenwald Fund. Beginning in 1913, Julius Rosenwald, CEO of Sears and Roebuck and a Jewish philanthropist, partnered with the prominent Black leader Booker T. Washington, who founded the Tuskegee Institute in Alabama, to build K-12 schools throughout Southern states.[42] The Rosenwald Fund offered cash assistance for building educational facilities for Black children if the Black community matched the funding with cash or in-kind contributions, such as land, lumber, or labor, and if the local school board approved the venture and agreed to administer the school. It was with the support of the Rosenwald Fund that the first Prince George's high school for Black students, Lakeland High School, was erected in 1928.[43] Twenty-three schools were built in Prince George's County through the Rosenwald Fund, and 153 Rosenwald-supported schools were established throughout Maryland.[44]

The Post–World War II Period to the Present in Prince George's County

In the two decades following World War II, both the national economy and the economy of the DC region expanded demonstrably. Washington, DC, as the nation's capital, is the hub of federal government activity. Federal government expansion across all sectors—from the military to social services—increased the number of white-collar civil service jobs available. For the first time in US history, thanks to enactment of antiracial discrimination laws, most notably the Civil Rights Act of 1964, which prohibits racial discrimination in education and employment, increasing numbers of Black people could access high-paying government positions. With the Civil Rights Act and other laws in place, more and more Black Americans earned college educations and attained white-collar jobs.[45]

College-educated African Americans in the DC region were especially well positioned to benefit from federal government expansion. Given the federal government's need to fill positions, and because it wanted to model anti–racial discrimination practices for private industry, the federal government enacted a range of affirmative action programs, such as college internships that trained Black people for full-time civil service positions and targeted recruitment at Historically Black Colleges and Universities.[46]

The private sector, in contrast, has generally lagged behind federal, state, and local government efforts to recruit and retain Black white-collar professionals, although this pattern varies by industry.[47] Differences in public and private industry efforts to integrate their ranks along racial lines help explain why Black people with college degrees are overrepresented in government civil service.

The overrepresentation of Black people in civil service positions leads to several challenges for the Black middle class today, and for the local governments that serve them. For one, government usually pays less than the private sector for comparable work.[48] Moreover, the rate of salary increase year to year is lower in government, and government workers are not eligible for cash bonuses or stock options.[49] The lower incomes of African Americans leave them with less money for daily expenses and their lower salaries and wages amplify the White-Black wealth gap. White Americans' additional earnings set them up to accrue more wealth-generating assets, from homes to stocks and bonds, thus reinforcing and extending their financial head start over Black Americans. Furthermore, higher income and greater wealth translate into housing options with greater market value, leading to greater wealth concentrations in White-majority neighborhoods, which, in turn, lead to greater property tax yields in majority-White jurisdictions.

Another challenge related to Black people's concentration in civil service jobs is that, as all levels of government have downsized since the Richard Nixon administration in the 1970s, Black Americans have been especially vulnerable to job loss.[50] Baby Boomer Black Americans (those born in the 1940s, '50s, and '60s) who lose their civil service jobs often cannot find comparable work in private industry. Younger Black Americans (those born in the 1970s or later) can no longer count on civil service work as a sure path to middle-class socioeconomic status. Government downsizing is one of the reasons Black middle-class Americans are less likely to attain their parents' socioeconomic status or higher—or in social science parlance, to "socially reproduce." Consistent with national trends in racialized sorting into the public and private sectors, a disproportionate share of African Americans in the DC region work for the federal government as well as in Maryland, Virginia, and DC state and local governments.[51]

The efforts of the first Black mayor of Washington, DC, Marion Barry, show the significance of civil service work for Black people's ability to attain middle-class status. Mayor Barry, first elected in 1978, focused on hiring

Black people for city jobs and sought to use Black contractors for government work.[52] Indeed, one of his signature programs was summer jobs for teens, which helped them gain skills for civil service work in adulthood.

Many Black civil servants who worked for the DC government were among the first African Americans to move to Prince George's County as they sought to realize their American dream of a house with a yard in suburbia. Indeed, as African Americans throughout the DC region sought to translate their rising incomes into suburban living, Prince George's became their destination. In the 1970s, 81 percent of the Black households that moved from DC moved to Prince George's County.[53] The migration of Black people into the county shifted the racial and class composition of Prince George's. In the span of about three decades—the 1970s through the 1990s—Prince George's went from majority-White and working-class to majority-Black and middle-class. While the majority of the Black people who have moved to Prince George's since the 1970s have had median or higher incomes, working-class and low-income families have also chosen to call the county home.

Other "pull factors" also drew African Americans to Prince George's County. In the 1970s, because most of Prince George's White residents were working-class, their neighborhoods were more financially accessible to upwardly mobile Black people seeking a suburban residence in a jurisdiction easily accessible to DC. Montgomery County, Maryland, and Fairfax County, Virginia, were majority-White and upper-middle-class and thus more expensive places to live.

As the proportion of Black Prince Georgians increased, White Prince Georgians resisted Black newcomers through county government funding allocations that privileged White neighborhoods, particularly schools. The Ku Klux Klan had branches in three municipalities in Prince George's— Mt. Rainier, Brentwood, and Hyattsville, and one of its leaders was known to chase Black people with dogs and to hand Black children "Back to Africa" leaflets.[54] Open White hostility was the primary response in the 1970s and '80s. Then White resistance shifted to White departure from the county to live in other parts of the DC region. By the early 1990s, Prince George's had become majority-Black owing to increasing Black in-migration and White out-migration.

Prince George's County also became the destination for the DC area's suburban Black middle class because it had more undeveloped land than

Montgomery and Fairfax Counties in the 1970s, as it still does today. With ample open land, builders could construct housing subdivisions rapidly in response to Black Americans' intensifying demand, and Prince George's zoning regulations made such rapid construction feasible. For instance, in 1973 Montgomery County enacted an adequate public facilities ordinance to ensure that public infrastructure in the county kept pace with the building of residential and commercial properties.[55] Prince George's did not enact a similar law. With more lenient zoning and public facilities requirements than in Montgomery County, construction of housing subdivisions in Prince George's has often not been coupled with sufficient investment in public infrastructure, from schools to roads and firehouses. Inadequate infrastructure investment decades ago created the intense need today in Prince George's for investment in the built environment not only to address wear and tear but to make up for the lack of investment in prior decades. Deferred maintenance, coupled with a fast-growing population, places ever greater pressure on Prince George's County's already well-worn infrastructure.

Despite these challenges, Prince George's County is a desirable jurisdiction for several reasons. Many of the affluent Black residents I spoke to called Prince George's the "Black Mecca." That is, the county is sought after by well-to-do African Americans seeking upscale suburban living in a Black space. Put another way, Prince George's is an example of Black "placemaking"—a geographic space with a Black population substantial enough to sustain a vibrant Black culture, from churches to entertainment venues, restaurants, and civic organizations.[56]

Certainly, Black places vary along regional, class, and ethnic lines, with ethnic variation especially pronounced in places with significant numbers of Black immigrants, such as New York City.[57] Yet there are shared rhythms and through lines across Black communities in the United States, given that most Black people in the country have cultural roots in the South.[58] Furthermore, in majority–affluent Black places, like Prince George's County, Black middle- and upper-middle-class people can create subcultures. These subcultures allow African American middle-class and upper-middle-class/elite parents to transmit cultural scripts to their children that they believe will anchor their kids in an affirming Black identity while also training their kids to navigate elite White spaces successfully.[59]

While it is true that Black people enjoy living among each other, the social science literature also shows that Black people prefer to live in racially integrated neighborhoods, those where the White population is about 50 percent and the other half is the total non-White population—Black, Latino, Asian, and Indigenous.[60] And African Americans generally do not want to "pioneer," that is, to be the only Black people, or one of only a few, in a White neighborhood. White people, on the other hand, show some openness to racial desegregation, but want to be the super-majority population, and they are especially sensitive to what they perceive to be "too many" Black residents. White Americans are more willing to live next to Asian and Latino Americans.[61] Therefore, the threshold that Black Americans desire for racial integration is far above the threshold that White Americans will accept.

Consequently, when Black Americans move into neighborhoods where the non-White population is growing and a significant share of those non-Whites are African American, such neighborhoods often transition to majority-Black spaces as White residents move out. White Americans with children are particularly apt to relocate to a place with a higher White population because they seek majority-White schools. Across the country, White parents use the racial composition of schools as a proxy for school quality.[62] White parents assume that the greater the share of White students, the higher the school's performance, irrespective of other factors.

Beyond the "pull factors" that attracted African Americans to Prince George's County, there were "push factors" in other DC-area jurisdictions that prevented Black people from moving in. Neighborhood and housing opportunity structures within and across jurisdictions of the DC region in the decades following World War II, like prospects for jobs in the private versus the public sector, were uneven along racial lines, and that variation generally worked to the advantage of White Americans. White upper-middle-class residents of Fairfax and Montgomery Counties were better able to leverage real estate agencies, banking and mortgage institutions, and homeowner associations to carry out anti-Black racial exclusion practices, equipping them to maintain White neighborhoods.[63] Racial exclusion occurred despite the Supreme Court's ruling prohibiting racial zoning through local government ordinances in the 1917 case *Buchanan v. Warley*, and the Court's outlawing of enforcement of racial exclusion provisions in home deeds in the 1948 case *Kramer v. Shelley*.[64] The Fair Housing Act of 1968 reinforced these court decisions by explicitly prohibiting racial discrimination in the rental and sale of housing. But White people remained resistant to Black people moving into their neighborhoods despite laws and court cases rendering racial discrimination illegal.

Meaningful and stable racial integration is elusive because the Fair Housing Act largely relies on individuals to recognize that they have experienced racial discrimination and then to invest the time, money, and energy to sue in court for redress. That is, the federal government largely does not systematically take proactive steps to investigate rental application processes, real estate sales, lending, and other practices already known to be a means of racial exclusion. When the US Department of Housing and Urban Development and researchers do conduct such studies, they usually find significant anti-Black racial discrimination.[65]

In the next section, I discuss the political and economic opportunities and constraints that Prince George's experienced from the 1990s forward—that is, after the county's population became majority-Black—in light of the regional trends just explained. It is critical to note at the outset that many of the structural constraints I discuss would be present irrespective of the racial status of decision-makers. While shared racial status between constituents and decision-makers yields some benefits, officials cannot overcome the structural limitations embedded in political economy arrangements through sheer force of will. Those sorts of changes require changes in policy, policy enforcement, and policy interpretation by courts.

Black Political Authority in Prince George's County from the 1990s to the Present

African Americans attained political control of Prince George's County in the 1990s, most of them by climbing the Democratic Party ranks in Maryland and Prince George's. Black Americans have held prominent positions across institutions, including the county executive's office, as well as seats on the county council and school board. Most developed their political acumen under White Democrats known to be "king-" and "queen-" makers across Maryland. Among the most influential of these White leaders were Paris Glendening, the Prince George's County executive from 1982 to 1994 and later the Maryland governor from 1995 to 2003; Steny Hoyer, a former Maryland legislator and a current US congressional representative serving Maryland's Fifth District since 1981; and the late Mike Miller, who served in the Maryland legislature for almost fifty years (1971–2020), thirty-three of which were as Senate president.[66]

In 1994, Wayne Curry became Prince George's first Black county executive. That year the county had a projected budget deficit of $107 million.[67]

Paris Glendening, Curry's predecessor, presided over the county as the shortfall developed. The deficit stemmed from two main factors: a tax generation limitation imposed by White taxpayers as the county transitioned to majority-Black (discussed in the next section), and the county's effort to serve a growing population without commensurate additional county and state investment in public goods and services, particularly public schools. Curry's experience of inheriting a budget deficit from his White predecessor mirrors the experiences of Black mayors who faced fiscal crises during their terms in office in the 1970s and 1980s, such as Maynard Jackson of Atlanta, Harold Washington of Chicago, and Coleman Young of Detroit. A key through line between Curry's and Black mayors' experiences is how the shift of the White population out of their jurisdictions contributed to significant loss of tax revenue in jurisdictions with Black political control.[68]

Among Curry's first actions upon taking office were to lay off one hundred county employees and to cut county services. In addition, Prince George's struggled to maintain the top bond rating of AAA. Curry fought to keep this rating by, among other things, meeting with Wall Street analysts to explain why the county should not be downgraded.[69] Were that to have happened, Prince George's would have paid higher interest rates to borrow money to build the public infrastructure the county sorely needed. By the time Curry left office in 2002, the county's fiscal health had recovered considerably. Prince George's was running a budget surplus, and the bond rating remained AAA, the highest rating.[70] Nevertheless, county leaders to this day must navigate the underlying currents prevalent during the first Black county executive's tenure.

Tax Generation Limitations and Prince George's County's Fiscal Footing

During Prince George's County's racial-majority transition, voters enacted several measures restricting the county's tax generation capacity. Given the timing of the enactment of these measures—when the county was still majority-White but Black people were about to become the population majority—these laws are embedded in racialized politics. Namely, they reflect White voters' beliefs about whether, and to what extent, the county government should continue to invest in public goods and services that supported White and Black residents. By restricting tax revenue generation, White residents, facing imminent loss of their population majority, could keep more of their household income as they prepared to leave the county. Less government revenue also restrained the county's efforts to invest in public goods and services. White residents' desire to reduce government efficacy was especially strong regarding investment in K-12 schools.

From the late 1970s through the early 1990s, three tax restriction laws were passed: the Tax Reform Initiative by Marylanders (TRIM), Question I, and the Homestead Tax Cap. TRIM, enacted in 1978, affects Prince George's property tax rate by setting it at $0.96 per $100 of assessed value. The only time the tax rate has been increased since 1978 was in 2016, when the rate increased to $1.00 per $100 of assessed value owing to a "supplemental education tax."[71] Prince George's property tax rate is comparable to or higher than those of nearby counties. But as discussed in later chapters, in serving more moderate- and low-income people who generally have greater public goods and services needs than those who are more affluent, the county experiences greater strain on its budget.

Additionally, because properties in Prince George's appreciate at a slower rate than those in neighboring wealthier and Whiter counties, its tax base is smaller. Thus, although Prince George's tax rates are close to those of Montgomery and Fairfax Counties, its smaller tax base yields less revenue. Prince George's would have to raise taxes significantly to garner a similar tax yield, but doing so, at least in the short run, would require residents to pay even more for public goods and services that are generally of lower quality than those of neighboring wealthier and Whiter counties. In chapter 5, I discuss the county's development opportunities and constraints.

Most homebuyers and owners, however, do not care only about the tax rate. They also care about what they receive for their tax contributions, and having a high-performing K-12 public school system usually tops residents' priority list. Homebuyers and owners also want to see their homes' values increase, enabling them to attain more equity: the difference between their mortgage and the market-appraised value of their home. Equity increases with increasing homebuyer demand in neighborhoods, and neighborhoods with high-performing schools usually experience the most demand.

Question I concerns taxes and fees for county services. In the wake of TRIM, county officials sought other sources of revenue and initiated new taxes and fees to garner income to offset losses in property tax revenue.

In 1996, Wayne Curry, the first Black county executive, pursued a ballot measure to end TRIM. That same year, voters, frustrated by the new taxes and fees, enacted Question I, which amended the county charter to state that any new taxes and fees required direct voter approval. Upon Question I's enactment, Curry told the *Washington Post*: "The voters of Prince George's have spoken and spoken emphatically. They have called for a smaller, leaner government. And that's exactly what they will get."[72] According to the Prince George's County Blue Ribbon Commission on the Structural Deficit, "No other Maryland jurisdiction has such a provision in law."[73]

Finally, the Homestead Tax Credit is designed to mitigate significant increases in property taxes on a principal residence, or a "homestead." This act spreads tax increases over a three-year period: one-third of the additional amount is assessed the first year, another third of the amount is assessed in the second year, and the full new assessment sets in the third year. The Homestead Tax Credit also caps the percentage increase of property taxes on homesteads to 10 percent. Counties across Maryland set the permissible credit for homeowners between 0 and 10 percent. In 1992, Prince George's County voters decided that the credit percentage would have a base of 0 percent, plus the percentage of increase in the Consumer Price Index (CPI) for the previous twelve months, but not more than 5 percent. While CPI-based increases within the 5 percent limit capture some additional revenue, the county loses revenue between the 5 percent county cap and Maryland's maximum of 10 percent. Through these three measures—TRIM, Question I, and the Homestead Tax Cap—Prince George's voters removed all tax and fee authority discretion from their elected officials and now control it directly themselves.

Question I and the Homestead Tax Cap were enacted after Prince George's became majority-Black. But TRIM was the first and most consequential measure because it destabilized the county fiscally. Question I and the Homestead Tax Cap are effectively voter responses to steps that officials took to mitigate the county's financial distress caused by TRIM's limitations. Therefore, it is important to consider what motivated Prince Georgians to enact TRIM in the first place.

The History of TRIM's Enactment

In the 1970s, the most prominent political concern among most residents of Prince George's—then still a majority-White county—was the federally enforced desegregation of the county's schools.[74] The court order took effect in 1974, after Black parents sued the county, with the support of the National Association for the Advancement of Colored People (NAACP) and the American Civil Liberties Union (ACLU). TRIM became law four years after the desegregation order, and thus at a point when White resentment had been building for years. Many White parents protested desegregation, at times violently. Notably, the same year TRIM was passed the majority of county voters supported George Wallace, an avowed segregationist, in the Republican Party presidential primary.[75] When I asked a Prince George's government civil servant in senior positions since the 1990s, "What do you think led to TRIM's passage?," he articulated the perspective I heard from most Black Prince George's officials:

> Can I tell you honestly? I think it was the transition and the color of the people that were getting into government. And I think also the desegregation [of county public schools] suit added a lot to it because people did not want to spend their money busing children from the inner beltway to the outer beltway. And we had a lot of people who did not have faith in Black people in general or Black elected officials. . . . People don't want to say it, but we have to be honest with ourselves. . . . I'll never forget I overheard a [White] council member say, "Oh my God, all the people with the brains are leaving Upper Marlboro [the seat of county government]."

A county council member similarly framed TRIM's enactment and its connection to the county's racial transition:

> It was just during a time when the change was happening between Whites, the White flight, and African Americans taking over. And as Whites still have a lot of remnants of power. It's what happens, right? We don't wanna pay for the other. If everybody looked Irish, and Italian, and German, and whatever, they wouldn't have minded paying for those kids to go to school.

A congressional representative whose district includes a portion of Prince George's County also shared the perspective that the racial transition from majority-White to majority-Black motivated TRIM's enactment:

> Quite frankly, while I don't believe in a conspiracy theory, I subscribe to what I think a lot of people believe, which was non-African Americans, who at one time were the majority, Whites, who were the majority, saw that they were losing the majority. And they said, "Shoot, you know what,

let's put on a tax cap. Because quite frankly, I don't think we trust African Americans with what they may do with taxes and how they're going to spend it." And then we were really hampered in our ability to invest in this county. Schools, infrastructure, the things that attract businesses and culture. And that's why we're a bedroom community. So I think the needs are the same, but we are coming out of this period of neglect during this transition.

Note that this federal official linked TRIM's enactment to the county's decades-long inability to fund its public goods and services adequately ("we were really hampered in our ability to invest in this county"). These three leaders' assessment of what led to TRIM's passage is that White Prince George's leaders and residents, foreseeing the looming loss of White political control in the county, sought to restrict county officials' "power of the purse," given that they themselves would no longer control it. More specifically, White Prince Georgians wanted to halt, or at least undermine, the school desegregation process by starving the school system of money. Schools are also the county's largest budget expenditure.

But not all leaders I spoke to agreed that White resistance to Black leadership and school desegregation motivated White Prince Georgians to support TRIM. Those who held this perspective contend that TRIM was embedded in a national wave of "tax revolts" that were not necessarily based in White domination and anti-Black racism. They noted the national-level political energy initiated by Proposition 13 in California, which was enacted in 1978 and imposed a statewide property tax limitation.

The county council chair during Curry's 1990s administration also served in 2018 as chair of the Business Roundtable of Prince George's corporations. This official stated the perspective I heard from most White leaders:

RESPONDENT: It started on the West Coast with Prop 13. You had California, which was very wealthy and was running a surplus in the billions of dollars. . . . And at the same time, they're increasing people's taxes, and they just had enough. . . . So you had this businessman and someone else who started a movement out there, put this Prop 13 on that froze the actual amount of money being raised from property taxes. . . . It started spreading east. We had an election cycle coming up here for county executive. You had a Republican, Larry Hogan . . . and another candidate, Democrat by the name of Winfield Kelly. The two of them kind of jumped on that bandwagon so that one couldn't outdo the other by saying they were for a tax limitation here that was similar to Prop 13. . . . There were a number of other counties that had similar bills. None of them passed to the extent that ours did. In 1978, the voters imposed a tax limitation here that was crushing. It literally froze our real estate tax revenue at the same rate as it was in 1978. . . . So no matter how much our assessments went up, no matter what we did, we couldn't raise any more money by property tax, our main revenue source, than we did in 1978. That's when our infrastructure fell apart, started falling apart. And we went from 1978 until 1984 before that was modified. And had it not been for the public safety workers and some of the teachers, that issue would not have been on the ballot. And we wouldn't have been in the position we're in today. And what they did, instead of freezing the absolute amount, they froze the rate. So you could take advantage of the assessable base going on.

AUTHOR: But just because something is coterminous does not mean it's causal. It's certainly interesting that it [the imposition of TRIM] was happening at the same time that the county was transitioning from being majority-White to majority-Black.

RESPONDENT: I don't really think that was it. I'll tell you why. Because African Americans have done the same thing in subsequent elections. You put a tax increase there, people are not going to vote themselves a tax increase. I don't care who they are. And that's more the issue. . . . I hate to use the expression, but we screwed ourselves.

A White county council member shared a similar narrative:

So TRIM was passed in the eighties [1978], and it was sort of a nationwide backlash. I mean, it just sort of caught hold, started in California with one of their propositions. It started this whole democracy by referendum movement that went from west to east. And I think voters had gotten fed up in Prince George's County with what they thought were high property tax rates and not a good return on their dollar. A very high crime rate back then. What people viewed as sort of substandard schools, lack of accountability in government. Where is our money going? Probably lack of transparency and understanding how are our dollars being spent? But just, people felt like their neighborhoods were declining, schools were declining, they were paying all this money in property taxes with no end in sight. And that movement and that belief that, okay, if you're not going to make good decisions, you're not going to be wise stewards of our tax money, well, then we're going to impose limits on you. And so it was citizen-driven, it was a grassroots effort to get the question on the ballot. And it passed pretty overwhelmingly.

This council member argues that Prince George's residents who supported TRIM wanted to limit government because they were not getting a "good return on their dollar" and because their "neighborhoods were declining, schools were declining." The frames of "returns on investment" and "decline" are thinly veiled references to race. First, the largest budget expenditure is public schools. The "return" that White residents likely did not want was tax revenue used to support the racial desegregation of schools, which the majority of White Prince Georgians opposed. Second, "decline" in neighborhood and school quality is unlikely to have occurred in a context where the increase in the number of Black Prince Georgians led to an increase in average class status in the county.

In addition, from a national perspective, trends in property tax restrictions stemming from California's Proposition 13 were also tethered to White voter backlash to school desegregation and other modern civil rights movement legislative and court case breakthroughs that sought to end anti-Black racial discrimination and allow Black Americans greater access to US opportunity structures.[76] According to historian Andrew Kahrl, author of *The Black Tax*:

> By the early 1980s, lawmakers and voters across the country were rushing to adopt versions of California's radical reforms. Between 1978 and 1983 alone, twenty states enacted limits on property assessment increases, tax-rate increases, spending increases, or some combination of them. By 1995, forty-six states had some law limiting local governments' ability to raise tax rates, upwardly adjust assessments, or increase local budgets.[77]

The early and mid-1970s were the brief period when federal courts enforced the US Supreme Court rulings in *Brown v. Board of Education I* (1954), which stated the legal reasoning and principles for racial desegregation, and *Brown v. Board of Education II* (1955), which stipulated enforcement measures.[78] The fact that TRIM received enough registered voter signatures to even be on the Prince George's ballot in 1978—the same year California's Proposition 13 was enacted—demonstrates that similar political sentiment probably existed in

Prince George's County prior to Proposition 13's passage. While it is certainly possible that Prince Georgians voted in favor of TRIM for reasons other than racial animus, such as "small government," "small government" itself is entangled in a desire to limit mechanisms for achieving racial and class equity through government policies.

Taxes are the lifeblood of governments. These dollars enable governments to carry out their responsibilities, including the provision of public goods and services. Anti-government sentiment and anti-tax sentiment work hand in glove. And politically conservative Americans apply this "small government" stance selectively; notably, they tend to support expanding military and police spending, but not spending on human services programs. Still, throughout the twentieth century and up to the present, a majority of White Americans, irrespective of party affiliation, support major federal social safety net programs, such as Social Security old-age pensions and Medicare-funded health care for elderly people.[79]

Though Question I and the Homestead Tax Cap became law when the county was majority-Black, the effects of TRIM created severe fiscal consequences. Prince George's officials, seeking to close budget shortfalls initiated by TRIM, passed licensing and permitting fees as well as other fees and taxes to prevent drastic cuts to county services. Thus, as county leaders adapted to the fiscal constraints created by TRIM, their revenue-raising strategies led to voter frustration, which Prince Georgians expressed by seeking—and attaining—direct control over all tax and fee increases.

TRIM's Downstream Consequences Today

Even with TRIM in place in Prince George's, the county's property tax rate is at parity with, if not higher than, the rate in nearby counties, including Fairfax and Montgomery. According to the Prince George's County Blue Ribbon Commission on the Structural Deficit:

> A close examination of the data shows that any property tax relief felt by residents is not due to TRIM, but rather is due to the lower property values in the County relative to neighboring counties. In fact, TRIM's real effect has been to keep the County's property tax rate at $0.96 per $100 of assessed value, which is relatively high compared to other counties without a tax cap during the period between 1978 and 2015.[80]

Because all taxes and fees require direct voter approval, the county's tax regime is locked in place, unless voters pass referendums allowing for tax and fee increases. Unable to tailor the tax regime to reflect economic cycles or the evolution of the county's economy, county leaders are left with few tools for crafting tax packages designed to maximize the county's tax generation capacity while minimizing reliance on property tax revenue. For instance, it is possible that the county could attain more net revenue by lowering property taxes and raising other taxes and fees.

Fallout from TRIM's enactment and subsequent tax restrictions contributed to Prince George's fiscal trajectory not keeping pace with public goods and services demand today. When Prince George's officials have tried to make the case that tax restrictions prevent the county from investing in public goods and services to the degree voters want, voters have essentially asked officials to do more with less—that is, to find ways to use the revenue they already have to maintain or improve public goods and services quality. Indeed, all of the residents I spoke to supported TRIM.

Yet it is important to distinguish between Black and White voters' support for tax generation restrictions. Furthermore, *even if* local taxes were increased, Prince George's fiscal limitations would most likely remain. The county's financial trajectory mostly results from the relative regional burden that the county carries for the DC metropolitan area; this burden highlights the county's economic capacity as shaped by its embeddedness with wealthier, Whiter neighboring jurisdictions, as I explain in chapters 3 and 4. Ultimately, Prince George's residents cannot tax themselves at rates high enough to overcome the cumulative effects of racial capitalism, which I call the exclusion-extraction 2-step. Yet it is still true that granting Prince George's officials latitude in setting tax and fee rates would probably alleviate some of the budget pressure the county government manages each fiscal year. Since that is the case, why do Black residents continue to support tax restrictions?

Current Resistance to Overturning Tax Revenue Generation Restrictions

County executives have tried to repeal the Tax Reform Initiative by Marylanders (TRIM) several times since the county became majority-Black in the 1990s. In each instance, Prince George's voters resoundingly rejected the proposed repeal.[81] The reasons voters support TRIM vary, but several themes emerged during interviews with residents and during my observations of the county's political processes: (1) Many residents, already struggling financially, do not want to raise their taxes and fees because they cannot afford them; (2) residents are frustrated that they do not have public goods and services and private amenities comparable to those of neighboring counties and thus view raising taxes as rewarding county officials for poor performance; and (3) high-profile corruption scandals have undermined public trust in the integrity of government officials' use of county funds.

In my interviews with residents, none said that they supported the outright repeal of TRIM, but some indicated support for its repeal under certain conditions. When I asked residents whether they agreed that TRIM should remain in place and about the basis of their position, about half knew what TRIM is. For those not familiar with the measure, I explained what TRIM is and then asked about their position on whether it was a good idea. When I reframed the question to one about raising taxes to fund public goods and services that residents cared about, not about TRIM per se, more than half said that they would support raising their taxes. The funding areas that residents named varied, but the issue that topped most respondents' list was education.

For instance, Mary, a Black woman over the age of sixty-five who owned a single-family home in an upper-middle-class retirement community outside of the beltway, stated her contingent support for raising taxes this way when I asked her, "Are there any conditions under which you would agree to have your taxes raised?"

> Yeah, and then it would have to be very, because you have to watch these people with loopholes. So, for example, the lottery money in California, when we all voted for the lottery out there, supposed to go to education. So you got all these hundreds and hundreds of millions, billions of dollars over time, going in there. Well, what it did is that it didn't, the legislation didn't say that you have to maintain this, the level of funding already in the schools and that this would be additional. . . . That's what they [Prince George's County officials] did with the MGM [casino], and I'm thinking, Anybody take a look at that to see if that was the case? . . . And I think there are things that I would pay more for. I would pay for education, I would even pay for healthcare. . . . If in fact it was there and that money was clearly earmarked and had an agenda that was good for the people of this county.

Mary's response showed her recognition that new funding did not nec-essarily mean that the revenue would supplement, not supplant, existing funding. Her impression of how California used lottery funds was that state officials promoted the lottery as a way to improve schools, but that when they allocated the revenue, decision-makers reduced the amount of revenue coming from funding sources outside of the lottery. The net effect was that funding for California schools did not increase. Mary was concerned that new revenue from raising county taxes would be spent on public services that were not residents' priority. Nevertheless, Mary was in fact open to raising her taxes, but that position had not been apparent when I asked her about TRIM directly.

Another example is John, a college-educated, married Black man in his thirties who owned a home near the beltway in northern Prince George's County. He responded as follows to the question regarding the conditions under which he would consent to having his taxes raised:

> I could consider it only after seeing some type of case study that has proved two, three times over that this type of investment in this thing—like, say for instance, if it were schools, if we raise taxes by blah, blah, blah, by $20 a household for the next ten years, for every paycheck that you get, which is a lot, actually, you will see this level of increase in student test scores. And that is going to have a direct connection to our ability to solicit startups and other economic development initiatives that will bring more businesses to the county that will all circle, continue to grow this ever-expanding net of funding that comes back into the county, that we can then use to pour back into our roads, our bridges, our public spaces, and things of that nature.

John wanted any new tax revenue to focus on evidence-based, strategic investments. Like Mary, he was concerned about what the revenue was earmarked for. Additionally, he sought data from county officials dem-onstrating that how they proposed spending new revenue had succeeded in other local jurisdictions. John wanted officials to prioritize investments with the greatest positive collateral effects—that is, investments that could increase the capacity of public services or private amenities. Overall, he evinced a belief that increased public spending had the potential to yield greater private investment that would improve the quality of life in Prince George's.

A final example is Melanie, a married Black woman with children who lived outside of the beltway in an upper-middle-class neighborhood in central Prince George's County. Her children initially attended public school. But when she became dissatisfied with the public schools, she decided to homeschool her children. She described the conditions under which she would consider consenting to tax increases:

> I think we pay a fair amount. I think we could possibly pay more. I would probably, maybe, be open to that if they were absolutely doing what they were supposed to be doing with the money. So I think the amount of tax we're paying right now, I'm good. I'm good with that . . . think making me pay more and I'm fighting the county left and right, no. So I will be open to paying more, if I thought we were getting our money's worth. I'm like, "What are you doing with the money now?"

Melanie evinced a deep reluctance to pay more in taxes but was still open to the idea. She was concerned that county officials might not spend the money the way she wanted them to and that the mechanisms for residents to hold county officials accountable for how the government allocated funds were insufficient. Melanie did not want to be "fighting the county left and right" regarding her public goods and services priorities. In her interview, she discussed the challenges she encountered in the public school system that eventually led her to homeschool her children. Like John, Melanie wanted a return on investment, indicators that she was "getting [her] money's worth" from paying additional taxes. And like Mary, she was concerned that new revenue would not be spent in ways she desired.

Overall, Prince George's residents are not necessarily opposed to paying more in taxes. But most do want to retain control over any tax and fee increases, and they want to decide how any new revenue is spent. This stance indicates that Black middle-class Prince Georgians are seeking neither "small government" nor limited government capacity. Rather, they are concerned about how revenue would be spent and seek tools for ensuring that government officials' spending priorities match their own. Some residents' openness to raising taxes, albeit with caveats, suggests that county officials seeking to raise taxes and/or to repeal TRIM and other tax restrictions need to focus on building public trust in their decision-making regarding investments in public goods and services.

Prince George's County residents' dissatisfaction with the quality of public goods and services and their lack of confidence in county officials' capacity to improve them are interrelated, like the strands of a braid. One strand of concern is about decision-making around the public goods and services that are prioritized for new funding. Another strand is skepticism regarding bureaucratic capacity to deliver public goods and services and to do so efficiently. And the third strand centers on the ethical behavior of elected officials.

For the first strand, voters' desire to shape the prioritization of funding for public goods and services, residents have several options. They can petition their council representatives and the county executive's office by contacting officials' staffs and testifying at policy and budget hearings. They can also decide who to elect and re-elect to office. But, to be sure, these options do not provide direct control over spending decisions.

Regarding the second strand, bureaucratic effectiveness and efficiency, the public's experience of government agencies often disappoints them. In chapter 3, which captures how the fiscal year 2018 budget was allocated and the trade-offs that decision-makers made between public goods and services, I discuss the severe staffing shortages faced by many county agencies. Insufficient civil servant labor usually translates into reduced quality of service to the public. For instance, with too few people answering 3-1-1 calls, residents wait longer to speak to someone about non-emergency issues in their neighborhoods and often wait weeks or months for their issues to be resolved.

Regarding the last strand, the ethical behavior of elected officials, certain high-profile cases in Prince George's County, including one in which a county executive was convicted of malfeasance in 2011, seemingly confirm residents' suspicions about the county government's lack of capacity to steward their tax dollars wisely.[82] But there is no indication from government or media reports that government corruption is pervasive in Prince George's County. Based on my observations, the county navigates challenges that are typical of large governing bodies, most of which will have a few individuals on staff who engage in wrongdoing. Bureaucratic agencies, the organizations that deliver public goods and services, are complex institutions. Agencies are responsible for equitable distribution of public goods and services across the county, the efficiency of goods and services delivery, and thorough and consistent enforcement of county regulations. The public's perception of what causes the county government to underperform in these areas often does not correspond to the root causes.

During my fieldwork, council members demonstrated great care in crafting laws and in carrying out agency oversight. The refrain the council chair and vice chair stated during dozens of work sessions to amend bills to reflect the feedback of residents, businesses, and experts on proposed legislation was: "measure twice and cut once." In his interview, the council chair noted that he assiduously incorporates voter education into his town hall and other meetings so that residents understand the basis of his decisions. As he put it: "I'd rather underpromise and overdeliver." When I observed a luncheon he gave for seniors at an assisted living facility, he peppered his remarks with statistics regarding the trajectory of Prince George's revenue and the logics he and his fellow council members used to determine public goods and services expenditures. Other council members, when hosting town halls or resident "meet and greets," took similar steps to educate residents about the constraints that county leaders faced as they allocated the budget.

Overall, Prince George's residents hold county officials accountable for matters that are outside of the control of their leaders. Yet, like most middle-class Americans, irrespective of race, they expect to have consistently high-quality public goods and services. The fundamental difference between Black middle-class and White middle-class jurisdictions is that they do not have the *same conditions* for garnering sufficient revenue for maintaining and improving public goods and services without raising taxes. Most importantly, majority-White jurisdictions can generally rely on tax bases that expand more quickly.

Under the current political economy arrangements of metropolitan areas, a tax base expands when the following factors are present in a local jurisdiction: a disproportionately greater share of the region's upper-middle-class residents; a disproportionately lower share of the region's moderate- and low-income residents; commercial investment in expanding industries that attract upper-middle-class workers, such as medical and technology-focused firms; and finally, a disproportionate share of the region's White residents. White-majority space garners a premium from banks, mortgage lenders, appraisers, and other institutions and actors simply for being occupied by White people, indicating the enduring role of the exclusion-extraction 2-step.[83]

Prince Georgians' Meaning-Making amid Revenue Constraints

Middle-class Black Americans rightly wonder, in colloquial language, "Why can't we have nice things too?" The "too" of that question reflects the perception of affluent Black people, as they move around the DC region, that other counties provide more to their residents. Prince Georgians' frustration with their government sometimes translates into beliefs that their officials are less competent or even corrupt. But there is no evidence that this is the case. African Americans, given the centuries-long history of White domination and anti-Black racism, enact mental strategies for persisting despite US political and economic systems that were never designed to enable them to thrive.

An adage capturing this perspective is "We'll make a way out of no way." And when Black officials fail to "make a way," they are held responsible by their constituents for structural conditions outside of their control. That is, middle-class Black Americans take White domination and anti-Black racism as a "given" of American society and expect their elected officials to be savvy enough to overcome the inevitable political and economic constraints. In other words, Black people effectively say: "There has never been a time when African Americans have *not* experienced systemic discrimination, so why haven't you anticipated it and found ways to overcome it?"

During my interviews with residents, the fact that Prince George's is a majority-Black *and* middle-class county usually came up as a point of pride among respondents. At the same time, residents I spoke to sought to explain why the quality of life in Prince George's lagged that of neighboring counties with fewer Black residents and more White residents. But few Prince Georgians I spoke to, whether formally or informally, evinced knowledge of how racial capitalism and anti-Black racism create unique financial challenges for Prince George's, relative to other counties in the DC region. Certainly, Prince George's officials are accountable for doing the most they can within their authority, but much of what ails the county is beyond their influence, let alone control. As I discuss in the conclusion, there are short-, medium-, and long-term steps that Prince Georgians—and all Americans—can take to create governance structures designed for all Americans to meet their material needs.

In the final analysis, even if Prince Georgians were to tax themselves more, the additional revenue necessary to address decades of under-investment in the county would be far greater than what can be generated through increased local taxes alone. Black Americans—as individuals and as members of households, neighborhoods, and local jurisdictions—have never received their fair share of government and private investment. This underinvestment has had the downstream effect of leaving Prince George's County in need of billions of dollars in additional revenue to both make up for underinvestment and attain parity with majority-White jurisdictions. In other words, Prince Georgians cannot tax themselves out of anti-Black policies and racial capitalism. In the next section, I show that Prince George's self-imposed tax generation constraints combine with those externally imposed through Maryland law and private actors to intensify the county's budget pressures.

External Structural Constraints on Prince George's Budget

The Prince George's County Blue Ribbon Commission on the Structural Deficit issued a report in 2017 identifying several factors that might cause the county to take in less revenue than what it needs to spend to maintain and improve county public goods and services.[84] Budget shortfalls were predicted to start as early as fiscal year 2018, with deficits growing larger in out-years. These funding gaps—if not filled by tax base expansion, tax rate increases, or funds transfers from the federal government or Maryland—would lead to Prince George's officials cutting or reducing public goods and services provision.

The Blue Ribbon Commission found that six factors are the most consequential for the county budget: (1) a protracted recovery from the Great Recession of 2009–2011; (2) reductions in state and federal transfers; (3) a commitment to make up for recession-related cuts in county employee salaries and benefits; (4) the need to compensate for state reductions in contributions to the county employee pension plan; (5) increased debt service, or interest, on bonds and other borrowing; and (6) pressure from bond rating agencies to increase funding for the Risk Management Fund (or "rainy day fund" for emergency expenses).[85] Prince George's County's bond rating in 2018 was AAA, the highest level. County leaders are committed to maintaining this status, which affords them the lowest interest rate on bonds. Taken together, these six fiscal challenges are dimensions of converging fiscal constraints, as each one is embedded in anti-Black policies and/or racial capitalism.

County Employee Pensions

Painting the full fiscal picture requires considering the county's financial obligations beyond the provision of public goods and services. One of those obligations is pension payments for retired county employees. When the council deliberated over the 2018 fiscal year budget, Prince George's Office of Management and Budget (OMB) noted systemic concerns regarding the county's contribution to its pension funds. The state of Maryland, like many states across the country, has been contributing less to these funds and requiring local governments to make up the difference to keep the plans solvent.

At a hearing where Prince George's OMB senior officials testified about the solvency of pension funds and workers' compensation funds (revenue set aside for county employees injured during activities related to their jobs), both these officials and the county council expressed concerns about Prince George's ability to meet the funds' obligations over the next five years and beyond:[86]

> COUNCIL MEMBER: My big question is—we've been talking very much about workers' compensation. We saw charts on [the pension fund] and our ability to cover our pensions. Do we do long-term forecasting?

> OMB OFFICIAL: Yes, that's reflected in the deficit number—starting with the FY 2018 approved budget, part of our spending affordability process. We do that for expenditures and revenues.

> COUNCIL MEMBER: I'm sure that gets us to a solution for risk management and workers' compensation. . . . There's a really big item on the table—in terms of how we're addressing workers' compensation. We do not do a centralized system, and that's costing us. Are you triggering conversations? There are some red flags here, and I'm not sure we're positioning ourselves well.

> OMB OFFICIAL: At this point, we're just recovering from the recession. We will put in $20 million. The OMB director sits on the

pension boards. We're considering changes, including with collective bargaining, decreases in fringe benefits.

COUNCIL MEMBER: I'm not convinced we're being assertive enough on workers' compensation. You institute a plan and don't realize gains until three to five years. We're not going to be able to sustain this. Same with the pension. I do have severe concerns about what the data is starting to show. It's interesting to me how everything gets very segmented. There are these other driving forces.

OMB OFFICIAL: For the pensions, the executive has made changes. We should see some stabilization soon. But with regard to workers' compensation, that's been on a downward spiral for years.

Faced with the looming insolvency of pension and workers' compensation funds, Prince George's County may soon endure even tighter financial constraints. Statutorily required spending is mandatory. That is, unless laws are changed, the county must make payments to people who qualify. If the retirement and workers' compensation funds do not have sufficient revenue, then payments owed to retirees and injured people would be deducted from the general fund, the primary fund through which agencies receive revenue for public goods and services provision. And reductions in agency appropriations would likely compromise the quality of public goods and services even more.

Furthermore, credit rating agencies would likely interpret insolvent retirement and workers' compensation funds as a sign of systemic fiscal distress in the county. They evaluate the financial health of local governments for the purpose of letting bonds and would be concerned that non-self-sustaining pension and workers' compensation funds may undermine the ability of Prince George's County to pay bondholders in full. Prince George's County is not the only local jurisdiction grappling with keeping workers' compensation and pension funds solvent. But because the county is majority-Black, it navigates more hurdles in generating revenue.

Bonds

Bonds are usually let to pay for major infrastructure projects, such as school buildings, bridges and roads, and firehouses. These projects cost hundreds of millions of dollars—too much for a county to allocate out of one year's budget. To pay for these projects over time, usually over ten to twenty years, counties issue bonds through municipal bond markets. Local jurisdictions receive the best interest rate from lenders if they maintain a AAA bond rating.

Asked during his interview about the significance of counties' bond ratings for a county's ability to invest in infrastructure, a senior Prince George's County official who focuses on economic development said:

> It doesn't take long once you're elected to realize that the most important thing for a manager or county executive is to make sure that you have a AAA rating. And that's true for Prince George's County, Westchester County, or any county in the United States. Because Wall Street's looking at your bonds, your borrowing power, and if you go down in your AAA rating, like your credit rating, your personal credit rating, if you have a poor credit rating, you're going to get charged more on interest because you're a risk versus if you're a good credit rating, then you don't pay as much.

Bond rating agencies, such as Moody's and Fitch, assess county governments' financial status based on several criteria. Moody's and Fitch are particularly concerned about two things: the level of debt the county is already carrying, and the amount the county government has in its reserve fund.[87] From lenders' perspectives, having too much debt could mean that when the bond period ends, the county will not have enough money to pay all of its creditors. Insufficient reserves could mean that if there is an economic downturn, or the county otherwise experiences financial challenges, the jurisdiction may not have an adequate budgetary cushion to meet all of its financial obligations.

Prince George's County's tax generation restrictions, which were explained earlier in this chapter, hurt the county's ability to demonstrate fiscal fitness. Rating agencies interpret these measures as limiting government officials' capacity to respond to budget shortfalls by increasing taxes. As a result, Prince George's must show it has other means for ensuring that bond obligations will be met. One of the primary ways the county does this is by keeping a robust reserve fund. Consequently, Prince George's officials are reluctant to use the rainy day fund for its intended purpose: to offset shortfalls in revenue by drawing from the fund to maintain the quality of public goods and services. Hence, the fund is largely a tool to signal to bondholders that the county prioritizes bondholder interests above those of residents.

Thus far, this chapter has discussed evidence for policy and political economy arrangements that work against Prince George's County's fiscal interests. But there is evidence that some state-level policies have helped the county overcome the effects of converging fiscal constraints and relative regional burden. It is to that evidence that I now turn.

Bi-County Public Goods Funding Structures That Overcome Racial and Fiscal Subordination

In addition to the county government in Prince George's, two other bodies wield significant authority over the county's public goods and services: the Washington Suburban Sanitary Commission (WSSC), which controls water and sewer systems, and the Maryland–National Capital Park and Planning Commission (MNCPPC), which plans subdivisions, recommends zoning classifications, issues building permits, and purchases, develops, and maintains park lands. Maryland created WSSC in 1918 and MNCPPC in 1927.[88]

Both of these commissions serve Prince George's and Montgomery Counties and are unique entities within the state of Maryland; there are no comparable governmental bodies in the state. In effect, these commissions acknowledge individual counties' limitations in providing consistent, reliable public goods and services in contexts where the best results stem from economies of scale and dedicated funding streams, among other factors. Both WSSC and MNCPPC have won national awards for quality. These governing bodies show that state ingenuity in governance and funding mechanisms can mitigate the relative regional burden endured by majority-Black counties.

When Maryland established WSSC and MNCPPC, it created a structure through which Prince George's and Montgomery Counties buttress each other's capacities. The two counties share risks, rewards, and costs and spread them out over a larger population than either of the counties could manage on their own. Both WSSC and MNCPPC have infrastructure-intensive responsibilities—from laying pipes and maintaining water treatment centers (WSSC) to maintaining dozens of recreation facilities and trails (MNCPPC). Thus, when each body lets bonds, its support by larger populations reduces its risk of default. Bond markets reward this lower risk with lower interest rates for borrowing. Furthermore, WSSC and MNCPPC save money for both counties because they can purchase inputs related to service delivery, such as water treatment chemicals, at bulk rates. The commissions also use civil service staff efficiently by reducing each county's need to hire its own staff.

At the same time, it is important to acknowledge that WSSC and MNCPPC have particular advantages compared to other public goods and services. First, WSSC and MNCPPC have authority to charge residents fees for their services. Generally, agencies do not have this authority. Indeed, the two agencies consuming the greatest share of most local governments' budgets, K-12 schools and police, cannot charge residents fees for the core services they provide.

Second, both commissions are governed by a board of commissioners, with half of their members appointed by each county's executive and approved by each county's council. The county councils approve these commissions' budgets, which consist of dedicated fees built into local government tax assessments, alongside what the commissions charge residents directly as they use water, parks, zoning and building permits, and recreation services. Additionally, WSSC and MNCPPC can let bonds separately from the Prince George's and Montgomery County governments.

Although WSSC and MNCPPC show the promise of regional solutions for delivering public goods and services, regional strategies are still constrained by federalism. Recall that each state confers authority on its local jurisdictions. And there are few regional entities that govern, or otherwise coordinate, state and local jurisdictions within regions, with the exception of some public transit and port authority organizations. As such, creating agencies like WSSC and MNCPPC is possible within a version of regionalism that is still confined to a specific state. For instance, when WSSC was created, given the flow of river and stream systems within Maryland and DC, it would have been most effective to create a water and sewer system that included Prince George's and Montgomery Counties and DC.

WSSC's and MNCPPC's ability to provide high-quality public goods and services demonstrates that state-county cooperation, rather than competition, improves the quality of life for a broader swath of people in a region. In Prince George's and Montgomery Counties today, each county's council and executive, and the state delegates and senators who represent these counties, are invested in WSSC and MNCPPC thriving. Thus, when needs arise, investments are less likely to be parochial and are more likely to focus on system-wide maintenance in ways that benefit both counties. Finally, because financial power—at the individual, household, and neighborhood levels—translates into political power, Prince George's County's interests are carried alongside those of its Whiter, wealthier neighbor, Montgomery County. This confers political influence on Prince George's County that it would not otherwise have.

What would happen were Maryland, and the DC region more broadly, to cooperate more in public goods and services delivery? For instance, imagine what would occur if the political boundaries separating Prince George's and Montgomery Counties were dissolved. Because local jurisdictions derive authority from state constitutions and laws, such a change is possible. Without political borders, majority- and plurality-White local jurisdictions would lose their primary tool for hoarding material resources. No longer would they so readily enjoy a market-value premium for White space. And the converse is true too—that premium would no longer be built on subsidization from Black spaces.

That is not to say that political borders are the only tool that White Americans have to concentrate their resources in specific geographic areas. Both places with political authority (counties and municipalities) and places without political authority (neighborhoods) wield considerable political influence because both concentrate wealth and other material resources in specific locations. Indeed, some scholars have noted that significant resource-hoarding happens within counties, indicating that White people use multiple mechanisms to cluster resources in specific places and take steps to prevent resources from being redistributed elsewhere.[89]

Still, I highlight local political boundaries because they are a particularly potent tool for material resource hoarding. For instance, not only are local jurisdictions and their borders recognized by states as distinct spaces, but pathways for conveying that official recognition are pre-established, enabling local jurisdictions to receive and petition for more funding, whether for building K-12 schools or maintaining roads. When states allocate funding for public goods and services, they often create funding formulas to determine how resources will be apportioned. Decisions about the amount of revenue appropriated to states' local jurisdictions is a core activity of state legislatures. Therefore, local jurisdictions have explicit channels through which they can pursue their interests. Moreover, the governments of local jurisdictions have staff dedicated to managing the interface with state governments.

Local governments do not just pursue what matters to them individually. They also organize to act collectively in effort to present a unified agenda to their state in ways that protect and expand local jurisdiction authority, from taxing authority to zoning authority. In Maryland, the body that represents counties is the Maryland Association of Counties (MACo).

Finally, federal courts have reinforced local jurisdictions' ability to hoard resources. During the period of contestation over school desegregation measures in the 1970s, in cases such as *San Antonio Independent School District v. Rodriguez* (1972), courts ruled that local jurisdictions cannot be forced by their state to redistribute revenue generated through property taxes because such action violates people's property rights.[90] These court decisions limit states' ability to distribute a primary source of local government revenue, property taxes. In Maryland, local jurisdictions also receive income tax revenue, alongside the state, but this authority is less common across other states.

The social forces of anti-Black policies and racial capitalism, as they have evolved since the founding of the United States, have deprived Black Americans—at the individual, household, neighborhood, and local government levels—of the conditions necessary for sound financial footing, irrespective of class status. This chapter has shown that from the point at which Prince George's transitioned to majority-Black in the 1990s to the present, the county has had to fight for a fiscal foothold within DC-area political economy arrangements, as well as those created by Maryland and private actors. In the next chapter, I highlight Prince George's County's unique fiscal constraints by comparing its fiscal fitness to that of two neighboring jurisdictions with smaller Black and larger White populations—Montgomery County, Maryland, and Fairfax County, Virginia.

CHAPTER 2

Converging Fiscal Constraints and Relative Regional Burden in the Washington, DC, Metropolitan Area

THE PREVIOUS CHAPTER explained the national (macro-level) and regional (meso-level) social processes shaping the fiscal capacity of Prince George's County and majority-Black jurisdictions more broadly. This chapter explains in greater depth the socioeconomic factors underpinning my two meso-level theories—converging fiscal constraints and relative regional burden. These theories identify the metropolitan-area political economy arrangements in the DC metropolitan area and the impact of these arrangements on the financial capacities and propensities of the region's households, neighborhoods, and local jurisdictions. The capacities I highlight are access to money and wealth-generating assets. The propensities I discuss center on the ability, or lack of ability, to leverage material resources to achieve and maintain financial health.

Local jurisdictions long inhabited by affluent White Americans generally have the greatest concentrations of material resources and benefit from the highest-performing public goods and services because these jurisdictions have larger and expanding tax bases. Prince George's County became the destination for the DC area's Black middle class in part because, while the county was majority-White in the 1970s, the majority of the population was lower-middle and working-class, whereas Montgomery and Fairfax Counties were majority-White and most residents were middle- and upper-middle-class. The high cost of living in affluent White jurisdictions insulates

https://doi.org/10.7758/bwmi8829.7867

them from a proportionate share of the region's moderate- and low-income households moving into their neighborhoods. While all local jurisdictions within the DC region have a cost of living above the national average, moderate- and low-income residents largely live in the *relatively* most affordable jurisdiction.

Interdependence Patterns in DC Local Jurisdictions, World War II to the Present

> We're behind, we start the race thirty years behind Montgomery County, thirty years behind everybody else. We start the race and we're different. They're driving a different kind of car than we are. They have a more monolithic reality than we do. We have a more multiethnic reality.
>
> —Prince George's County council member

In the United States, the majorities of all racial and ethnic groups live in suburbia. But there is significant variation across suburban jurisdictions in terms of the quality of life they offer residents, as manifested in public goods and services and in private amenities.[1] The patterns in the DC region are consistent with this national trend. My terms "converging fiscal constraints" and "relative regional burden" capture how the variation in the quality of public goods and services offered in Prince George's, Montgomery, and Fairfax Counties reflects the cumulative weight of the "exclusion extraction 2-step." By analyzing the per capita and per pupil spending in these three counties, I show how the economic trajectories of these jurisdictions are fundamentally interconnected. And I argue that this interdependence leads to Prince George's County *subsidizing* wealth accumulation in richer and Whiter DC-area jurisdictions.

In terms of population expansion, the DC metropolitan area is among the top five fastest-growing regions in the United States.[2] And the city of Washington has undergone intense gentrification across its neighborhoods, especially over the past twenty years. From 1970 to 2020, DC lost about sixty-one thousand Black residents and gained about fifty-four thousand White residents.[3] Most of the White people moving in have had median or higher incomes.[4] And many Black people have left DC because they can no longer afford the cost of living in the city.[5] The high number of Black people leaving the city of DC has had significant collateral consequences in other DC metropolitan-area jurisdictions, especially those with borders nearest to the District of Columbia. Displaced people have family and friends, employment, and other ties to geographic space. Thus, if they move for economic reasons, they usually seek a less expensive place to live that is proximate to their former home. And as noted, Prince George's County has the lowest cost of living among the counties contiguous with DC.

Population churn in the DC region has led to some jurisdictions garnering more tax revenue than others as people of different racial and class statuses sort into the region's jurisdictions, creating clusters of wealth or disadvantage in certain neighborhoods. As the council member quoted in the epigraph of this section states, there is considerable variation in the quality of life across DC-area local jurisdictions. Prince George's County, according to the council member, is "driving a different kind of car." The "different cars" are the economic conditions in each county that determine tax revenue generation capacity. Extending the analogy, some counties have four-cylinder engines in their "cars" and others have eight-cylinder engines. When counties press the gas pedal of economic growth, it is no surprise that the eight-cylinder cars win the race. Jurisdictions with more affluent households and greater commercial investment stand to collect more of the property and income tax revenue that enables them to invest in public goods and services. Moreover, present-day DC-area political economy arrangements reflect the cumulative effects of decades of population sorting and public and private investment patterns.

My research not only highlights interconnections between local jurisdictions within metropolitan areas but also shows the importance of specifically assessing the spillover effects in suburbia stemming from city-based gentrification. Metropolitan spaces are constellations of economic (and social) networks that include city-suburb and suburb-suburb relationships. I show that Prince George's location next to a city that is rapidly gentrifying makes the county more likely to absorb the displacement of moderate- and low-income residents priced out of gentrifying DC neighborhoods. Most studies on gentrification focus on one or a few neighborhoods. This study demonstrates the importance of examining how jurisdictions' embeddedness within regional economic processes leads to some jurisdictions gaining more economically than others owing to the racial and class composition of the dozens of neighborhoods within locales' borders.[6]

Because Prince George's County is geographically proximate to DC and is more affordable than the District, yet offers a similar set of social offerings, the county is the jurisdiction that bears the greatest fiscal burden as DC gentrifies. Prince George's shares the longest border with DC and is seamlessly connected to the city through subway and bus transit lines. The staffs and memberships of many organizations, such as churches, are drawn from neighborhoods that span the DC–Prince George's border. Increasing inflows of moderate- and low-income people from DC heighten Prince George's County's fiscal constraints because the jurisdiction continues to receive a greater share of the DC region's families who earn median or lower incomes and, on average, have a greater need for public goods and services. Inflows to Montgomery and Fairfax Counties, in contrast, include a greater share of upper-middle-class families.

Contemporary gentrification and neighborhood succession patterns are rooted in sociohistorical processes that took shape after World War II. In the 1950s, African Americans across the United States experienced significant displacement stemming from the construction connected to provisions of the Housing Act of 1949. One of those provisions established "Urban Renewal" programs. As Urban Renewal projects took shape across US cities and metropolitan areas, they were nicknamed "Negro Removal," owing to their disproportionate displacement of Black people.

Under Urban Renewal, city officials were empowered by federal law to determine whether neighborhoods were "blighted," defined as containing insufficient material conditions for habitability and/or economic growth potential.[7] Black neighborhoods were more likely than White neighborhoods to receive this categorization because they had endured the starkest levels of underinvestment by government and market institutions for the longest periods of time. Once neighborhoods were deemed "blighted," city officials had the right to use "imminent domain" to seize private properties for public use, such as highway construction.[8] Altogether the Urban Renewal Program displaced about 1.36 million individuals between 1950 and 1970. And about 60 percent of those displaced were non-White, when the non-White population was less than 20 percent of the US population.[9]

In Washington, DC, major construction projects were initiated not only in the name of Urban Renewal but also through the auspices of the District of Columbia Redevelopment Act of 1945.[10] One of the most significant postwar redevelopment sites was the Southwest DC waterfront and nearby neighborhoods. During this period, the Southeast and Southwest Freeways and Interstate 695 were built, connecting Virginia, DC, and Maryland.[11] In her book *Right to Suburbia*, planning scholar Willow Lung-Amam notes that

> the 1944 and 1956 Federal Highway Acts contributed massive federal funds to create a national interstate system. These acts prompted the NCPPC [National Capital Park and Planning Commission], headed by planner and avid segregationist Harland Bartholomew, along with powerful suburban stakeholders, including shopping center developer James Rouse, to adopt a regional plan in 1950. The plan called for a highway network radiating out from DC's core to promote decentralization. Between 1952 and 1972, thirteen major highways were constructed in the Baltimore-Washington area to serve its growing suburbs, including the Capital Beltway, which allowed suburbanites to bypass the city altogether. Many freeways displaced and divided long-standing Black communities.

Many of the people displaced from Southwest DC, and from elsewhere in the DC region, did not move back. Over the years of highway and other construction, many people, trying to stabilize their lives, relocated to other parts of the city or to DC-area suburbs, including Prince George's County. Redevelopment projects, like those just discussed, significantly shaped where racial and class groups could afford to live after World War II. These infusions of public and private investment set in motion differing, and often divergent, "economic engines" in different neighborhoods and local jurisdictions of the DC region.

Differing and divergent economic trajectories for neighborhoods and local jurisdictions within regions create a greater likelihood of a concentration of development benefits for some places and a greater share of development burdens for others. The jurisdictions that benefit most are those that attract and retain affluent White residents, who generally pay higher property and income taxes. Jurisdictions that benefit the least attract and retain economically distressed households, who generally pay less in taxes and usually have greater needs for public goods and services due to their material constraints.

Many of the moderate- and low-income households increasingly pushed out of DC move to the apartments in the inner ring of Prince George's County: the area between the DC line and the Interstate 95 Capital Beltway (see figure 1.1). Prince George's leaders often indicated that they under-stood their county's economic interdependence with DC. For instance, I frequently heard officials in informal settings jokingly refer to the part of the county along the DC border as "Ward 9," thus describing that portion of Prince George's as an extension of the city. Furthermore, Prince George's County sits next to the District's two most economically distressed wards—Wards 7 and 8.

The concentration of low-income households along the Prince George's–DC border stems from government and private investment decisions in the late 1970s and 1980s, when Prince George's County was still majority-White and White people held most elected positions. During those decades, most Black people moving into Prince George's were middle-class, but some were working-class or poor. Thus, the county needed to build new housing to accommodate White and Black working-class and poor households. But it was also clear that, within a decade or so, the county was likely to tran-sition to majority-Black. White Prince George's decision-makers approved the construction of low-rise, garden-style apartments consisting of three or four stories. Because these multi-family units were not high-rises, zoning laws did not require that they be constructed with the most durable materials, like brick. Most of these buildings were made with siding that deteriorates more quickly than brick.

In the ensuing decades, the racial and class composition along the DC–Prince George's border shifted from White working-class and poor residents to Black working-class and poor residents. These apartments were the most affordable places to live within a few miles of the DC border when compared to Montgomery and Fairfax Counties, which also share a border with DC. Because Prince George's apartments along the DC boundary line largely house people with moderate- or low-incomes, landlords have lim-ited financial incentive to invest significantly in the maintenance of their buildings, let alone to take steps to improve the quality of life for residents. Most of the apartment buildings are now over forty years old, and many are in need of significant repairs. As I explain in chapter 3, residents and county officials struggle to hold landlords accountable for providing hab-itable residences because the county government agency responsible for code enforcement is understaffed.

Montgomery County also experienced population growth during the 1970s and '80s, but responded differently than Prince George's. A higher proportion of apartment buildings along the Montgomery-DC border are brick high-rises, most of them ten stories or more. These buildings have attracted and retained residents from a wider range of socioeconomic and racial statuses, including White, Asian, and Latino middle-class people.

In his interview, a person who served as Prince George's chief budget officer and as chief of staff to then-governor Paris Glendening discussed the contrast between Prince George's County's and Montgomery County's development strategies during the 1970s:

> What you are right on is the presumption that now this redneck backwater town county was beginning to see this influx of [Black] folks in the region and in Prince George's specifically. And what they fail to understand is that instead of doing Montgomery or some other places where there would be a proliferation of estate or single-family homes, they allow basically because of, in my opinion, probably some visit at that time, political contributions, allow developers to build all of these apartments. So we end up having at one point more apartments than anybody else in the region. Now, the problem with that is when you got that kind of density and you might not have had them build, if you will, the top of the line because they weren't serious high-rise. So they were three- and four-story. So the quality of the work, therefore the longevity on it in some cases, wasn't there. And so you then had the turnover because in the initial wave of that there were Whites in those units, they got older, and that was the same upkeep, and then Blacks took it over, and because that was a cheaper place to live as they were rolling out of the District coming into the area.

According to this respondent, private investors' development strategies differed between Prince George's and Montgomery Counties in terms of the type and quality of the housing they built in inner-ring neighborhoods. And local and state officials enabled investors' plans to come to fruition through local zoning laws and state infrastructure investment and development incentives. In the 1970s, it was clear that Prince George's was likely to become majority-Black—and market and government officials effectively created conditions that reinforced this trajectory by investing more in Montgomery County.

Overall, Montgomery County and Maryland state officials worked to extend Montgomery's socioeconomic head start. As a result, many inner-ring apartment buildings in Montgomery County have been recently refurbished and building owners charge middle- and upper-middle-class residents higher rents, reinforcing Montgomery's tax generation capacity and thus the quality of its public goods and services. These state and local policy decisions are constitutive of political economy dynamics that create relative regional burden for Prince George's County. In the next section, I explain how relative regional burden can be measured by comparing per capita and per pupil spending in Prince George's, Montgomery, and Fairfax Counties.

Per Capita and Per Pupil Spending in Prince George's, Montgomery, and Fairfax Counties in Fiscal Year 2018

I begin by establishing that Prince George's County is a solidly middle-class local jurisdiction by comparing its socioeconomic indicators to those of Maryland and the United States as a whole. Table 2.1 shows that Prince George's County is solidly middle-class. The county's median household income is about $20,000 above the national median and virtually identical to Maryland's. Median home value in Prince George's is about $85,000 above the US median and about $12,000 below Maryland's. Residents of Prince George's County are also well educated: a slightly greater percentage of residents than the US average have received postsecondary education, though the share of well-educated Prince Georgians is about seven percentage points below the average percentage for all residents of Maryland, one of the wealthiest and most educated states in the country.[12]

When Prince George's is compared with Montgomery and Fairfax Counties, however, Prince George's County's economic disadvantage is striking. The DC region is majority-minority with a White plurality; White Americans account for about 47 percent of the population. But racial and ethnic groups are not evenly distributed across local jurisdictions, nor are household-, community-, and neighborhood-level poverty and wealth.[13] Examining racial group settlement patterns in the DC region at a granular level, including by census tract and neighborhood, indicates that "segregated diversity" is the primary pattern.[14]

Table 2.2 shows that in 2018 both Montgomery and Fairfax, compared to Prince George's, had almost double the percentage of residents with a

Table 2.1 Comparison of Prince George's County, Maryland, and the United States, 2019

	Prince George's County	Maryland	United States
Total population	909,327	6,045,680	328,239,523
Race and ethnicity			
Black (not Hispanic/Latino)	64.4%	31.1%	13.4%
White (not Hispanic/Latino)	12.3%	50.0%	60.1%
Hispanic/Latino (any race)	19.5%	10.6%	18.5%
Income and wealth			
Median household income	$84,920	$84,805	$62,843
Median home value (owner-occupied)	$302,800	$314,800	$217,500
Median gross rent	$1,475	$1,392	$1,062
Persons in poverty	8.7%	9.3%	11.4%
Educational attainment			
College degree or higher	33.1%	40.2%	32.1%
High school diploma or GED	86.7%	90.2%	88.0%

Source: Simms 2023. Reprinted with permission.

Table 2.2 Comparison of Prince George's, Montgomery, and Fairfax Counties, 2019

	Prince George's	Montgomery	Fairfax
Total population	909,327	1,050,688	1,147,532
Race and ethnicity			
Black (not Hispanic/Latino)	64.4%	20.1%	10.6%
White (not Hispanic/Latino)	12.3%	42.9%	50.0%
Latino (any race)	19.5%	20.1%	16.5%
Income and wealth			
Median household income	$84,920	$108,820	$124,831
Median home value (owner-occupied)	$302,800	$484,900	$563,100
Median rent	$1,475	$1,768	$1,881
Persons in poverty	8.7%	7.3%	6.0%
Educational attainment			
College degree or higher	33.1%	58.9%	61.6%
High school diploma or GED	86.7%	91.0%	92.5%

Source: Simms 2023. Reprinted with permission.

college degree or other advanced postsecondary education. Median household annual income in Montgomery was about $24,000 higher than in Prince George's. In Fairfax, it was about $40,000 more than in Prince George's. Median home value in Montgomery was $182,000 more than in Prince George's, and Fairfax's median home value was $260,000 greater. Also significant is that Montgomery and Fairfax Counties had much smaller Black populations. Montgomery had about one-third as many Black residents as Prince George's, and Fairfax about one-sixth as many. Comparing Prince George's to its neighboring counties highlights the underlying economic conditions shaping the three counties' tax bases, most notably, residents' incomes and home values. These disparities reflect that Montgomery and Fairfax are less responsible for navigating the fallout of anti-Black policies and racial capitalism than Prince George's.

The economic and social conditions creating fiscal disparities are evident visually. The four maps in figures 2.1 to 2.4 depict the class and race distribution of four local jurisdictions in the DC metropolitan area: Prince George's, Montgomery, and Fairfax Counties, and the District of Columbia.

Let us interpret what the maps depict. Class and race variables are binary: Black versus non-Black, and median income or higher versus lower than

Figure 2.1 The DC Region, 1990

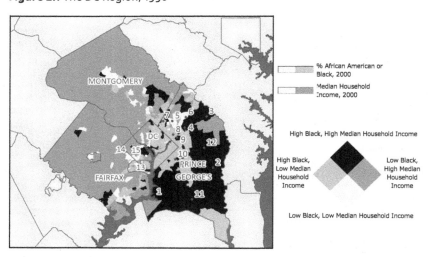

Source: Map by Dr. Dirk Kinsey.

Figure 2.2 The DC Region, 2000

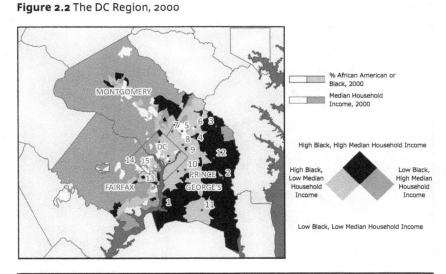

Source: Map by Dr. Dirk Kinsey.

Figure 2.3 The DC Region, 2010

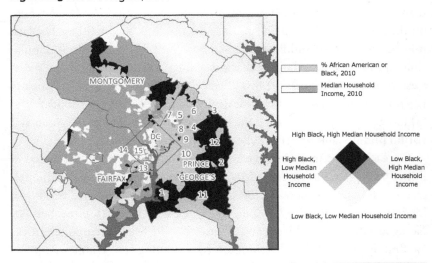

Source: Map by Dr. Dirk Kinsey.

Figure 2.4 The DC Region, 2018

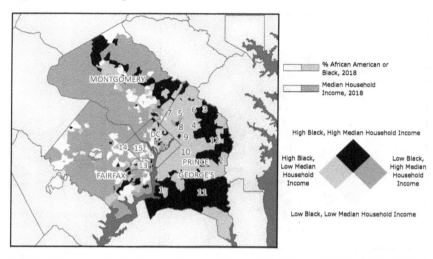

Source: Map by Dr. Dirk Kinsey.

median income. The maps would be difficult to interpret were I to show more than two overlapping variables. There are four population cluster categories on these maps: (1) high Black population and high income (largely Black middle- and upper-middle-class neighborhoods); (2) high Black population and low income (largely Black working-class and economically distressed neighborhoods); (3) low Black population, low income (mostly Latino working-class and economically distressed neighborhoods); and (4) low Black population, high income (mostly White and some Asian and Latino middle- and upper middle-class neighborhoods).

On each of the maps in the four figures, twelve places are numbered in Prince George's County. Some locations are incorporated areas, or municipalities, and some are not. The seven municipalities are numbered as follows: Bladensburg (7), Bowie (2), Cheverly (8), College Park (4), Greenbelt (5), New Carrollton (3), and Upper Marlboro (10). The five unincorporated areas are Brandywine (11), Fort Washington (1), Kettering (12), Langley Park (6), and Suitland (9). In addition to Prince George's locations, three places in Virginia are included to orient you to other counties and municipalities in the DC region: city of Alexandria (13), city of Falls Church (14), and Arlington County (15).

Maryland municipalities offer residents an additional layer of political representation. For instance, municipalities sometimes petition for Maryland state resources over and above what the county distributes to them. Some municipalities also provide additional public goods and services, such as a police force. Of the municipalities labeled, two of them, Bowie and Greenbelt, share zoning authority with Prince George's County. (The other municipality, not shown, that has zoning authority is Laurel, which sits just north of College Park.) Overall, however, the Prince George's County government still retains the most local political authority. Notably, none of the municipalities have their own school system. Public schools are generally local governments' largest budget expenditure and the public service with the greatest impact on homes' market value.

Starting with 2018, one of the years I conducted my ethnographic research, notice that Prince George's County has by far the greatest number of neighborhoods with Black middle-class majorities. (For the purposes of this analysis, "neighborhoods" are roughly US census blocks.) There are pockets of Black middle-class people in DC, Fairfax, and Montgomery Counties, but Prince George's County is clearly the Black middle-class haven among local jurisdictions contiguous with the District of Columbia.

Second, notice that Prince George's County's Black middle class is almost entirely in the county's outer ring—that is, beyond the I-95 Capital Beltway. Conversely, people with lower incomes are concentrated inside of the beltway. The 2018 map (figure 2.4) also indicates that Fairfax and Montgomery Counties mostly consist of neighborhoods with households earning median or higher incomes and that they have non-Black majorities. Most of these neighborhoods are majority-White, -Asian, or -Latino.

Observe in the other three figures—maps of the DC region in 2010, 2000, and 1990—that the clustering of Black middle-class people was already substantial in 1990, the point at which Prince George's tipped from majority-White and working-class to majority-Black and middle-class. The Black and middle-class share of the Prince George's population expanded considerably between 1990 and 2010, but shrank between 2010 and 2018. This contraction probably reflects fallout from the Great Recession of 2009–2011, given that the recession precipitated a home foreclosure crisis that harmed middle-class Black neighborhoods disproportionately. Later in this chapter, I explain the fiscal consequences of the Great Recession for Prince George's County.

From 1990 to 2018, DC and Fairfax and Montgomery Counties maintained some Black middle-class neighborhoods, though these neighborhoods had smaller populations and there were fewer of them, when compared to Prince George's County. By 2018, there were even fewer affluent Black neighborhoods in DC. The figures also show that DC and Montgomery and Fairfax Counties experienced steady growth in their non-Black and high-income populations from the 2000s forward. On the other side of the class continuum, the figures indicate that households with below-median incomes were increasingly concentrated in Prince George's County. These working-class and low-income communities are mostly between Prince George's border with DC and the I-95 Capital Beltway. Except for Langley Park in northern Prince George's, which is majority-Latino, these neighborhoods are majority-Black.

Altogether, figures 2.1 to 2.4 show that, from 1990 through 2018, the city of DC lost thousands of Black households across the class spectrum, while the city's share of non-Black and high-income households, most of them White, increased. DC retains a sizable Black working-class and low-income population in part because of its public housing complexes. The city offers housing vouchers to residents, and other federally supported financial assistance is available to families with below-median household income. Families without these supports, however, such as those on wait-lists for these programs, are at risk of being priced out of the city as the cost of living—particularly rent—continues to increase precipitously. Many of the families displaced from DC will move to Prince George's, as it is the most affordable place to live among the local jurisdictions that border the District. And as already noted, Metro buses and subways run seamlessly between Prince George's and DC, enabling people to stay connected to their former communities.

These figures equip us to see that Prince George's County is indeed a solidly middle-class jurisdiction. At the same time, Prince George's has been responsible over the past thirty years for a greater and greater share of the DC region's working-class and economically poor residents because the cost of living in other parts of the region has increased faster than in Prince George's. The primary fiscal implication is that Prince George's, with fewer affluent residents contributing tax revenue and a greater share of high-needs residents to serve than are found in Whiter, wealthier counties, is experiencing greater demand on its budget.

Table 2.3 Per Capita and Per Pupil Spending and Student Poverty in Prince George's, Montgomery, and Fairfax Counties, Fiscal Year 2018

	Prince George's	Montgomery	Fairfax
Spending per capita	$4,263	$5,187	$6,616
Spending per pupil	$14,322	$15,499	$14,813
Low-income students	61%	34%	29%

Source: Author's compilation.

To crystallize the fiscal capacity disparity between DC region suburban counties in dollars, I compare the fiscal year 2018 per capita and per pupil spending in Prince George's, Montgomery, and Fairfax Counties. These spending levels are proxies for how much each jurisdiction invested in their public goods and services that year. I calculate per capita spending by dividing each county's total budget, including all sources—what they generate through their own taxing authority plus transfers from state and federal governments—by the number of residents in each jurisdiction.[15]

Table 2.3 shows that both Montgomery and Fairfax Counties spend more than Prince George's per person annually—Montgomery County about $1,000 more and Fairfax County about $2,300 more. Although these numbers may not seem significant in and of themselves, when they are multiplied by about one million residents—roughly the number of people in each of the three counties—the orders of magnitude of difference in public spending is striking: about $924 million more in Montgomery County than in Prince George's, and over $2.3 billion more in Fairfax County. In percentage terms, Montgomery County spends about 18 percent more than Prince George's County on public goods and services and Fairfax County spends about 36 percent more.

Having another $1 billion or more to spend on public goods and services each year is consequential for timely maintenance of public goods and services and creates conditions for improving quality still further. Additionally, because Fairfax and Montgomery Counties have more affluent residents and fewer moderate- and low-income residents than Prince George's, they experience less demand for public goods and services. The gaps in public goods and services investment and demand are dimensions of the relative regional burden that Prince George's carries for the DC metropolitan area.

Table 2.3 shows a similar logic applies to per pupil spending across the three counties. In 2018, Prince George's had about 130,000 students,

Montgomery County about 160,000, and Fairfax County about 190,000. Montgomery County spent about $1,000 more per student than Prince George's and Fairfax about $500 more.[16] When these amounts are multiplied by the number of young people in these counties' school systems, the additional revenue is about $190 million more for Montgomery and about $95 million more for Fairfax.

As shown in this table and discussed further in chapter 4, what is most consequential for public school expenditures is that Prince George's serves twice as many students from economically distressed households. Students from low-income households usually need more resources than students from high-income households to excel academically. Therefore, schools serving concentrations of low-income students are generally more expensive to operate and place more pressure on local jurisdictions' budgets. State and federal transfers offset some of Prince George's higher costs, but not all of them.

Per capita and per pupil spending, combined, reveal the downstream cumulative effects of the exclusion-extraction 2-step and anti-Black policies, as well as how these cascading consequences shape local government tax revenue generation and budget expenditures. Because Prince George's County is home to a greater share of the DC region's economically distressed residents, it, in effect, subsidizes Montgomery and Fairfax Counties' budgets. The revenue Montgomery and Fairfax Counties would have to allocate to high-needs residents can be apportioned to other purposes, including investing in their already higher quality public goods and services.

In other words, while public choice theorists argue that White affluent suburban households and businesses tend to locate in places with lower taxation and are generally averse to high taxes, especially if the revenue is used to support lower-income households' needs, I argue that this theory misses the conditions enabling White wealthy residents and businesses to "have their (fiscal conservatism) cake and eat it too." That is, White elites can levy low tax rates on themselves and still yield sufficient revenue for high-quality public goods and services because they leverage political borders to cordon themselves off from responsibility for the needs of moderate- and low-income households.[17] A thorough examination of White Americans' tax rate preferences, and the quality of life these rates support in majority-White jurisdictions, must consider the asymmetrical economic relationships between majority-White and majority-Black local jurisdictions within metropolitan areas. Two of my theory contributions—converging fiscal constraints and relative regional burden—fill this analytical need.

The per capita spending and per pupil spending I discuss here are consistent with fiscal capacity measures created in 2021 by the National Academy of Sciences Commission on Reimagining Our Economy (CORE).[18] CORE measures the well-being offered by counties across the United States. The commission explicitly chose to focus on well-being, rather than on market growth, the more common measure. After all, an expanding economy in and of itself does not necessarily translate into improved quality of life for the majority of Americans. And when quality of life does improve substantially, the degree of improvement varies by race, class, and geography.

CORE's quality of life score is based on four measures: economic security, economic opportunity, health, and political voice. The economic security measure is most closely related to my analysis of local governments' public goods and services provision. Economic security is evaluated based on the following indicators: a credit bureau index, which reflects household income, and disposable income, savings, assets, debts, and measures of credit behavior. Economic security also captures whether people pay more than 30 percent of their monthly income for housing and whether they rent, own, or carry a mortgage.

The credit bureau metric the commission used to develop its score is an individual-level measure and my focus is jurisdiction-level capacity. Nevertheless, all levels of social organization are interdependent: households' income, wealth, and other aspects of their financial well-being drive the financial health of local jurisdictions. Furthermore, because wealthy Americans have more private resources, they generate greater tax revenue for local jurisdictions and reduce the demand for public goods and services.

Economic security is measured on a scale from 1 to 10, with 1 denoting the least secure and 10 the most. In 2021, Prince George's score was 4.59, Montgomery's 6.37, and Fairfax's 7.07. Thus, Prince George's County's score was about two points lower than its neighbors' scores. Since 2017, when I initiated my fieldwork, and through 2021, Prince George's score has decreased, while those of Montgomery and Fairfax Counties have increased.

The interdependent relationships between Prince George's, Montgomery, and Fairfax Counties are similar to what geographer and legal scholar Danielle Purifoy and sociologist Louise Seamster call "creative extraction," a term that describes how White jurisdictions use political and economic tools in their relationships and interactions with Black jurisdictions in ways that lead to monetary, health, and other quality of life benefits for White areas.[19] "Erosion," one of the forms of creative extraction Purifoy and Seamster identify, aptly describes the relationships and interactions between Prince George's, Montgomery, and Fairfax Counties. Purifoy and Seamster define erosion as "robbing Black places of the ability to thrive from the full use of space, while unburdening white places to pursue other forms of desirable development."[20] The nuances of the relationships and interactions between Prince George's, Montgomery, and Fairfax are not as overt as those found by Purifoy and Seamster in their study, but as the logic underlying their theory highlights, the subordination of one jurisdiction to another is often not obvious, but rather is executed through ostensibly "race-neutral" mechanisms that are legal and embedded in regular business and political activity.

In the DC region, Prince George's County bears disproportionate responsibility for moderate- and low-income residents. This responsibility reduces the county's tax base growth potential and thus its capacity to raise sufficient revenue for public goods and services provision. By absorbing a greater share of the region's harder-to-serve populations, Prince George's enables nearby counties to expand their tax bases by attracting ever-greater shares of the region's middle- and upper-middle-class residents. This is a form of fiscal erosion.

I am not arguing that Montgomery and Fairfax County leaders have an explicit agenda seeking to undermine the fiscal capacity of Prince George's County. What I am arguing is that Montgomery and Fairfax, regardless of intent, benefit financially from their geographic proximity to a majority-Black county, and that routine government and market policies and practices regularize and reinforce fiscal advantages for Montgomery and Fairfax at Prince George's expense. That is, Montgomery and Fairfax Counties' *virtuous* fiscal cycles are partly enabled by Prince George's *vicious* fiscal cycles.

In a political context of decreasing state and federal support for public goods and services and greater focus on market-oriented public policy, developers often pit local jurisdictions against one another, forcing counties to offer tax concessions as a condition for development.[21] Black jurisdictions, like Prince George's, even with a majority-middle-class population, already endure the long-standing effects of systemic underinvestment by government and market actors simply because they are Black spaces, and their residents experience the cumulative effects of anti-Black policies and racial discrimination as they pursue employment and otherwise seek access to US opportunity structures.

As I discuss in chapter 5, given long-standing material resource deprivation, majority-Black jurisdictions must expend effort to be legible to developers of middle- to high-end commercial enterprises in the first place, a tax in itself. When investors do show interest, leaders in majority-Black counties, like Prince George's, often experience pressure from investors to offer greater tax concessions to win competitions with wealthier White counties, reducing the amount of tax revenue the majority-Black county receives. The decision to take less revenue now is a gamble with the future in a context where the exclusion-extraction 2-step still mediates Americans' access to material resources at the household, neighborhood, and local jurisdiction levels.

Racialized Relationships Among DC Region Local Jurisdictions: Converging Fiscal Constraints and Relative Regional Burden

Interlocking social processes stemming from anti-Black policies and racial capitalism lead to variation in local jurisdictions' capacities to generate sufficient revenue for high-quality public goods and services. I call the interlocking social processes shaping majority-Black counties' financial health "converging fiscal constraints." This term captures the confluence of three currents creating financial precarity, or vicious fiscal cycles, for local governments serving majority-Black populations: (1) the cumulative weight of anti-Black racism and anti-Black policies; (2) racialized and classed flows of people and capital into the metropolitan area's local jurisdictions; and (3) shared authority across levels of government—federal, state, and local. In contrast, Montgomery and Fairfax Counties' race and class composition advantages enable them to experience virtuous fiscal cycles.

A "virtuous" fiscal cycle is one that yields adequate revenue each year for a local jurisdiction to provide high-quality public goods and services. The converse, a "vicious" fiscal cycle, leads to local jurisdictions not having adequate revenue for high-quality public goods and services. The two core factors shaping these cycles are: tax generation capacity and demand for public goods and services. As I show in the next chapter, Prince George's garners too little revenue from its own sources and receives too little from higher levels of government. Additionally, the county absorbs a greater share of the DC region's moderate- and low-income residents, who are more likely to depend on public goods and services because they have fewer household material resources. Prince George's County's disproportionate responsibility for more high-needs residents shows that these cycles are not just the converse of each other but complements. Virtuous fiscal cycles in neighboring counties are enabled by the vicious fiscal cycles in others.

For example, while Latino families are distributed throughout DC region jurisdictions, Prince George's has the largest concentration of low-income and undocumented Latino immigrants among the counties contiguous with the District. Most of these Latino Prince George's residents live in Langley Park in the northern portion of the county. Certainly, these families contribute to the county's community and economy. At the same time, however, these immigrants tend to have significant need for public goods and services, particularly the children who attend Prince George's County Public Schools. Many Latino students in Prince George's schools, most of whom are from immigrant and/or economically distressed households, require above-average learning support, as well as significant social and health services to enable them to achieve their learning goals.

Suggesting the scale of the need that Prince George's navigates as it educates these children is the fact that, in 2019, the county was the fourth-largest recipient of unaccompanied undocumented children coming from the US-Mexico border.[22] Prince George's provided 1,558 children with classroom instruction and trauma care after it had made budget allocations for the public schools that year. The county reallocated money from other school programs to meet the needs of these young people who unexpectedly enrolled that year.

I argue that counties bearing the greatest financial weight from the negative economic fallout of classed and raced flows of people and capital into metropolitan-area jurisdictions experience relative regional burden and thus provide a relative regional benefit, or subsidy, to more affluent counties. That is, jurisdictions with the most robust economies have a dual advantage: the conditions for generating sufficient revenue for high-quality public goods and services, and insulation from the responsibility of caring for their proportionate share of high-needs populations.

The metropolitan area political economy dynamic between relative regional burden and relative regional benefit is a mechanism for "opportunity hoarding" by White Americans.[23] As DC region residents decide where to live, work, shop, and enjoy recreation, they often do not do all of these things within the same jurisdiction. But it is the *residents* of local jurisdictions who have the greatest impact on jurisdictions' tax income trajectories. Where race and class groups cluster drive local government tax generation and expenditures because people are eligible to draw down certain public goods and services, such as public schooling, only in the jurisdiction where they officially live. For instance, many of those who earn low wages, such as nannies, retail store cashiers, line cooks, and day laborers, work in the fastest-growing areas of the DC region, which are largely affluent, White-majority or -plurality spaces. But low-wage workers usually cannot afford the cost of living in these locations. These low-income workers tend to live in jurisdictions that are already revenue-starved. Under these circumstances, White, wealthy counties benefit from a proximate low-wage labor pool without bearing responsibility for these workers' and their families' material well-being through the provision of public goods and services.

To be clear, Prince George's generally provides its residents with decent public goods and services. But as the next chapter shows, the county struggles to offer *consistently high-quality* public goods and services across ethno-racial and class groups and across neighborhoods. Prince George's County endures chronic fiscal precarity, irrespective of global, national, and regional economic cycles and other macro-level patterns. Even during periods of expansion on any of these economic scales, Prince George's is fiscally fragile.

The Great Recession of 2009–2011: Converging Fiscal Constraints and Relative Regional Burden During an Economic Shock

The Great Recession of 2009–2011 was the most significant national economic downturn since the Great Depression of 1929.[24] Individual Americans, families, neighborhoods, and local governments experienced hardship as people lost jobs and the market value of residential and commercial properties plummeted. But, as was the case prior to the recession, the people, neighborhoods, and local governments serving them were differently positioned to respond to and recover from this shock. Those with more wealth and other material resources recovered faster than those who had less. And because the recession was deeper and more protracted among groups and locations already economically marginalized, racial disparities in material resource access grew during the Great Recession and the years that followed.

Nationwide, mortgage lenders targeted Black neighborhoods with mortgages containing adverse mortgage terms, such as variable interest rates—and Prince George's County was not an exception.[25] Prince George's County, as one of the wealthiest majority-Black jurisdictions in the United States, likely had more fiscal margin than most Black jurisdictions in the country. Yet the county endured significant fiscal harm. Not only did Prince George's have extensive Black wealth, but the economy of the DC region was also buoyed by federal government employment. The federal government did not lay off workers when many private industries did. When I began my fieldwork in Prince George's County in 2017, more than six years after the recession officially ended, the county was still reeling from it. Government leaders regularly spoke of "budget recovery" strategies as they sought to make agencies and county employees whole from recession-related cuts. At the height of the foreclosure crisis in 2011, Prince George's foreclosure rate was about 5.5 percent of households with mortgages, while the overall rate for the DC region was 2.5 percent. Montgomery County's rate was about 2.3 percent and Fairfax County's was about 1.7 percent.[26]

According to a former congressional representative whose district included a portion of Prince George's, signs of mass foreclosure were evident as early as 2006, over two years before the Great Recession officially began. In her interview, she stated:

> While I was on the campaign trail, I heard it over and over again, people saying, "I'm losing my home." By the time I got to Congress in 2008, I had to have a person on my staff full-time who did nothing but try to mitigate home foreclosures. And we couldn't save every home and we just couldn't do it. Some we did, and good for them, but a lot of them we couldn't because it was so far down the line—there were no protections at all. The banks held all the cards.

As the representative's remarks indicate, the foreclosure crisis started earlier and was more pervasive in Prince George's County than elsewhere in the DC region. In the lead-up to the official beginning of the recession, mortgage lenders had leveraged the fact that Black people were less likely than White people to own their homes but were no less interested in achieving this part of the American Dream. Lenders, like Wells Fargo, preyed upon African Americans' long-standing home-buying desire and their limited information about the lending landscape. Furthermore, mortgage brokers did not offer Black homebuyers the same mortgage terms they offered to White homebuyers with comparable credit scores and other indicators of financial fitness.[27] In 2012, the US Justice Department found that Wells Fargo deployed racist practices when determining the types of mortgages to offer homebuyers.[28] Wells Fargo paid $184.3 million to compensate borrowers, but it was restitution incommensurate with the harm the corporation had caused.

It is also important to note what the federal government did *not* do to account for the full scope of the foreclosure damage and what it did *not* do to prevent such actions from happening again. For instance, Congress and the president could have sought legislation empowering the Department of Housing and Urban Development and/or the Justice Department to investigate racism in real estate markets. It stands to reason that the behavior of Wells Fargo and other lenders relied on or created racialized structures.

In addition, the sum Wells Fargo paid did not account for the collateral effects of foreclosures on local jurisdictions' tax revenues. As the market value of residential properties plunged, foreclosures were concentrated in the neighborhoods of local jurisdictions whose governments served majority-Black populations, like Prince George's County. At a time when demand for public goods and services was increasing because households were seeking help meeting their material needs, given that their private means had been depleted, majority-Black jurisdictions were weathering deep revenue losses that undermined their budgets for public goods and services.

Together, the Neighborhood Stabilization Act of 2008 and the American Recovery Act of 2009 offered state and local governments about $6 billion to attenuate the negative effects of home foreclosures.[29] This funding could be used to acquire, rehabilitate, or convert properties to rentals. Local and state governments could also use the money to demolish structures and to create land banks for longer-term redevelopment. These two federal laws indicate that the national government understood that state and local governments experienced severe negative consequences from the recession, and that household financial strain led to state and local government revenue strain. But in the end, the federal government did not match its recognition of state and local government harms with commensurate assistance. Six billion dollars was a fraction of what was needed.

None of the Prince George's officials I spoke with indicated that Maryland or the federal government was providing significant financial support to the county in light of its disproportionate foreclosure rate. In fact, the same former congressperson quoted earlier lamented that she did not press the president for more aid to homebuyers:

> But when the administration came in, their principal goal was to get the banks in order and to shore them up. And so most of the money that was in TARP [Troubled Assets Relief Program of 2008] went to shore up the banks. It didn't go to help homeowners and consumers. And I regret that we didn't put language in the TARP that required that with a specific dollar amount, that instead many of us as Democrats were relying on the president to get that done.

The contrast between the federal government's level of support targeted at homebuyers and state and local governments and what it offered the financial industry—the institutions and actors who precipitated the financial crisis—is stark. In 2008, Congress and the president established a dedicated office within the US Department of the Treasury to administer the Troubled Asset Relief Program, the primary vehicle facilitating financial industry solvency during the Great Recession. There was no comparable commitment of funding, nor of bureaucratic support, to state and local governments. Hence, the financial industry created "troubled" financial instruments through unscrupulous and racist mortgage terms on the front end, and on the back end, the federal government rescued the institutions that had perpetrated the harm to a much greater degree than it did those who endured the harm.

Not only were fewer White Americans hurt by the recession, but many benefited from it. Through the Troubled Assets Relief Program, or TARP, the federal government offered banks tens of trillions of dollars in loans and enacted "liquidity" supports to ease investor access to capital. These measures equipped financial actors to rebound quickly and to be in position to make future investments.[30] What is more, the government did not enact regulations to prevent the behaviors that led to the recession.

The federal government's response to the Great Recession is yet another instance of the national government allowing market actors to engage in "predatory inclusion" of African Americans in the housing market, to use Keeanga-Yahmatta Taylor's term from her book *Race for Profit*.[31] Scholars have also found that governments themselves deploy unjust financial practices in Black neighborhoods.[32] Legal scholar Bernadette Atuahene, in her book *Plundered*, coins the term "predatory governance" to describe how Wayne County, where the city of Detroit is located, assessed Black people's properties beyond the legal limit and created barriers to prevent Black residents from activating property tax exemptions for homesteads.

"Predatory inclusion," "predatory governance," and "creative extraction" demonstrate that when Black people "play by the rules" of US government and market institutions, they are less likely to be treated fairly than White people. Not only that, Black Americans are at greater risk of losing what gains they have attained despite the headwinds of White domination and anti-Blackness. Race-based targeting by core government and market institutions shows that middle-class status and home buying in suburbia do not confer to Black Americans the same financial foothold they confer to White Americans.

Consistent with my theory of the exclusion-extraction 2-step, White-dominant institutions and actors use racial residential segregation to acquire resources and wealth from Black people and communities. Racial residential segregation also facilitates isolating harm in Black neighborhoods and local jurisdictions. In Detroit, Black people have recovered some of their losses through policy activism.[33] But without concerted efforts to hold bad actors accountable, Black people who endure racial discrimination are usually forced to absorb their losses with no compensation or other forms of support, and many eventually experience downward mobility from the middle class.

Household-Level Fallout from the Great Recession Foreclosure Crisis

As the economy expanded nationally from 2011 onward, many White Americans experienced economic gains, including from the marked upward swing in the value of homes and other real estate, as well as stocks and bonds. European Americans, even during the height of the recession, owing to their cumulative wealth advantages, were better positioned to use their savings to buy homes, stocks and bonds, and other assets, at "bargain prices." The racialized impact of the recession is also evident in the racial disparities in losses in home equity—the amount of market value one realizes beyond one's mortgage. According to the US Department of the Treasury, "from peak to trough prior to and during the Great Recession, total housing equity wealth for white households in the United States fell by 41 percent. In contrast, housing equity wealth fell by . . . 53 percent for Black households."[34] Loss in home equity is a loss of wealth. Indeed, the Black-White wealth gap grew after the Great Recession.[35]

Many Black people who experienced foreclosure also endured downward socioeconomic mobility from the Black middle class. Black Americans, irrespective of the state of the economy, are more likely to be downwardly mobile and less likely to attain upward mobility in their lifetimes and intergenerationally than White Americans.[36] As adults in Black families lose middle-class status and the material and social resources that come with that status, so do their children, who are then less likely to achieve middle-class status themselves. In an economic context driven by racial capitalism, it is not surprising that home values in Fairfax and Montgomery Counties were largely unscathed by the Great Recession. A congressperson whose district includes a portion of Prince George's amplified this point when he said:

> I've lived here for twenty-five years. I've owned, bought and sold a number
> of properties, not for investment purposes, but I've lived in a number of
> places, and from the earliest townhouse that I bought in Bowie—and then
> went to sell that—I experienced firsthand how everything in Prince George
> County seems to be delayed or sluggish. The housing market goes down,
> we are slower to recover.

County-Level Fallout from the Great Recession Foreclosure Crisis

While Prince George's County was still recovering from the recession in 2017, Fairfax and Montgomery Counties were in much better fiscal positions. Not only could these two counties continue to meet the public goods and services needs of their residents, but they also had fiscal latitude to capitalize on development opportunities already underway and on the horizon in the DC region when the recession set in. Post-recession fiscal capacity gaps between Prince George's County and Montgomery and Fairfax Counties made Prince George's even more "affordable," owing to the erosion of household and neighborhood wealth within its borders, while Montgomery and Fairfax enjoyed increasing demand for housing from affluent households. These Whiter, wealthier counties also had greater developer investment interest as developers sought to provide private amenities to elite households.

Interjurisdiction differences in recession experiences were further heightened by the rapid gentrification in Washington, DC, that continued unabated during the recession. Many moderate- and low-income families displaced from the District moved to Prince George's County. Racial and class group migration patterns during the recession and in its immediate aftermath amplified the virtuous fiscal cycles of Montgomery and Fairfax Counties and the vicious fiscal cycle of Prince George's.

At the neighborhood level, as foreclosures mounted in Prince George's communities, remaining residents suffered too. Appraisers assess homes' market value in part by considering what nearby homes have recently sold for. Concentrations of foreclosed homes drove down home values for neighboring properties. Banks and other mortgage lenders were often willing to sell at prices lower than the homes' value prior to the Great Recession because these institutions focused on recouping their sunk costs as quickly as possible.[37]

Additionally, as banks wait for a buyer, they do not have a strong incentive to maintain the homes and their yards. Peeling paint, dilapidated siding, shattered windows, and overgrown grass were common among bank-owned properties. Poor property upkeep compromised quality of life for remaining residents, not only because these unoccupied properties became eye sores but because they detracted from the aesthetic beauty of the neighborhood, its "curb appeal," thus making the neighborhood less attractive to would-be homebuyers.[38] In the worst-case scenario, those in communities with foreclosure clusters experience "underwater" mortgages—home loans that are more than the market value of their homes.

In my interview with a county council member whose district was a foreclosure "hot spot," her assessment of her district's Great Recession experience echoed that of most other county leaders:

> There's a rule of thumb in the community development world . . . if more than 60 percent of your block is rental or non-home-owner-occupied, then you can start to experience quality of life changes in your community. I think there are some neighborhoods where we're seeing data points that

are like that, and part of it is we had an intense amount of foreclosures in Prince George's County. We still have a lot of foreclosures in Prince George's County. There was a moment in time when I came into office [2016] where every neighborhood that I door-knocked as I was running for elected office there was hands down a vacant house in every one of them, and you could obviously detect it. The grass was growing high. Maybe it was boarded up. It was clearly poorly maintained. Nowadays, we still have vacant homes in our neighborhoods. I'm not sure it's on that scale as it was, but we had two of our zip codes in my district were hot spots for foreclosures in the peak of the crisis.

This council member described the recession as "intense" and referred to the many "hot spot" neighborhoods throughout the county that created conditions that led to a longer recovery in Prince George's than in neighboring jurisdictions. Furthermore, because Prince George's County is a majority-Black jurisdiction, most prospective home buyers are African American. And given that Black people were disproportionately harmed by the recession, fewer African Americans were in a financial position to buy homes than were European Americans.

Tepid demand for homes in Prince George's County led to another deleterious outcome. Consistent with national trends, investment firms purchased foreclosed properties in bulk from banks—and even from the federally sponsored organization Fannie Mae.[39] These firms rent the properties they own, thus reducing the number of owner-occupied units in Prince George's neighborhoods. Generally, homeowners and buyers in neighborhoods are more willing to invest in their neighborhoods' social and physical well-being, such as by participating in beautification projects.

Linking the Acute Shock of the Great Recession to Prince George's County's Chronic Fiscal Fragility

As the foreclosure crisis unfolded, Prince George's officials experienced a two-pronged budget burden—less tax revenue alongside increasing demand for public goods and services—and responded by making severe budget cuts that Montgomery and Fairfax Counties did not have to make in the wake of the recession.[40] Montgomery and Fairfax Counties, which have smaller Black populations and few majority-Black neighborhoods, were not targeted with toxic mortgages by lenders. These two counties also had fewer moderate-income and economically distressed households to support prior to the economic crisis and during it.

Prince George's County suffered more severe recession-related scarring than neighboring Whiter, wealthier jurisdictions for at least three reasons: (1) the magnitude of the foreclosures in Prince George's was greater; (2) the county already managed more of the cumulative effects of anti-Black policies and racial capitalism, and, relatedly; (3) the anti-Black social processes that caused the county to experience greater harm from the recession were the same structural barriers hindering the jurisdiction's recovery. The Prince George's leaders I spoke to were exasperated by how long it was taking the county to return to pre-recession fiscal capacity, let alone increase revenue to improve public goods and services. A council member offered this perspective on the county's fiscal situation, capturing what I heard from most county elected officials:

> It took us longer than anyone in the region to dig out. . . . We're still digging out, and it affected our African American middle class in the worst way. People lost their homes, and that's how you build wealth in this country, is by homeownership—and it hit us hard. There's a consequence to that that I think we're still trying to figure out.

Recession-related financial harms discussed in this chapter indicate that converging fiscal constraints led to a greater relative regional burden on Prince George's during the Great Recession. Racial capitalism logics and anti-Black public policies were evident in the actions and inactions of government and market institutions in the months leading up to the recession, during it, and in its aftermath. Market actors preyed upon Black households and neighborhoods. Yet Black people, and the local jurisdictions serving them, were largely left to navigate the financial fallout by themselves, given they received insufficient federal and state government support. The Great Recession was an acute shock that intensified Prince George's County's chronic fiscal constraints. In the next chapter, I discuss the county's revenue generation limitations and the implications for public goods and services provision in fiscal year 2018.

CHAPTER 3

Fiscal Subordination Fallout: Prince George's County's Fiscal Year 2018 Budget Deliberations and Allocations

In the words of former Vice President Joe Biden, "Don't tell me what you value, show me your budget, and I'll tell you what you value." Take a careful look at this budget. You will see our shared values reflected in continued investments in education, public infrastructure, economic development, improved human service delivery, safe communities, and support for the county's most vulnerable residents. Revenues are improving, in part because of a full year of MGM National Harbor [casino]–related receipts, but we still have miles to go before we sleep. Laying the groundwork for the future, the council approached this year's budget process with cautious optimism, making very modest and prudent investments and adjustments in FY [fiscal year] 2018. Continuing to lead the region as the economy grows will depend greatly on the *fiscal prudence* we exercise today. That is why the work of the Blue Ribbon Commission is so critically important. The commission's recommendations for addressing the *structural deficit* and related fiscal challenges were factored into our FY '18 budget considerations and will also play an important role in all future county spending decisions as we work to safeguard our financial health. The adopted spending plan is not only a budget for the new fiscal year— it is part of a multi-year, measured, and long-term *financial strategy* that will require structural balance to succeed. (emphasis mine)

—Remarks of Prince George's County council chair
at the County Administration Building,
Upper Marlboro, Maryland, as the council approved
the fiscal year 2018 budget on May 25, 2017

https://doi.org/10.7758/bwmi8829.7504

THIS CHAPTER EXPLAINS the consequences of Prince George's County's experience of converging fiscal constraints—the cumulative effects of White domination and anti-Black racism, raced and classed flows of people and capital into local jurisdictions, and shared authority between levels of government. I also discuss how the county carries relative regional burden for the DC region. By focusing on the development of Prince George's County's fiscal year 2018 budget, we see that the county takes in too little revenue to invest at levels adequate for maintaining consistent high-quality public goods and services.

With severe revenue generation challenges, Prince George's officials must make hard trade-offs as they distribute funds to the agencies responsible for public goods and services provision. Funding for Prince George's County Public Schools (PGCPS) represents the greatest share of the county budget at about 60 percent. Yet PGCPS needs more revenue to meet students' learning needs, pay teachers and staff competitive salaries, and repair school infrastructure and build new schools in the fastest-growing portions of the county. But given that schools already receive the lion's share of the budget and other public goods and services are underfunded, it is difficult to increase school funding without causing serious harm to residents by reducing allocations for other public goods and services to even lower levels. This chapter addresses the implications of insufficient funding for a range of public goods and services, except for public schools. The next chapter is dedicated to the budget constraint consequences for PGCPS.

I begin by discussing the amount of revenue the county received through its own revenue generation authority and through transfers from state and federal governments. Then I turn to the apportionment of the revenue across spending categories. Next, I explain the budget deliberation process, during which county government agency leaders, residents, business owners and their associations, developers, and other stakeholders made their case for how funding should be allocated. This deliberation process was not partisan; neither Democrats nor Republicans nor other political parties offered different policy agendas. The county executive and all council and school board members were Democrats. But they often disagreed about which public goods and services to prioritize.

By examining the budget deliberation process and the appropriations trade-offs that policy officials made, I show that the majority-Black county with the highest concentration of middle-class African Americans in the

United States does not have the capacity to fund high-quality public goods and services consistently. Prince George's County's fiscal challenges were regularly discussed during elected officials' town hall meetings with residents, in candidate debates, and in other election and civic activity. But in most cases, these convenings did not address the upstream factors leading to the county's inadequate revenue for maintaining high-quality public goods and services. Ultimately, this chapter reveals that the Black middle class receives fewer returns to its class status than middle-class Whites. This finding reinforces and extends research based outside of the DC region and within it, which shows that White Americans, on average, are more likely than Black Americans to achieve middle-class status and to transfer it intergenerationally.[1]

Prince George's County's Structural Deficit

The council chair's discussion of "fiscal prudence" and a "financial strategy" in the face of a "structural deficit" in the epigraph for this chapter alludes to the hard budget trade-offs that Prince George's officials make as they seek to fund public goods and services each year. A *structural* deficit is more severe than an occasional year-to-year revenue shortfall due to over-estimating revenue intake. A structural deficit is also not tied to economic recessions. Recessions and national and global economic growth contractions occur cyclically, and local governments generally recover after economic growth resumes. As I explained in chapter 2, Prince George's County took longer to rebound after the Great Recession because this acute shock compounded the chronic relative regional burden the county bears for the DC metropolitan area, irrespective of economic cycles.

Structural deficits indicate that there are foundational problems with the tax regime in place. With such deficits, the county will regularly struggle to meet public goods and services demand, and if all factors remain constant, the county will not garner enough revenue to maintain current levels of public goods and services. Every year the county must balance its budget. Unlike the federal government, local governments, as stipulated in state law, can borrow only for a narrow set of needs, usually those connected to major infrastructure projects, such as building new schools and roads and bridges. Inflation alone compels governments to invest more each year simply to maintain public goods and services at a consistent quality over time, let alone demonstrably improve public goods and services provision. The 2018 spending plan, or budget, was where the action was as Prince

George's County officials decided how to move forward in a fiscal context where the demand for public goods and services from residents exceeded what officials could afford to supply.

What Is a County "Budget"?

The county budget is a document stating the amount of revenue the juris-diction approves for each agency in a fiscal year, given expected revenue from county taxes and state and federal funding transfers. Prince George's County agencies—from those implementing K-12 education to those enforcing civil and criminal laws, to those delivering health and social services—are the bureaucratic units that create and deliver the public goods and services sought by residents. A strong bureaucratic foundation, which is essential to maintain the quality of public goods and services, is the base upon which the county coordinates the human activity and material resources that become public goods and services.

The Prince George's County Council approves the next fiscal year's budget by no later than June 30 each year, the last day of the fiscal year. "Budget season" commences in March, when the county executive proposes a budget for all agencies and submits that proposal to the county council, which has appropriations authority. Then, from March through June, the county council holds a series of committee and full council hearings to learn the budget priorities of a range of stakeholders, including, among others: res-idents; agency administrators; municipal leaders; civil servant unions; civil society groups, like churches and nonprofit organizations; business owners; developers and prospective investors; and industry lobbyists.

Maryland law only authorizes council members to appropriate revenue expected during the next fiscal year, plus any surpluses from prior years, as projected by the county's Office of Management and Budget. As the fiscal year unfolds, if the county takes in less revenue than expected, it must cut public goods and services or borrow money from its "rainy day" fund.

Prince George's Revenue Sources and Expenditures for Fiscal Year 2018

Prince George's County's general fund budget, out of which most public goods and services receive their allotment, was about $3.3 billion in fiscal year 2018. The three largest sources of revenue based on the county's own tax generation authority were: property taxes ($847 million, 26 percent of the budget); local income taxes levied on residents' salaries and wages ($632.7 million, 19.5 percent); and other local taxes and receipts, such as hotel taxes, ($419.7 million, 12.9 percent).[2]

The majority of the total budget, including revenue from all levels of government, went to public schools (61 percent), followed by law enforcement (21 percent). All other county public goods and services, from health clinics to trash collection, were paid for with the remaining 18 percent of the budget.[3] Maryland provides the greatest funding support for K-12 public schools. In fiscal year 2018, the state transferred about $1 billion to Prince George's County Public Schools (PGCPS). And the county added another $1 billion, creating a $2 billion budget for PGCPS. I focus on the implications of budget constraints for Prince George's schools in the next chapter.

During the budget deliberation period, Prince George's officials and stakeholders negotiated how to ration the county's revenue. That the county could devote only 18 percent of its budget to non-school and non-law-enforcement expenditures required that elected officials make hard budget trade-offs between core public goods and services. Prince George's County's fiscal strain illustrates how converging fiscal constraints create unique financial burdens in majority-Black jurisdictions, irrespective of their class composition.

Fiscal Year 2018 Budget Deliberation in a Context of Converging Fiscal Constraints

To understand the consequences of Prince George's County's budget limitations for public goods and services provision, I start by examining converging fiscal constraints in terms of Prince George's revenue *inflow* and *outflow*. Inflow is the amount of money the county garners through its own taxing authority, in addition to funds transferred to it from federal and state governments, in a single fiscal year. Outflow captures the county's budget expenditures across public goods and services each fiscal year.

Tax revenue inflow and budget outflow are significantly shaped by local jurisdictions' race and class compositions. Prince George's County has a smaller proportion of the DC region's upper-middle-class and elite residents than Montgomery and Fairfax Counties. Prince George's also serves a greater share of the DC region's residents who are lower-middle-class, working-class, or economically distressed. Therefore, Prince George's receives less revenue through property and income taxes than do its Whiter and wealthier neighbors, Fairfax and Montgomery Counties. Roughly equivalent tax rates across the three counties lead to Montgomery and Fairfax Counties generating more revenue in large part because their residents have higher incomes and their properties have higher market value.[4]

Additionally, businesses in Prince George's County generally cater to middle-class, working-class, and poor residents, not upper-middle-class and elite residents. As a result, the businesses in Prince George's generally do not have the same profit generation potential as those serving affluent residents in Montgomery and Fairfax Counties. Prince George's County's disadvantage in garnering commercial tax revenue is compounded by "retail redlining," whereby prospective investors with high-end businesses assume that a majority-Black county, irrespective of class composition, cannot generate the profit they seek. I discuss retail redlining and the county's other private development challenges in chapter 5.

Since the 1970s, federal and state governments have provided increasingly less revenue to local jurisdictions to support their noncarceral public goods and services.[5] Consequently, local jurisdictions have largely adopted an "entrepreneurial stance," or "hustle-mindset," in their pursuit of sufficient revenue.[6] Their main strategy is recruitment and retention of wealthy residents and businesses; the corollary strategy is seeking to serve the fewest moderate- and low-income residents. Insufficient federal and state funding leads to competition between local jurisdictions.

Even in a context of reduced state funding, states can still mandate that local jurisdictions carry out the same public goods and services functions. For example, all state constitutions require their local jurisdictions to educate every child. But states do not guarantee that local governments will have the resources to educate all children within their jurisdiction well, nor do states guarantee that their local jurisdictions will generate the same amounts of revenue through local tax authority.

Many states, including Maryland, compensate for uneven local government tax yields by creating funding formulas that transfer more revenue to lower-yield local governments. This is especially the case for K-12 public schools, the largest budget expenditure for most state and local governments. While these formulas offset some of the disparity between counties and school districts with high and low tax yields, they are inadequate to meet the scale of need in majority-Black jurisdictions. These jurisdictions carry the cumulative effects of underinvestment in Black people and their households and neighborhoods.

Furthermore, funding formula allocations to local governments usually fluctuate based on state revenue intake. During economic downturns, local jurisdictions need even more state revenue to balance their budgets. But in these instances, states often transfer less revenue to local governments because they too have garnered less revenue. Whereas the federal government regularly borrows from the private sector through Treasury bonds to meet operating costs, state and local governments are required by state constitutions to balance their budgets each year.[7]

Fiscal Year 2018 Budget Development in Prince George's County

As council members deliberated budget allotments to agencies, two main parameters shaped their thinking: the total spending limit for the year, and how appropriating money to one public good or service necessarily constricted the amount they could invest in another. The Prince George's Council considers different types of legislation each year. Budget-related measures are "appropriations" bills—they state how much money will be given to each agency in a fiscal year. "Authorization" bills are the other major category of legislation. They stipulate what government agencies may spend money on and the maximum amounts agencies can receive for program areas.

In general, agencies do not execute all of the authority conferred on them to the fullest extent possible, in large part because they do not receive the full level of funding authorized. Agency administrators, in consultation with the county executive and county council, use their discretion to distribute funding to spending categories—from salaries and benefits to commodity purchases, like salt for roads.

The council also conducts oversight hearings of agencies to determine the degree to which agencies are carrying out local laws based on the council's interpretation of them. Council members also convene weekly to vote on bills voted out of committees. During committee hearings, council members amend, or "mark up," draft legislation based on testimony and other input from constituents and interest groups.

Finally, the council hosts briefings on issues facing the county. Briefings inform council members about topics that are significant to Prince George's but over which the county government has limited or no influence. For instance, council members were keenly interested in the solvency and investment patterns of the Washington Metropolitan Area Transit Authority (WMATA), which operates the Metro subway and bus systems servicing Prince George's County, other Maryland and Virginia counties, and the District of Columbia. Prince George's residents rely on Metro for their work commutes, and the council wanted to anchor development projects at Metro stations as part of its "smart growth" agenda, which I discuss in chapter 5. Thus, it was important for the council to understand WMATA's trajectory and to factor WMATA's status into decision-making.

Using appropriations, authorization, oversight, and briefing hearings, I explain how the council made decisions regarding public goods and services funding in a constrained fiscal context. The gap between Prince Georgians' public goods and services needs and the county's capacity to meet them demonstrates how converging fiscal constraints create unique financial challenges in majority-Black jurisdictions, even those that are majority-middle-class.

County Executive "Listening Sessions": Residents Voice Their Need for Improved Public Goods and Services

In 2017, prior to submitting his budget to the council, the county executive held three "listening sessions" with constituents across the county in January and February. These gatherings began at 7:00 PM and usually ended at 9:30 PM. One hundred to 150 people attended each session. Many of those present did not testify themselves but were there to show solidarity with particular groups through the T-shirts they wore or the signs they held. Energy was high, a mix of earnestness and camaraderie. This was an opportunity for residents not only to petition for resources but also to reconnect with neighbors and friends. People near where I sat talked about daily life—traffic, their children's achievements and challenges, what they had for dinner—along with the issue or issues that had brought them out to the meeting. When residents testified, others in attendance often encouraged and affirmed them with "Yes," "That's right," "Go 'head," in tones and cadences reminiscent of call-and-response in Black church services.

At all three county executive listening sessions, residents explicitly called for increased government funding of public goods and services. Spending requests encompassed nearly every facet of public goods and services provision—from repairing and building schools, to increased pay for county civil servants, to stricter enforcement of housing code violations, among many other domains. This wide range of requests is expected, given that the meetings are designed to discuss the entire budget. Moreover, residents who were satisfied with county public and goods services provision probably did not find it worth their time and energy to come to meetings to offer county officials gratitude. At the same time, it is also likely that the listening sessions only captured a fraction of residents' concerns about public goods and services provision. After all, attending public hearings costs residents time and energy, as well as money, since attendees might need to hire someone to watch children or elders in their care.

What is particularly noteworthy is the range of significant hardships that residents identified related to inadequate public goods and services. These hardships are evidence that Prince George's County's revenue is significantly below what is necessary to meet residents' material needs. The following excerpts from each of the three listening sessions show the range of public goods and services that disappointed residents, as well as the consequences for their lives.

Listening Session 1

> County Executive: I'm always delighted to hear how to spend your tax dollars, but I'm also happy to hear ideas on how to save dollars. (*He said this at the beginning of each budget listening session*)
>
> Resident #1 (*Black woman, early fifties*): I'm pretty well known to you—I've made over two hundred complaints about roads, but nothing done.
>
> County Executive: After the final budget hearing, we finalize and submit the budget to the council. Let's make sure we get your information on the roads.

RESIDENT #2 (*Black woman, late fifties*): Don't forget us seniors—please fund our programs.

RESIDENT #3 (*Black woman, mid-forties*): Since 2000, we've borrowed $343 million for public safety, but it took until a year ago to get a District 7 police station (*referring to bonds county let in 2010, 2012, and 2016*). Another example, $146 million for libraries, yet when you go to the website for New Carrollton, until this year, for over one year, it was not available. Similarly, for public works—$718 million, yet I call 3-1-1 for roads to be repaved. Money coming in from MGM [casino]—we don't want that to replace money already being spent. We don't want to supplant, we want that money in addition to.

RESIDENT #4 (*Black woman, late seventies*): Garbage collection should be twice a week, not once—we have picnics on Monday and Friday.

RESIDENT #5 (*Black woman, early thirties, real estate agent*): It's ridiculous—everything is cut, schools, roads. We have to give them money to use. It's a deadly highway (*suggests speed cameras on 210 for safety and revenue generation*). In DC, speed cameras brought in $37 million. Second idea is a bag tax—helps with the environment, plus income. Montgomery County brought in $10.4 million. 210 can't handle the traffic. People in this area have the same businesses—four Chinese carryouts, two McDonald's. We need more businesses here. Why should I have to go to another county? I've started a website called MD 4-1-1—we're being proactive. Stop being reactive, start supplying.

COUNTY EXECUTIVE: We've put the bag tax up for the past four years, but it's been shot down by our delegation (*state legislators with Prince George's districts*), let alone the legislature. By the way, she's talking about the state budget—the governor's budget—what he said in the State of the State. (*The governor's annual speech on the status of Maryland's government and the governor's spending policy priorities*)

Listening Session 2

RESIDENT #1 (*Black man, seventies*): Taxes are a way of life. They should not take our life—seniors need money for food and medicine.

We voted to ask you to stop this runaway train—that is, taxes. We expected you to stem the tide of tax increases. When will the financial infidelity stop?! (*States that he lives on a fixed income and also wants more frequent trash collection*)

RESIDENT #2 (*Black woman, thirties, with special needs twins and a husband who needs organ transplant*): I could not make it without him [her home health aide]. This man comes every day, every single day. I don't know how he does it. I'm surprised he hasn't left. It's because of his love. . . . Help us, they deserve it.

RESIDENT #3 (*Black woman, late thirties*): I want increased litter pickup and enforcement. People dump mattresses and trash. In Lanham, we have the smallest community center and not much green space. The county should build new schools in that area. Route 4 and Pennsylvania Avenue has been on the books, but no action yet—push it through. At Suitland and Pennsylvania, install a red-light camera.

RESIDENT #4 (*White Latino man, late thirties, testifying in Spanish with a Black Latino man translating*): I have lived in Prince George's County for nineteen years. I want better housing quality. My apartment is a health hazard to children. I have waited three months for my pipes to be fixed. With the Purple Line [a new train that will run east to west between Prince George's and Montgomery Counties], I like the idea of more transportation near my house, but I worry my rent will increase. I want the county to work with apartment owners to improve apartment quality and for the county to think about how to help low-income people stay in place once the Purple Line is built.

RESIDENT #5 (*Black woman, forties*): "I'm (*states her name*), the one and only elected by the people to speak for the people. Enforce litter laws. Prince George's County is not going to get business if they see the trash. You can't get quality business without a quality county. I want more money for schools, libraries—more recreation should be connected to schools. Invest in older communities. Seniors can't afford to fix up their homes. If you want great and gorgeous, then give the county a facelift. Stop pimpin' my people—don't have us coming to meetings when you've already made decisions in back rooms.

Listening Session 3

RESIDENT #1 (*representing Friends of the Library*): The library budget was cut ten years ago by 40 percent, and to date the budget has not been fully restored. As a result, libraries have short hours—eight-hour days, seven of eight have Sunday hours, some six and some four hours. Please help us keep our libraries open.

RESIDENT #2 (*executive director of nonprofit for adults with developmental disabilities*): I'm here again because I can't meet the minimum wage. The state is not funding us. We're competing with fast food for staff.

RESIDENT #3 (*Black man, twenties, resident of adults with disabilities facility*): Sir, when I was at Mom's house, I had no social life. I couldn't go where I wanted to go. I took classes at PGCCC [Prince George's County Community College], but online. I wondered why my staff kept coming and going. Then I realized the pay, they [adults with disabilities caregivers] couldn't live off of it. I just want to have my workers paid what they're valued.

RESIDENT #4 (*Black man, late thirties, local business owner*): We're looking for fair inclusion. Metrics for MGM [casino]. You look at construction, but not operations. How do we get past 30 percent at build to ongoing when they have national contracts? (*Referring to increased oversight for Prince George's–based minority-owned business opportunity contracts at MGM Casino*)

Residents raised concerns across a host of public goods and services. Those who spoke spanned the generational spectrum of adults. And the range of issues identified across age groups and throughout the county indicates that Prince Georgians do not receive consistent high-quality public goods and services.

A portion of the concerns residents raised, however, were not related to public goods and services per se. That is, for some of the issues residents spoke about, local government has a limited and/or indirect role. This is especially true for matters concerning private development. The county can only intervene in particular ways at particular times, such as during the permitting phase of a new project.

For instance, one of the residents stated a grievance about contracts with MGM Casino. This person highlights a limitation of relying on commercial development as a strategy for generating new tax revenue. The economic activity that casinos and other businesses create for Prince George's County is to some degree conditioned by the extent to which they conduct significant business transactions with enterprises based in the county. Major corporations often have established relationships with vendors who produce at a scale allowing them to offer discounted pricing that small businesses cannot afford, given that their profit margins tend to be narrower. Certainly, one of MGM Casino's main contributions to the county is tax revenue. But as discussed further in chapter 5, part of the rationale for seeking increased commercial investment in Prince George's is the desire to create synergies across small and large businesses and across sectors. Such synergies lead to more money circulating in the county and more business transactions yielding tax revenue.

Residents' petitions for improved public goods and services provision is one way to see the fallout from inadequate locally generated revenue. Another perspective on revenue constraints is agencies' point of view on whether they have the money and other inputs to function optimally. I now shift to how agencies described the effects of budget constraints on their ability to achieve their missions.

Budget Constraint Consequences in Prince George's Agencies

Agency employees facilitate public goods and services provision. Some civil servants work behind the scenes, like technologists who maintain computers; others are public-facing, such as teachers and police officers. During hearings where agency administrators testified before the Prince George's council regarding their agency's fiscal year 2018 funding request, all administrators requested significant levels of increased funding to carry out their *core* functions. That is, agency leaders were not seeking additional revenue to expand or improve services, but rather to meet current public goods and services demand, and they explained the impact of inadequate funding on public goods and services delivery. Those who testified also stated that the lack of adequate funding overburdened employees and led to employee burnout, causing some people to leave their positions. Many agency administrators also noted that their staffing challenges worsened during the Great Recession and its aftermath.

During the Great Recession, Prince George's County froze civil servants' pay. When I arrived in 2017, about six years after the recession officially ended, the county was still in the process of bringing civil servant salaries up to what they would have been had they increased as expected, based on cost-of-living adjustments and merit pay. Before the recession, Prince George's County struggled to compensate its workforce at levels comparable to neighboring local jurisdictions. Across agencies, Prince George's County's pay scale is often lower than what it is in neighboring Whiter, wealthier counties, such as Montgomery and Fairfax Counties. Thus, even when Prince George's civil servants were made whole from recession-related pay cuts, they were often still earning less than they would for similar work in other counties and municipalities in the DC region. In addition to other local jurisdictions, Prince George's County competes with the Maryland and Virginia state governments and the federal government for the most experienced and well-trained government workers. Prince George's agency leaders stated that many civil servants use the strategy of gaining experience and training in Prince George's as a springboard to better-paid positions in other governments.

The thresholds at which agencies' performance suffers because of under-staffing varies across agencies. For instance, by automating some tasks, like sending alerts to residents regarding emergencies, the county has reduced the need for personnel. But, in general, staff shortages force county employees to manage too many assignments for optimal public services provision. This section highlights the consequences of agencies' understaffing, other than for the public school system, which is the subject of the next chapter.

A prime example of how staffing shortages affect public goods and services provision is the experience of the Department of Permitting, Inspections, and Enforcement (DPIE). One of DPIE's main responsibilities is enforcing housing codes, such as ordinances pertaining to property maintenance, both residential and commercial—from apartment buildings, to single-family homes, to office complexes, to shopping centers. At a hearing related to property standards, a DPIE administrator testified: "We have a 6.5 percent increase [in turnover], but the region pays 15 percent more. So that's going to continue to be an issue."

At another hearing related to code enforcement, the council considered a bill that sought to improve the living conditions in apartment buildings through mechanisms that would reduce the need for additional revenue allocations to DPIE. The bill tethered the zoning code to the housing code.

Current law required apartment building owners whose structures did not meet present-day building standards to apply for an exception to continue to operate. Many of these apartment buildings had been granted waivers because they were built decades ago when the zoning laws were more permissive. Under the proposed bill, building owners needing exceptions would not be able to renew their housing permits if they had any outstanding DPIE violations.

County leaders recognized that while many of these apartment buildings were in ill repair, they were an affordable place to live for working-class and low-income residents. At the same time, officials wanted apartment owners to refurbish their buildings, as residents often complained about unlivable conditions, such as broken pipes. Since the council has the right of final review on zoning matters, it sought to use that authority to improve the habitability of older apartment buildings, while not adding significant new responsibilities to DPIE.

At the hearing where the bill was "marked up" in committee, apartment owners countered that habitability issues were not pervasive in their properties and that they made timely and sufficient repairs. Apartment owners also stated that they met a vital need in the county—providing affordable housing for economically strained families. This bill, they testified, would jeopardize their ability to continue meeting that need. In addition, apartment owners argued, because DPIE was understaffed, owners could have remedied an issue but DPIE might not have updated the status of the violation in its database; as a result, apartment owners in good standing could be denied a permit. The following excerpt from the hearing captures how council members, apartment owners, and developers articulated their interests and responded to each other:

SPEAKER #1 (*White man, sixties, Apartment and Office Building Association (AOBA) representative, lobbyist for apartment owners*): AOBA remains opposed to CB-49 in its draft 2 form. Due to the uncertainty and significant negative impact the bill would have on our members that own properties with nonconforming uses. As you can appreciate, most of the rental housing was built before 1970, and this housing is often the most affordable. In the county, as the county zoning code has changed, they have become nonconforming. It does not mean they are problem properties. Nonetheless, this bill subjects nonconforming properties to a higher level of scrutiny and uncertainty when obtaining a certification of nonconforming use or a use and occupancy permit. Our members have invested hundreds of millions of dollars in acquiring and maintaining and improving these properties. I think the council wants to continue that type of activity . . .

SPEAKER #2 (*White man, fifties, president of Southern Management Corporation, developer*): We own several properties in the county. They're vintage apartments, value-added apartments. . . . I'm opposed to this bill because this bill is really about code enforcement. I've seen DPIE stepping up their game in a big way, but if there's anything added or needed at this point, it should all be done with DPIE.

SPEAKER #3 (*White man, forties, president of Kay Management Company*): I represent almost six thousand units in Prince George's County that we own and/or manage. About three thousand are under nonconforming UNOs [use and occupancy orders]. I'd like to vote against this bill as it stands. We see it as overly burdensome, driving up costs, with increase in administration, overhead, and legal costs. . . . The vagueness of the bill jeopardizes a certification based merely on a complaint that has not yet been determined, whether or not it's valid. . . . We provide affordable housing. It's a great market in Prince George's County, and we certainly don't want a situation where we can't continue to offer that product.

COUNCIL MEMBER #1: I give special recognition to Southern Management properties, which are in my district, and they do maintain their properties very well. . . . But you know who the culprits are. You have to take care of your properties—this county deserves better—stop putting it on our inspectors. Our staff are overworked and underpaid—they can't do your job for you all the time. You know if you have properties that are not being maintained, that are not being kept up. The county residents deserve better; take care of your properties.

COUNCIL MEMBER #2: . . . Thank you, (*speaking to council member who spoke before her*). One of the things we experience in all of our districts is that there's a few bad actors. Coming out of PZED [Planning, Zoning, and Economic Development], I did not support this because of legal issues. Apartment buildings are not the only things affected by nonconforming use. The amendments address my concerns, while addressing [another council member] and others' concerns, ensuring that properties applying for nonconforming use do not have pending violations.

COUNCIL MEMBER #3 (*bill sponsor*): Thank you, everyone, for your support. We've compromised—this bill has a strong industry voice. We have many property owners who do the right thing, but a lot of people are riding the coattails of AOBA. . . . I'm trying to tackle all these issues in our community.

In this exchange, apartment owners and developers acknowledge the county's dependence on them to provide affordable housing and assert that they are "good actors" whose permits should effectively be automatically renewed. These industry representatives recognize that the county has limited capacity to verify that their actions are in keeping with county law and said little about the specific steps they take to ensure their compliance with housing code requirements. Rather, industry representatives effectively told county officials to "keep up the good work." Indeed, one speaker offered an explicit performance review: "I've seen DPIE stepping up their game in a big way, but if there's anything added or needed at this point, it should all be done with DPIE." Recall the resident who testified at the county executive budget listening session that pipes in his building had long needed repair. This man's complaint is an example of the stakes of (in)effective code enforcement. County leaders regularly hear concerns of this sort regarding older apartment building maintenance.

The Homeland Security director also discussed severe staffing shortages during the budget hearing for his agency. In his exchange with council members, the administrator said that his agency struggled to recruit and retain emergency call dispatchers:

COUNCIL MEMBER: A couple questions about staffing and compensation. Why do you have a vacancy rate of 25 percent? It makes me wonder whether you need them.

AGENCY DIRECTOR: We need them, but we can't keep up with attrition. That's why we're increasing the salary by 10 percent.

COUNCIL MEMBER: Is the 25 percent a high, typical?

AGENCY DIRECTOR: We were competing with Bowie [a municipality within Prince George's County] when they put out $40,000. DC was recruiting from us too.

COUNCIL MEMBER: Yes, but we should have anticipated that.

The Office of the State's Attorney for Prince George's County offers another window into the consequences of staffing shortages. At the budget hearing for the agency, the state's attorney explained how insufficient funding shapes her ability to adjudicate criminal and civil cases and the number of cases lawyers manage:

> When I started, we needed to increase the budget. We've gone from $13 million to $19 million. . . . If you compare us to Baltimore, they had 200 attorneys for the same level of crime, minus the homicides. We now have 100. Our salaries are still comparable to Baltimore and Montgomery—each attorney handles 4,300 cases per year. It's not necessarily sustainable. The increases in the budget have been on grant dollars [from the federal and state governments], but that's not sustainable. Our salaries are comparable, but we're a huge recruitment ground for the federal government—we can't compete with them. Our attrition rate was higher this year than expected. We're finding that midlevel lawyers are leaving.

While the salaries for lawyers in the State's Attorney's Office are competitive with those in neighboring counties, Prince George's lawyers usually handle more cases than their counterparts in other local governments. Prince George's attorneys can find jobs in a nearby jurisdiction with a lighter workload for the same pay. The reduced stress of a lighter workload is effectively a pay raise, since the attorney would be doing less work for the same compensation. Beyond that, Prince George's competes with the federal government for lawyers, and as the state's attorney said, "We can't compete with that." Under these circumstances, it is not surprising that the attrition rate for lawyers in the Office of the State's Attorney is high.

The budget listening sessions and agency staffing shortages show the fallout from having too little revenue to maintain high-quality public goods and services. But some Prince George's County residents experience more harm than others because they vary in their ability to substitute private resources for public goods and services, as well as in their ages and physical and mental capacities.

Budget Constraint Consequences for Prince George's County's Most Vulnerable Residents

As Prince George's County manages budget limitations, the effects are felt across constituent groups. But people with disabilities, school-age children, and others who are dependent on government-provided care to meet their basic daily living needs, endure the direst consequences when there is insufficient revenue for maintaining high-quality public goods and services. County officials are keenly aware of these residents' needs and seek to meet them, but the scale of need outpaces county financial capacity. In this context of constraint, even county officials' actions undertaken in good faith to help vulnerable populations sometimes create unintended consequences that they cannot easily counteract without hurting public goods and services provision in other ways.

For example, when Prince George's officials sought to improve the quality of life for residents by raising the county's hourly minimum wage in 2017, they inadvertently caused harm. While this pay increase helped many low-wage earners, it hurt institutions that provided care to adults with disabilities.[8] Workers employed by Adults with Developmental Disabilities (ADD) providers were reimbursed at Maryland's minimum wage level, which was lower than Prince George's County's new minimum wage. When the county's new minimum wage became law, Prince George's officials allowed ADD providers to pay their workers Maryland's minimum wage.

The following year, ADD providers complained that this county decision undermined their ability to attract and retain staff because workers could make more by working virtually anywhere else in the county. Leaders in the ADD community requested that Prince George's offer $3.5 million in "gap funding" to cover the difference between the county and state minimum wages. After holding several hearings to learn stakeholders' concerns, the Prince George's council provided the additional money by shifting funds from economic development incentives programs.

Recall that during the county executive listening sessions, parents of adult children with disabilities and providers testified regarding "gap funding." Both Prince George's County's inability to cover the pay differential out of its health services budget and the overall health services funding level indicate the inadequacy of the county's investment in health services. Indeed,

Prince George's mostly relies on state funding for health services, appropriating less than $10 million each fiscal year in this spending category.

Montgomery County, in contrast, enacted a similar minimum wage increase in 2017 and offered gap funding for its ADD providers without significant deliberation. The county simply increased its social services spending for 2018, without cutting other programs or holding hearings about the matter.[9] The difference in how Prince George's and Montgomery Counties managed the need for gap funding demonstrates that local jurisdictions with more robust tax bases, and thus more revenue, can more readily protect and invest in their residents without making hard trade-offs between constituent groups. Residents in wealthier counties also benefit from having leaders who have more time to focus on constituent needs not related to the fallout from rationing revenue.

Another instance of budget constraints reducing the quality of life for some residents more than others in Prince George's is limited funds for maintaining the county's public spaces. Some neighborhoods have significant amounts of discarded materials, especially in wooded areas. Recall from the introduction that, at a neighborhood association meeting, residents and a representative from the Prince George's Department of the Environment had this exchange regarding trash in the community:

DoE REPRESENTATIVE (*Black woman, thirties*): As a community, we have to take back our community. We can pick up the litter that's getting on our nerves—help me with that. If you've called County Click and your issue was not addressed, it's time for you to act.

RESIDENT (*Black woman, fifties*): What about cleanup of illegal dumping of furniture and mattresses in the neighborhood?

DoE REPRESENTATIVE: That sounds like a comprehensive community cleanup. There's a four-year wait-list—it's really popular. I'll connect you with my colleague.

This discussion shows that in a context of budget scarcity, some county services are thinned to the point of nonexistence. A four-year wait-list for items left in people's neighborhoods is effectively nonresponsiveness to the community's need for cleanliness. For smaller forms of rubbish, the county representative tries to shift the burden to residents by creating a community cleanup day. While encouraging people to work together to take care of their neighborhood is laudable and reinforces community solidarity and efficacy, it is a different matter when community cleanup days are substituted for sufficient public service delivery.

Furthermore, most of the people at the meeting appeared to be older adults, between the ages of fifty and eighty. While people of advanced age tend to have more physical limitations, people of any age could have a physical disability. Later in the meeting, the DoE representative seemed to acknowledge that not all people are physically able to participate in a community cleanup day when she suggested that people at the meeting try to persuade the teenagers in the recreation center to do the project to earn volunteer hours, which are required for graduation from Prince George's County Public Schools. Some neighborhood associations may choose to hire a private cleanup service and thus use their class resources to maintain their quality of life. If they do, they bear an additional financial cost when they ostensibly already pay taxes for trash pickup service.

The Bottom Line on the Budget Bottom Line

Prince George's officials, residents, and other stakeholders navigate revenue constraints in various ways—and some have more material and social resources to mitigate harm than others. Material living conditions in Prince George's County are shaped by budget needs of a few million dollars, as was the case with the "gap funding" requested by adults with disabilities providers, as well as budget needs of tens of millions of dollars, as was the case when county agencies sought to hire more workers. Thus, even the US county with the highest concentration of middle-class African Americans—and therefore the majority-Black local jurisdiction best positioned to overcome anti-Black racism and racial capitalism—still struggles financially. Prince George's County's fiscal challenges illuminate how national and regional political economy arrangements reinforce and extend racial inequity in material resource access at the household, neighborhood, and local jurisdiction levels and how these levels of social organization shape each other's financial capacities. In the next chapter, I show how budget shortfalls shape Prince George's County's ability to provide high-quality K-12 education, the county's largest budget expenditure.

CHAPTER 4

Prince George's County's Fiscal Distress and K-12 Public Schools

THE CONSEQUENCES OF Prince George's County's budget constraints are nowhere better revealed than in the challenges the county experiences as it seeks to provide high-quality K-12 education. Public school funding levels are important to examine because schools have direct and indirect effects on county residents' quality of life, regardless of whether they have day-to-day contact with the school system. Starting with the explicit role of public education, schools provide fundamental academic and life skills training for the youngest generation of residents, ideally equipping young people to be economically and socially stable adults.

K-12 education is also Prince George's largest budget expenditure, constituting about 60 percent of the budget. The challenges of Prince George's County Public Schools (PGCPS) have ramifications for other public goods and services funding because schools already capture the majority of the budget and yet still need more funding. Given the amount the county already dedicates to schools (about $1 billion) and the scale of investment needed to improve learning conditions (hundreds of millions of dollars), the county would need to spend the equivalent of some agencies' entire budget to increase funding for schools to levels necessary for large-scale improvement. Therefore, as schools consume more of the county budget, other public goods and services are further compromised.

https://doi.org/10.7758/bwmi8829.6665

Beyond the direct role of schools, they are the most common metric that current and prospective residents use to measure the quality of public goods and services and the overall quality of life in Prince George's. This reality has implications for the raced and classed sorting of people into and out of the county and for how county residents relate to the school system—including whether they choose to send their children to public schools and whether they support tax increases intended to provide additional revenue for schools. In Prince George's, the county and the school district are one and the same, but there is significant variation in the performance and reputations of its schools, depending on neighborhood and school type. Options outside of neighborhood schools in Prince George's County include specialty, magnet, and charter schools.

Demographics of the PGCPS Student Body

In 2018, PGCPS served about 132,000 students, making the system one of the twenty largest school districts in the United States, and the second largest in Maryland (Montgomery County has the most populous school system in Maryland).[1] African Americans were the majority student population at 52 percent. Latinos of any race were the second-largest and fastest-growing ethno-racial group at 39 percent. Twenty-four percent of students were English language learners, and about 10 percent were in special education programs. PGCPS youth came from a wide range of socioeconomic backgrounds, but economically distressed students were the largest and fastest-growing proportion. About 60 percent of the county's students qualified for free and reduced-price meals, an indication that their households are financially strained. Taken together, the population served by PGCPS tends to require above-average levels of per pupil investment to enable all children to excel academically.

Many Prince George's schools provide excellent academic instruction and co-curricular programs, even as the system faces the challenges already noted. PGCPS' primary constraints center on providing a high level of education across all schools within the county's five hundred square miles of rural, suburban, and urban densities and across ethno-racial and class statuses. Students attending schools outside of the beltway, in places like Upper Marlboro and Bowie, where middle- and upper-middle-class neighborhoods are concentrated, generally have the greatest variety of high-performing options. Youth living inside the beltway, where the densest and most economically distressed neighborhoods are located, and students living in rural portions of the county have fewer high-performing schools nearby. Beyond that, schools in northern Prince George's, where the Latino population clusters, experience severe overcrowding and need significant repairs. Schools in the southern portion of the county generally have sufficient space for students but also have significant deferred maintenance.

The range of high schools is exemplified by two secondary schools in northern Prince George's County. On one end of the spectrum is High Point High School in Beltsville, a neighborhood school that manages overcrowding and stands in sore need of maintenance. High Point mostly serves students from immigrant families, most of whom face household-level economic distress. On the other end of the spectrum is Eleanor Roosevelt High School in Greenbelt, a science and technology magnet school and one of the DC region's most renowned secondary schools. Its population consists mostly of affluent Black and White students.

PGCPS offers a range of instructional opportunities for elementary, middle, and high school students.[2] School types include traditional neighborhood schools alongside myriad specialty options, such as foreign language immersion across grade levels and high school International Baccalaureate (IB) and magnet schools for STEM (Science, Technology, Engineering, and Math) and the arts. PGCPS also has career academies for culinary arts and automotive technology, among other trades, and some of these programs include industry certification. And there are thirteen charter schools in PGCPS.

Students sort into schooling options based on their place of residence and interests and aptitudes. But their class and race backgrounds also shape where they attend school. The uneven geographic distribution of high-performing schools plays a role in school selection as well. Overall, students from affluent households and those who live outside of the I-95 Capital Beltway are disproportionately enrolled in specialty schools.[3] Furthermore, as I discuss later, county elected officials—the executive and the council and school board members—prioritize funding for specialty schools because they are one of the primary means of attracting and retaining middle-class and upper-middle-class students in the school system. With affluent parents already tending to opt out of the public school system and into private and parochial schools, county officials are acutely aware that unsatisfied middle- and upper-middle-class parents are likely to withdraw their children from the public school system.

Prince George's County's struggle to provide a high-quality education to all students, irrespective of their social status categories and where they live, stems from sociohistorical processes that began in the 1970s. In that decade, Prince George's initiated school desegregation. And this decade was when the number of Black Americans in the county was increasing dramatically.

The Sociohistorical Context of Prince George's County Public Schools

Prince George's County Public Schools' challenges are embedded in the race and class settlement patterns of the DC region specifically and in US settlement patterns more broadly. Nationwide, children largely learn in race- and class-segregated settings because racial residential segregation persists and students are assigned to schools designated for their neighborhoods.[4] Furthermore, students are eligible to attend schools only within their school district. For Prince George's County Public Schools, the boundaries of the school district and those of the county are the same. In many states, there are several school districts within a county or municipality, and setting district boundaries has become a core tool used by White parents to attain majority-White schools. Therefore, even with the explicit desegregation efforts from the 1950s to 1980s, and the growth of "school choice" from the 2000s forward, most youth in the United States still attend their neighborhood school and learn alongside those who share their race and class statuses.[5]

Additionally, once students are enrolled in a school, they are often tracked into different classes. Tracking leads to race and class advantages for some and disadvantages for others. While students are assigned a remedial, average, or advanced curriculum based on their aptitude, as demonstrated on standardized tests and through class grades, teacher assumptions about and expectations of students, along with parental advocacy, make White students more likely to be in advanced classes.[6] Teachers generally have higher expectations for White and Asian students than they do for Black and Latino students.[7]

White and Asian parents are also more likely to have the financial resources to prepare their children for tests and to pay for them to take multiple tests to increase their likelihood of achieving the scores necessary for advanced placement (AP) classes.[8] And these parents usually have the time and institutional knowledge required to appeal placement decisions. Schools are also more receptive to advocacy from White parents. At the school and school district levels, Whiter and wealthier schools and districts generally have more money to invest in the human and material resources required to offer a wide range of advanced courses, recruit qualified teachers, build state-of-the-art facilities, and buy sophisticated technological equipment.

In Prince George's County, most students are Black and Latino, so resource rationing in the county's schools largely falls along class, ethnic (Latino/non-Latino), immigration status, and geographic lines. Education scholars have found that Black students in well-resourced, multiracial, and majority-White suburban districts receive fewer resources than their White peers, on average.[9] I find that Black middle-class parents in PGCPS, a majority-Black school district, attain significant resources for their children and that school officials focus on their children's needs. At the same time, these Black middle-class parents have fewer high-performing school options than White middle-class parents in Montgomery and Fairfax Counties. What I found in Prince George's County is consistent with research on the heterogeneity of the quality of life in suburban jurisdictions generally and the performance of public schools in suburban jurisdictions specifically.[10]

Given these national trends, Prince George's County's challenges in providing adequate educational resources should be seen through two lenses: (1) a US-wide struggle to provide a high-quality, culturally relevant education to Black and Latino students; and (2) local jurisdiction fiscal constraints reflecting national, state, and regional political economies that determine the amount of tax revenue local jurisdictions generate and thus what they can distribute to school systems. Prince George's County, as the suburban jurisdiction with the largest share of middle-class Black Americans in the United States, is best positioned to overcome these challenges—yet it does not. The county's experiences highlight that variation in the quality of the education that school districts provide is, in large part, a function of whether districts are burdened by or benefit from anti-Black policies and racial capitalism.

Prince George's County's struggle to provide a high-quality education, and that of other majority-Black jurisdictions, are constitutive of Black Americans' centuries-long quest for equitable K-12 and postsecondary educational opportunities.[11] During the slavery era, it was unlawful in most states where slavery was legal to teach enslaved people to read, so most Black people did not receive a formal education until after the Civil War, which ended in 1865.[12] From the mid-nineteenth century through the mid-twentieth, Jim Crow segregation prevailed across the country and most states tended to fund White children's educations at higher levels than Black children's.[13] After the *Brown v. Board of Education* decisions in 1954 and 1955, the funding gap between Black and White children's educations closed to some extent, as did the racial gaps in reading and math achievement.[14] Nevertheless, racial achievement and funding disparities persist to this day.[15]

While Black Americans' education opportunities have been limited throughout American history, their pursuit of high-quality education has never waned, whether in K-12 schools or postsecondary institutions, including Historically Black Colleges and Universities and those initially established for White students.[16] Core goals of modern civil rights movement actors included ending racial discrimination in education, employment, and public accommodations. The most famous case regarding school desegregation was *Brown v. Board of Education I*, which was decided in 1954.[17] This case combined five plaintiffs who sued school districts for providing unequal resources to Black and White schools, in violation, they argued, of their Fourteenth Amendment right to "equal protection of the laws." The second *Brown* decision, in 1955, established how the principles stipulated in *Brown I* were to be implemented.[18] Importantly, in *Brown II* the Supreme Court did not set a specific timeline for desegregation. Rather, *Brown II* required desegregation "with all deliberate speed," and it gave federal courts the authority to determine whether state and local desegregation plans met *Brown I* principles.

Beyond the *Brown I* and *Brown II* decisions, two federal laws increased national government involvement in K-12 education. The Civil Rights Act of 1964 prohibited racial discrimination in education and employment. And the Elementary and Secondary Education Act (ESEA) of 1965 provided federal funding for schools. These laws, alongside the *Brown* decisions, not only outlawed intentionally racially segregated schools but also empowered the federal government to invest billions of dollars in K-12 public schools, augmenting state and local contributions. Even with substantial federal funding, however, state and local governments still provide the majority of K-12 school revenue. The federal government provides about 10 percent of the budgets of most school districts, with the majority of funding targeted toward low-income students through Title I of the ESEA.[19]

But laws are not self-enacting. Unrelenting White resistance to school desegregation led most state and local governments to delay implementing meaningful desegregation processes until the 1970s. Indeed, federal court orders are what prompted the desegregation of many school systems.[20] And this was the case in Prince George's County, which initiated desegregation after Black parents sued the county. Hence, despite federal legislative and court breakthroughs, federalism—shared authority and funding across levels of government—has enabled states and local jurisdictions to evade meaningful desegregation.

Desegregation failures have fiscal implications for school districts. As I explain later, state funding formulas, including the one in Maryland, usually offset disparities in property tax revenue generation across school districts to some extent. But these formulas do not ensure that every school district has the resources it needs for educating all students well. And this is especially the case in school districts that experience the scarring effects of underinvestment during formal desegregation processes and therefore must account for not only present-day needs but also that long-standing lack of investment.

Furthermore, today's school financing structures were created during the de jure, or explicit, segregation period. Property taxes are the primary locally generated source of revenue. Property ownership and the market value of properties are inherently racialized. Since the post–Civil War Reconstruction period, Black youth across the country have usually lived in jurisdictions where Black students and their schools do not receive their proportionate share of investment, regardless of whether the jurisdictions garner sufficient revenue for public goods and services, including public schools.[21] Altogether, three mutually reinforcing social processes have led to Black children not attaining the K-12 resources they need to excel academically: (1) assigning children to schools based on where they live (schools have a catchment area) concentrates race-based structural disadvantages; (2) racial residential segregation persists and is most acute for Black children; and (3) White-dominant institutions and actors systematically undervalue properties in majority-Black neighborhoods, irrespective of other factors, thus undermining property tax revenue yields in majority-Black jurisdictions.

The *Brown* decisions ostensibly decoupled where students live from their access to high-performing schools by prohibiting explicitly racially segregated schools in all states. Accordingly, state and local officials were required to devise plans for ensuring that Black and White students did not learn in racially homogenous classrooms, irrespective of their neighborhoods' racial demographics.[22] Proactive desegregation reduced racial homogeneity in schools, but meaningful desegregation was short-lived.

In 1968, in the face of continued White resistance to racially desegregated schools, the US Supreme Court affirmed its commitment to desegregation in the case *Green v. County Board of Education of New Kent County, Virginia*. The court ruled that it intended to remove all dimensions of racial discrimination in access to public education "root and branch," and granted states and locales "wide latitude in shaping desegregation remedies."[23] A few years later, in the US Supreme Court case *Swann v. Charlotte-Mecklenburg County Board of Education* (1971), the court upheld busing as a tool to achieve racial desegregation in schools.[24] Together, *Brown I*, *Brown II*, *Green*, and *Swann* created important pathways for short-circuiting White Americans' K-12 educational advantages by not only mandating that Black and White children attend the same schools, but also by devising mechanisms to prevent White parents from evading desegregation efforts by moving to all-White neighborhoods and local jurisdictions. In the early 1970s, busing students to schools outside of their neighborhood was the primary desegregation method.[25]

But White Americans' strong opposition to desegregation never waned, and in the end the US Supreme Court acquiesced to White Americans' resistance. First, in the case *Milliken v. Bradley* (1974), and again in 2006 in the case *Meredith v. Jefferson County Board of Education*, federal courts ruled that regardless of whether school districts are contiguous or within the same metropolitan area, only within-district desegregation is required. With these rulings, it became virtually impossible to merge urban and suburban student populations or students in adjacent suburban districts.[26]

The final death blow to enforcing racial desegregation was the US Supreme Court case *San Antonio Independent School District v. Rodriguez* (1972), which reinforced the political significance of the political boundaries of local jurisdictions.[27] At issue in *Rodriguez* was the use of property taxes to fund schools because the variability between districts of the assessable market value of properties led to communities with higher-valued properties generating more revenue than those with lower-valued properties. The Court ruled that states are not required to ensure "equal" K-12 school funding across their local jurisdictions and schools. States must only ensure "adequate" funding. As noted previously, most states, including Maryland, offset disparities in revenue generation between local jurisdictions by using funding formulas ensuring that more money is offered to jurisdictions that raise the least revenue on their own.[28] In this way, states mitigate disparities between jurisdictions, but still do not guarantee that the same investment is made in the education of all students within the state.

Currently, Prince George's County manages the scarring effects of a failed desegregation process. The county, even though it is majority-middle class, also serves more students from economically distressed households than do neighboring wealthier, Whiter counties. The present-day challenges of Prince George's County Public Schools are rooted in the county's racial transition from the 1970s to the 1990s and its school desegregation processes during that period.

Racial Desegregation in PGCPS from the 1970s Through the 1990s

As the Black middle class burgeoned in Prince George's County from the 1970s onward, the rate of increase of Black students in the county's schools rose too. White county leaders resisted desegregating PGCPS until a federal court order compelled them to do so.[29] Before the court order, White Prince Georgians circumvented meaningful desegregation through policies that were race-neutral on their face but that maintained racially homogenous schools.

African American parents in Prince George's County, with support from the National Association for the Advancement of Colored People (NAACP) and the American Civil Liberties Union (ACLU), challenged Prince George's County's school assignment policy in 1972. This lawsuit led to the US District Court of Maryland devising a desegregation plan for PGCPS. The plan established a process for monitoring compliance and it remained in place until the mid-1990s.

Prior to court-ordered desegregation, Prince George's County officials maintained school segregation through what county leaders called a "freedom of choice policy," under which students were still steered to schools based on their racial status.[30] The court order led to significant social unrest among many White Prince Georgians, including acts of violence. According to a current congressperson who has represented a portion of Prince George's County since the 1970s, Maryland's political leaders, including those in Prince George's County, have implemented anti-Black policies throughout the state's history. Therefore, the desegregation order had to confront deeply entrenched White-domination and anti-Blackness:

> This county [Prince George's] was Southern-sympathizing [and] would have clearly joined the Confederate army, as would [have] all of southern Maryland and much of Maryland. I don't know whether you're familiar with the Maryland song, but one line—it was written by a guy named James R. Randall, "Maryland, My Maryland." He was in New Orleans when he wrote it. And the song, one of the first lines is "The despot's heel is on the shore of Maryland, my Maryland." The despot was Lincoln's army sent to Baltimore to stop Maryland from seceding from the Union. So this was a tobacco-growing, slave-holding conservative Democratic state in the old sense, when the Democratic Party was the segregationist party. And when I went to high school, it was a segregated high school in '57. *Brown versus Board of Education* '54. We didn't transition really until '72, when we had the big busing work.

Similarly, the political appointee who chaired a committee central to executing the federal court's desegregation plan explained that White Prince Georgians' anti-Black racism led to their virulent opposition to desegregation:

> It was very just raw, rank prejudice and racism—that's at the parent level. At the leadership level, it's the economics of it. This is 1973. Prince George's County, particularly, is a very George Wallace area—it's the Upper South, like Alabama. People don't know each other, live together, et cetera, so when you start talking about putting the kids together, that simply wasn't going to work. So, there was massive resistance . . . school buses being turned over, White mothers throwing eggs at the school buses. Also it [Prince George's County] abuts the nation's capital that is becoming significantly what we call a "chocolate city." So that Black dynamic caused a great deal of fear out here among the Whites.

Despite White resistance, the PGCPS desegregation plan moved forward. Executing it resulted in major changes for students and parents, both Black and White. The first year of the plan, 1972, about thirteen thousand additional students were bused to school than had been bused the prior year.[31] While busing was controversial, the provision PGCPS found the hardest to implement was the one requiring all PGCPS schools to have student bodies at least 10 percent—but no more than 50 percent—African American. European Americans left Prince George's in droves once desegregation took effect, leaving fewer and fewer Whites with whom Blacks could integrate. When desegregation began in 1972, Black students constituted about 25 percent of PGCPS; a decade later, their proportion had more than doubled to about 52 percent.[32]

Resistance to desegregation was not limited, however, to White parents. Some Black parents also opposed the process. The Black Coalition Against Unnecessary Busing (BCAUB), a parent-based organization, stood against sending their children to non-neighborhood schools.[33] BCAUB was mostly composed of middle-class parents living in racially integrated outside-the-beltway neighborhoods. They did not want to send their children to inside-the-beltway schools, nor did they want children from those schools sent to their schools. BCAUB members argued that their children, more than White children, bore untenable logistical costs, such as long school commutes.

Black students experienced disproportionate desegregation burdens in part because one of the strategies for desegregation was closing Black schools and then busing displaced Black students to White schools.[34] Prince George's officials, like school leaders across the United States, justified these closures by claiming that Black schools were lower-performing than White schools. They made this claim even in the presence of a clear record of state and local governments systematically underinvesting in Black schools—from teacher pay and training, to books and other school supplies, to school building maintenance. County officials had created the very conditions that led to lower achievement outcomes in Black schools.

Notwithstanding pervasive, cross-racial opposition to busing, a contingent of Black and White parents, along with other stakeholders, were committed to resolving the core issue at stake: racial *equity* in access to educational resources. Equity is distinct from equality in that equity accounts for differing needs based on learning capacity and historical and contemporary disparities in access to resources, whereas equality distributes the same resources to everyone, regardless of other factors.

Consternation over desegregation in Prince George's County, from the 1970s through the 1990s, was akin to concerns raised in local jurisdictions across the United States during this period. The late legal scholar Derrick Bell argued in a 1980 *Harvard Law Review* essay that while *Brown I* found racial segregation in schools to be a violation of the equal protection clause of the Fourteenth Amendment, the court's willingness to overturn the "separate but equal" doctrine of *Plessy v. Ferguson* (1896) was always tenuous and contested.[35] Bell contended that this was because the ruling reflected what he called "interest convergence."[36] He argued that interest convergence emerged in the 1950s between Black people—who had always sought equitable educational resources—and segments of White decision-makers. Bell posited that some White leaders' openness to desegregation stemmed from their economic and foreign policy agendas.

Black people, often under the aegis of the NAACP and other civil rights organizations, have petitioned the courts for increased funding of their schools since Jim Crow segregation in public accommodations was imposed in the 1800s. Black litigants called on states to live up to the *equal* in "separate but equal." That is, the legal strategy was pragmatic: Black plaintiffs accepted racial separation in schools, but sought to have resources equivalent to those available to White schools. After World War II, however, Black litigants paired this pragmatic argument with a direct challenge to segregation. They contended that "separate but equal" violated the equal protection clause of the Fourteenth Amendment because racial separation conferred on Black children a badge of inferiority to White children, thus undermining Black children's sense of self-worth.

According to Bell, courts were sympathetic to this more expansive opposition to *Plessy* because overturning that case advanced the interests of some White Americans, who, broadly speaking, fell into three camps. One group objected to racially segregated schools on moral grounds, just as some Whites had always opposed slavery. This group was emboldened in the wake of the defeat of the Nazi regime, which had an explicitly racist agenda.

Another group sought to dismantle single-race schools because they believed that such a system was a barrier to economic growth, given that two school systems are less efficient than one, and that Black children received a less robust education than White children. In Southern states, in particular, business leaders foresaw that industrialization and technological development related to the military installations built to fight the Cold War would be a boon to Southern economies. And these installations required a more skilled workforce. Systematically under-educating Black people, who were nearly half of the population in many Southern states, was "bad for business."

A third camp contended that racial segregation undermined the US ability to make a strong case for democracy and capitalism in countries where the United States competed with the Soviet Union for allegiance.[37] The recently decolonized countries in Africa, Asia, and Latin America were often the sites of proxy battles in the bipolar world order anchored by the United States and the Soviet Union. Countries that had non-White population majorities and were emerging from White Western (explicit) dominance saw a contradiction between US claims that capitalism and democracy necessarily expanded freedom and economic opportunity and the living conditions of Black Americans, who were systematically deprived of state resources and largely could not realize upward socioeconomic mobility.

But, as Bell argues, the interest convergence the *Brown* court case reflected was neither a full-throated repudiation of anti-Black racism nor a disavowal of Whites' commitment to retaining disproportionate access to and control of US material and social resources. For most White Americans, the "psychological wage" of supposed White superiority, to use W.E.B. Du Bois's term, was still central to their identity and political ideology.[38] And for working-class and poor White people, the "wages of Whiteness" were especially valuable because they were a mental salve, a means of attaining dignity and self-worth in the face of meager economic conditions.[39]

Applying the "wages of Whiteness" logic to Prince George's County's White population in the 1970s, we can see that these residents, most of whom were working-class, were aggrieved that Black people, many of whom had college degrees and middle-class incomes, not only moved into their neighborhoods but sought to send their children to White-majority schools. In other words, affluent African Americans' expectation of equal access to educational resources defied White Prince Georgian's "sense of group position."[40] Like most White Americans, White Prince Georgians believed that Black people's "proper place" was always in subordination to White people, irrespective of Black people's class and other social statuses.

That is not to say that the White residents of Fairfax and Montgomery Counties were racially inclusive. In fact, these wealthier jurisdictions used various means to resist Black people moving into their neighborhoods and, by implication, attending their public schools. For instance, homeowners and homeowners associations (HOAs) worked with real estate brokerages to steer White people toward their neighborhoods when homes were put up for sale and to steer Black people away. Moreover, the cost of living in Montgomery and Fairfax Counties, including housing prices, was higher than in Prince George's in the 1970s—as it is today—thus limiting the number of Black people who found these jurisdictions financially feasible, given racial disparities in income and wealth.

In light of persistent White resistance to desegregation, Derrick Bell surmised that desegregation in and of itself does not enable Black children to attain the resources required for a sound K-12 education. As Bell wrote in his 1980 *Harvard Law Review* essay:

> The question still remains as to the surest way to reach the goal of educational effectiveness for both blacks and whites. I believe that the most widely used programs mandated by the courts—"antidefiance, racial balance" plans— may in some cases be inferior to plans focusing on "educational components," including the creation and development of "model" all-black schools.[41]

In Prince George's County, the Council of 100 was a group of county stakeholders assigned to develop a plan for "educational effectiveness," to use Bell's term. Importantly, The Council of 100 did not solely focus on desegregation but sought to enable all students to attain the material and relational resources they needed to excel academically and socioemotionally, regardless of the racial composition of the school they attended. Members of the Council of 100 included Black and White parents, county government employees, and others with school system interests. The federal judge overseeing the county's desegregation plan convened the group. But despite the Council of 100's efforts, since the 1970s, when Black in-migration started to increase markedly, Prince George's County has struggled to provide a consistently high-quality education to all children irrespective of race, ethnicity, class, and geographic location.

Indeed, contentiousness over desegregation scarcely waned during the nearly two decades the desegregation order was in place. In 1980, when the school board approved a plan reducing the number of students bused by 25 percent, the NAACP filed suit against PGCPS a second time. In response, the school board argued that the dramatic increase in the Black student population rendered it impossible to prevent some schools from exceeding 50 percent Black student enrollment, the court's ceiling. The US district court found Prince George's County in violation of the desegregation order, but permitted schools with Black student populations greater than 50 percent.[42]

The primary remedies the court approved involved a combination of reduced busing; magnet schools with competitive admissions and specializations in subject areas, such as the arts or sciences; and "Milliken II schools," so named after a second case involving the *Milliken* plaintiff.[43] Under *Milliken II*, the US Supreme Court permitted majority-Black schools if they received compensatory funding and other additional resources.[44] Prince George's County's Milliken II schools included the following measures, according to the political appointee who headed the Council of 100:

> What the judge ultimately came up with was desegregation that did not involve school assignment. We called them Milliken Schools, where you don't try to put kids on the bus from the inner beltway, put them on a bus at 6:00 in the morning, drive them all around the beltway just to put them next to a White child. That just doesn't work anymore. Black parents didn't want it. White parents didn't want it. But the Black child still was not whole, still not complete from the years of segregation and denial, and so we came up with an equal distribution of resources.

In the mid-1980s and early 1990s, Prince George's County schools, consistent with the *Milliken II* ruling, focused on lowering student-teacher ratios; providing new instructional programs, including summer enrichment; and offering wraparound social services, by, for example, adding full-time nurses and social workers to school staffs. Additionally, schools with the lowest standardized test scores received more resources. And because the Black population in Prince George's increased significantly during the twenty-year period the desegregation order was in effect, the plan simultaneously sought to provide spending equity across schools, while accounting for racial composition changes in the county. Altogether, over the desegregation plan's twenty-year span, activists, the courts, and ad hoc committees had the greatest influence on PGCPS policy. Throughout the desegregation period, a cross-class, countywide Black agenda never solidified regarding how to achieve educational equity. And in 1998, federal district court approved ending mandatory busing for the purposes of racial desegregation in Prince George's County.[45]

While there was no consensus among Black Prince Georgians regarding the best strategies for pursuing school resource equity for Black children, White parents who remained in the school system championed specialty schools. Not only could these parents enroll their children in specialty schools, but they could then petition for resource allocations that favored these schools. Through this strategy, White parents could comply with court mandates while creating a path for resource concentrations that benefited their children. Presently, White children are less than 5 percent of the PGCPS student population, and the White children who remain in the public school system, along with Black middle-class children, are concentrated in specialty schools.

A senior official in the Prince George's teachers' union described the history of specialty schools and their current role in PGCPS:

> We are faced with the vestiges of segregation. Prince George's County was the last county in the state to desegregate the schools. And it was a fight. And the county's response in desegregating the schools, there was some fallout that came from that. One was they [White parents] did not want the White kids to be bused to the urban schools. And they really didn't want the kids from the urban schools to be bused out. And so, there was a lot of consternation about how to handle it. And that's where the Magnet Programs come from, because they were to attract White kids by having better programming, or programming period. So, you had your French immersion, you had the Montessori program, you had the Arts Magnet . . . you had all these little caviar programs that were 80/20, 80 percent White, 20 percent African American or minority. . . . I taught in the comprehensive program, where the kids weren't in a special program. Class sizes were much larger.

Presently, the ratio of White to Black students has flipped from what it was thirty years ago. PGCPS now serves mostly Black and Latino students. And it is mostly Black middle-class students who have access to the "caviar programs." This tiered school system, established during the official desegregation period of 1972 to 1998, was never designed to achieve meaningful equity across ethno-racial, class, and geographic lines, but rather was a tool for rationing resources in a context of funding scarcity. Furthermore, establishing magnet and other specialty schools was a strategy used in court mandates seeking to reconcile divergent interests: Whites' resistance to school desegregation and Blacks' desire for greater access to school resources.

On its face, creating a variety of schooling options increases parents' ability to select the educational opportunities best suited to their children's needs and interests. But given the sociohistorical context in which "school choice" is offered, it is no surprise that already advantaged groups navigate the school choice landscape more effectively than other groups, thus reinforcing and extending racial and class inequities. Or, as is the case for the majority of White Americans, having the option of school choice is not necessary because White Americans are usually satisfied with their neighborhood public schools. Satisfied with their default option, they do not feel compelled to consider alternatives.[46] And this makes sense—optimizing one's school choices takes time, energy, and money, all of which are limited. Consequently, parents who do activate school choice, most of whom are non-White, pay a "parenting tax."[47]

Because the courts have retreated from enforcing meaningful racial desegregation and economic and racial segregation persists, majority-Black and -Latino school systems, like PGCPS, bear more and more responsibility for educating higher-needs students. The scarring effects of protracted desegregation in Prince George's County fractured the system's foundation. In the next section, I show this fractured foundation is unable to support the weight of all of its students' needs.

Resegregation in PGCPS from the 2000s Forward

Current Prince George's decision-makers have inherited the resources and school type configurations created in the 1990s as the desegregation period drew to a close. County leaders deploy those resources to meet the needs of increasing numbers of students from working-class and poor households and decreasing numbers of students from affluent households. *Milliken II*'s premise—with which many scholars and activists concur—is that school systems can create high-performing schools without racial desegregation. Systems just need to allocate sufficient resources to all schools, regardless of their ethno-racial and class compositions.

The *Milliken II* stance is sound to some degree. What is underappreciated, however, is that the equitable distribution of resources across districts, among schools within districts, and between students within school districts is shaped by two highly racialized processes: (1) tax revenue generation as a function of residential and commercial property values within school districts, and (2) the clustering in certain school districts of harder-to-serve students, who generally require greater levels of investment. The negative effects of concentrated economic disadvantage on schools' performance have been documented at least since 1966. That year, the US Department of Health, Education, and Welfare (now the US Department of Health and Human Services) published its report on equality of educational opportunity, commonly known as the Coleman Report, so named for its lead author, James Coleman.[48] One of the report's main findings is that student outcomes improve when classrooms have students with a wide range of socioeconomic backgrounds. Said differently, concentrating students from low-income families in classrooms usually has a downward pull on student achievement.

Subsequent government and academic research continues to document relationships between economic and racial segregation in schools, achievement gaps between racial and class groups, and school system funding disparities.[49] These patterns indicate that White and Asian students are more likely to attend well-resourced schools, as measured by per pupil investment, teacher qualifications, curricular and co-curricular offerings, and school facility quality, among other factors.[50] And all of these conditions are associated with high levels of academic achievement. White students generally also attend schools where they are the population supermajority, and Asian students are more likely than Black and Latino children to attend mostly White schools. Prince George's County Schools' (PGCPS) constraints are consistent with these national trends. In the following section, I discuss the implications of funding constraints for PGCPS operating and capital expenditures.

PGCPS: Operating Budget and Expenditures

The county council appropriates funds to K-12 schools, just as it appropriates revenue for other public goods and services. But policies regarding how funds are distributed within the school system are managed by a school board composed of elected members from districts across the county and those appointed by the county executive. Maryland's contribution to PGCPS is driven by enrollment and a statutorily driven funding formula. Although the formula allocates funding on a per-pupil basis, according to measures of student need, such as socioeconomic status and English language proficiency, annual state funding levels are not guaranteed each year.

Regardless of state funding levels, the county council faces annual pressure to increase the amount it apportions to the school system. This pressure is especially acute and consequential when the state appropriates less money than the county anticipated, such as has happened during recessions. If Prince George's does not close the gap with its funds, the school system experiences a budget cut. To the extent that it provides these funds, however, the county must make hard budget trade-offs with other public goods and services. Furthermore, each year Prince George's must satisfy Maryland's "maintenance of effort" requirement by appropriating at least the same amount to the school system as it did the prior year, accounting for inflation. This requirement does not apply to other public goods and services.

Prince George's combines its apportionment of locally generated revenue with state funding to create its annual K-12 school budget. In 2018, the school budget was just under $2 billion, with Maryland and Prince George's each contributing about half of the revenue. Yet budget demands exceeded the funding that PGCPS received. As noted earlier in this chapter, about 60 percent of the system's students come from low-income households and 24 percent are English language learners. Students in these populations have a disproportionate need for educational and social and health services, among other material needs.[51]

Because Prince George's generally appropriates less to PGCPS than it requests, the school system often reduces or cuts programs and refrains from increasing its staff at sufficient rates; meanwhile, the student population continues to grow. A school board member representing inner beltway communities in southern Prince George's spoke about the rationing of school system funds:

> It's tough. We just celebrated negotiation contracts [with teachers and other school staff]. But you know, you're not given $150 million more. You have to make the decisions. Do we not have this or do we not have that? Do we not have twenty literacy coaches? Instead, we only have eight. So things have to be cut. Of course, our priority is going to be the education of students. But we also have to weigh the operations of schools. We have to weigh the payment of staff. And those all get weighed, and it's a difficult boat.

A county council member made similar comments about funding levels for county schools:

> Every school should be teaching a foreign language. Every school should have some vocational program that the student—you may not be able to do all of them, because we have so many different programs now, but the majority they should be able to, especially in the elementary school and middle school levels. They should have equity all across the board, so that every child has the same opportunity as a next child, and we don't have that.

As these comments demonstrate, decision-makers want to invest more in the school system to provide a wide range of educational options at every school. Were there equitable opportunities in all county schools, there would probably be less demand for admission to specialty and other selective schools. In this context of too few high-performing schools, the parents and guardians who are most adept at navigating the school system and who have the resources to live in certain neighborhoods have the most options. Thus, Black middle-class Prince Georgians endure education opportunity constraints that their White class peers in neighboring counties generally do not. But Black middle-class families in Prince George's do, on average, gain more access to educational resources than African Americans with lower socioeconomic status in the county.

County leaders have limited options for seeking additional revenue. Their two main funding streams are county and state tax revenue. The federal government contributes about 10 percent of funding to public schools, with most revenue targeted toward students from low-income families through Title I of the Elementary and Secondary Education Act. And for reasons explained in chapter 2, Prince George's County officials cannot raise taxes without direct voter approval.

In 2018, the PGCPS school board chair was well aware of these funding dynamics. But he asserted that even if he could not attain all of the money desired, it was still critical to propose a budget that accurately captured all school system needs. Throughout his tenure, he worked with other school board members, the county executive, and the PGCPS CEO (superintendent) to craft a "game change" budget for public schools—the amount that he believed was necessary to realize significant systemwide improvement. He described his strategy this way:

> What we said to the CEO [school superintendent] is, "Give us a budget. Give us a game-changing budget. What would it take to significantly increase academic achievement in our schools?" Not moderately, but significant increase. And those budgets were asking for $100, $150 million more than what the county had given us in previous years. And it was effective in kind of changing the discussion about what we needed, and it led to one year the county executive said, "Okay. The only way I can give you this is through a tax increase." So the county executive tried to propose a property tax increase to pay for education, and it crashed and burned really bad. We went out and we fought hard for it, and we thought that the citizens and at least policy leaders were ready for it, and they weren't.

School system leaders, like the school board chair, regularly seek to increase the PGCPS budget, but they encounter significant structural constraints in revenue generation. Despite budget limitations, the county council consistently prioritizes school system funding. In 2018, and in the five years prior, the council appropriated $20 to $40 million more to schools beyond the state "maintenance of effort" requirement.

Long-deferred spending dating back to the county's racial transition in the 1990s is now exacerbated by an increasing high-needs student population, the majority of whom come from economically distressed Black or Latino households. Given that the students served by PGCPS have many unmet material needs at home and in their neighborhoods, schools provide students with core resources, such as food and health care. County leaders seek to streamline and coordinate provision of health and human services to students, parents, and other neighborhood residents through "community schools." Under this model, county officials recognize that schools are usually the most trusted, widely known, and conveniently located local government institutions within neighborhoods.

Community schools' provision of health and other services shows significant promise, but in 2018 they were still in a "demonstration" phase, and therefore not widely available throughout the county. A school board member, reflecting on the board's role in managing PGCPS budget constraints, said this during her interview, capturing what I heard from most school leaders: "That's been very challenging for us, to try to make sure that all our kids are coming up and they all have the same level of resources to bring them all up to where they need to be. I'm really proud of the work that we have done as a board."

A core dimension of operating costs is compensation for teachers, whose pay and benefits are the greatest proportion of the school budget. Instructors are also the primary personnel managing students' learning. As discussed in chapter 3, in 2018 the county was still making county civil servants whole from recession-era pay freezes, and teachers were not exempt from those freezes. Although money was allocated in 2018 to increase teachers' pay, they still had not been made whole yet from the recession-period freeze.

Even before the recession, Prince George's teachers were generally paid less than their counterparts in neighboring wealthier, Whiter jurisdictions, like Montgomery and Fairfax Counties. A senior official in the Prince George's teachers' union noted that teacher pay was one of the main reasons for the higher-than-expected turnover rate of teachers year to year. She also noted that lower pay contributed to the presence of provisionally certified teachers in many classrooms, especially in the schools with the most high-needs students. Teachers with seniority have greater influence on their school assignment, and many of the most experienced teachers choose to work in well-resourced schools. During my interview with this teachers' union senior official, she spoke about teacher retention and compensation challenges:

> We had a 15 percent turnover of teachers last year. We're the training ground for the rest of the region. And we actually walked out—he [the county executive] came to speak to the Maryland State [Education] Association convention. And the reason why we walked out was because so many of our members are not on step where they should be. And we had to fight and march and picket just to get two steps.

This teachers' union official noted that teachers had to press hard to gain the raises they received in 2018, "just to get two steps." Furthermore, not only did she identify a 15 percent turnover rate, but she described how Prince George's County effectively subsidizes neighboring jurisdictions— "We're the training ground for the rest of the region." Later in her interview, she stated that Prince George's teacher pay is about comparable to compensation levels in neighboring local jurisdictions in teachers' early years.

The pay disparity with nearby locales expands considerably after teachers have five years of experience. Therefore, at the point where teacher effectiveness improves demonstrably, many teachers move to nearby counties for higher salaries and often easier work conditions, such as smaller class sizes and more school resources.

The county council chair made a similar observation about teacher turnover:

> When they start to be feeling like they're vilified because of all of that [referring to school performance levels and scandals reported in the local news], they can make a decision to go to Anne Arundel, Howard, Montgomery, DC, Arlington, Alexandria, anywhere else in this region, and live. They might live there already; they might live here. But they only have to drive an extra ten miles to get to where they have to go, make more money, and have less public scrutiny and probably a smaller class size. Why in the world would I stay?

Given its high levels of teacher turnover, Prince George's County, in effect, subsidizes neighboring Whiter, wealthier counties' school systems. Prince George's pays the up-front costs of recruiting, training, and mentoring newly minted teachers. But after making this investment, the county does not reap the reward of a well-trained and experienced teacher workforce commensurate with its investment. Rather, counties that are already more advantaged enjoy additional benefits at Prince George's expense.

To maintain a high-quality school system, Prince George's must consistently invest revenue in several major expense categories, one of which is operating costs, including those discussed in this section. Another major category of spending is capital expenditures, such as the maintenance of school buildings and the construction of new schools. In the next section, I discuss the county's capital needs and the constraints it faces as it seeks to meet them.

PGCPS Funding Constraints: Capital Expenditures

Garnering adequate revenue for capital investments is perhaps even more challenging than attaining sufficient operating revenue. Capital projects take significant time to come to fruition—several years—and the scale of revenue required for one project is significant, often tens of millions of dollars. The two main types of capital expenses are (1) repairing and improving existing buildings and (2) constructing new schools.

At county council and school board hearings, school officials frequently petitioned for substantial increases in dedicated capital funding. In a 2017 report, PGCPS stated that it needed $3 billion for capital expenses between 2017 and 2022.[52] "Those are the ones that are the most intractable for us. If your school is fifty years old, it's going to be fifty years old until we can build you a new school," remarked the school board chair when I asked him about the greatest challenges facing the school system.

Building new schools requires millions of dollars at the elementary and middle school levels and tens of millions at the high school level. Under the current funding arrangement for erecting schools, Maryland and the county share the cost, with the state usually paying at least half.[53] County leaders regularly stated that the long game involves increased state funding for capital expenditures. A council member representing a district with significant school overcrowding underscored the urgency of new school construction when she made this statement to Maryland legislators prior to the state's 2018 legislative session:

> One of the issues I have is overcrowding. I have whole schools in travel trailers. This cannot continue. Not only do I need four new schools, we're having discussions about split schools, night school. This is all over the northern parts of the county. The last time I heard this is in developing countries. We need to go beyond politics to address all the needs of all the children in the county. I don't want to funnel money to just one part of the county.

This council member's comments highlight what happens when resources are rationed. Her constituents, most of whom are Latino and working-class or poor, struggled to receive their share of resources. While all Prince Georgians experience the consequences of underfunded public goods and services, people with the most marginalized social statuses tend to fare worst, as these residents usually have few alternative ways to meet their material needs.

At the state level, Prince George's is one of twenty-four counties competing for educational resources. Maryland's education trust fund is the primary source of state revenue for county schools. Schools may also apply for state grants and other forms of targeted funding. And at the federal level, Title I of the Elementary and Secondary Education Act supports schools serving students from economically distressed households. Therefore, school districts with greater numbers of students from economically strained households receive more funding than districts with students from more economically affluent households.

Deferred maintenance has put most schools in Prince George's in need of investment and thus created a long queue of schools requesting increased capital funding each year, but only a subset of their requests receive meaningful attention. Therefore, how money from local and state revenue is allocated is particularly contentious, given that most schools' projects have been waiting for years. Council and school board members, the county executive, parents, and other stakeholders all have their own criteria for what they believe should have priority. The main axis of disagreement centers on being responsive to the areas with the fastest-growing student populations in the northern section of the county, while accounting for schools in the central and southern parts of the county that have longer-standing maintenance needs. That is, some groups claim length of time waiting for funds should take precedent, while others prioritize population density and growth.

Some southern Prince George's schools are losing population or are under-enrolled. In neighborhoods with shrinking student populations in their schools, one cost-saving strategy would be for the county to transfer students from the worst-maintained schools to the better-maintained ones and close those in the poorest condition. But closing schools is a lightning rod issue in most neighborhoods, as residents view schools as sacred community institutions. And given Black Americans' history of having less access to education than White Americans, African Americans are particularly concerned about projects that reduce educational touch points.

A key driver of the population growth asymmetry between northern and southern Prince George's is the age distribution of the Latino population compared to that of the Black population: Latinos have a younger average age than the Black population. This pattern is consistent with the national population distribution of these two groups. That is, many of the African Americans in the county, especially those who are middle class, are beyond childbearing age and thus do not send children to PGCPS. Yet the African Americans who are in the school system have long-standing unmet needs, including those related to school building maintenance and improvements.

For instance, some Black Americans in Suitland and Oxon Hill, neighborhoods in the southern part of the county, are concerned that their needs are neglected as the county seeks to respond to the needs of northern Prince George's. Valerie, an upper-middle-class parent of two children who lives in a single-family home in Temple Hills, an inside-the-beltway neighborhood, made these remarks during her interview, which are similar to what I heard from other African American parents living in the southern tip of the county:

> AUTHOR: If you were to speak to the county executive or the county council, are there any things you'd want to share with them about your experiences as a resident? Or things that you'd like to see them focus on? If they gave you ten minutes, what would you say to them?
>
> VALERIE: That definitely that they need to invest more in the southern half of the county . . . more resources down this way. . . . The schools, definitely the schools—they need to invest in their schools. Because I know that they have an earmark for a couple of schools that will get renovated. . . . There's some schools that are in dire need. . . . Actually, our neighborhood high school—it was brought to our attention that they were having, the paint was chipping from the walls, and that the school is just crumbling. But the money is being focused on another school that's in another part of the county. It's like, "Well, what about our schools down here in southern PG?"

Valerie knows that resources for school maintenance and construction are rationed owing to revenue constraints. Nonetheless, she is concerned that her neighborhood's high school is not receiving its fair share of attention: "Well, what about our schools down here in southern PG?"

On the other hand, the Latino population is growing faster than the Black population, and the rising number of Latino students puts inordinate pressure on an already frail infrastructure. Hence, the wear and tear on buildings with majority-Latino populations is even greater than it would be if these buildings served the number of students they were designed to serve. High Point High School, mentioned earlier, is a quintessential example of a majority-Latino high school in sore need of repair. The area where High Point sits could easily sustain another high school. As the council member noted earlier, because there are not enough schools in the district she serves, many schools accommodate their student populations by adding trailers to their campuses.

In this context of revenue scarcity—where African Americans have been petitioning for sufficient educational resources for years and the Latino population is the fastest-growing—there is significant ethno-racial tension between Black and Latino residents regarding capital investment priorities. Rationing is a short-term response to the constraints of too little revenue, but the long-term solution is generating more revenue. That is, this ethno-racial tension between African Americans and Latinos regarding school funding is a symptom of uneven material resource distributions across local jurisdictions within states and metropolitan areas—and that unevenness is anchored in mechanisms enabling White domination and resource hoarding. If local jurisdiction revenue were an apple pie, Black middle-class people have barely attained a sliver, yet they are disproportionately responsible for sharing their meager slice with economically distressed Black and Latino people. White middle-class Americans, in contrast, have a larger slice of the pie and are not required to share it with less affluent groups to the same extent as middle-class Black Americans.

Ultimately, given the cost of school maintenance and construction, Prince George's County needs significantly more fiscal support from Maryland. Current state provisions should account for the scarring effects of the desegregation processes of the 1970s through 1990s and the current challenges of race and class resegregation. In the next section, I discuss Maryland's role in supporting counties' school maintenance and construction.

Maryland's Contribution to Prince George's County Public Schools

Maryland's funding formula allocates money to counties based on their ability to raise locally generated revenue and based on student-related factors, including students' socioeconomic background, English language proficiency, and learning capacity, among other factors.[54] But even with the state formula weighted to support economically disadvantaged students and majority-minority counties, PGCPS struggles to provide the resources students need to excel. State aid's insufficiency reflects the depth of the county's unmet needs and thus the scale of increased revenue that Prince George's requires to fund operations and make capital investments.

Before Maryland's 2018 legislative session, the Prince George's County Council met with state delegates to discuss the county's policy priorities—and education topped the list. Council members explained that the strain that the county faces in trying to generate sufficient revenue for public goods and services often prevents the county from setting aside adequate revenue for state "matching funds" requirements. To activate state funding for school construction, Maryland requires that local jurisdictions demonstrate they have revenue to fund half of the cost of the project. At the meeting, county council members and state legislators explored options for accessing state funds without having to meet the matching requirement:

> COUNCIL CHAIR: We want to begin to have a brief dialogue. The lead is education, next is transportation, and the next is the distribution of resources and to create revenue. Sometimes we don't have authority. With regard to education, we need help with our capital improvement plan. Baltimore city was able to bond to do more work with their CIP [capital improvement plan]. We're wondering how we in PGC can do just that. We have one of the oldest and largest school systems, only eclipsed by Montgomery County, but they have far more resources than we do. Lastly, a desire to push for early education— early education is the best education we can give our children.

> MARYLAND HOUSE DELEGATE: With regard to Baltimore, they're not free schools. They pay some of the highest taxes in the state. We're moving in the right direction. I'm setting up an education council. If Prince George's County saw the taxes Baltimore residents pay, they may be resistant. For universal pre-K, I think we should use gaming funds. Governor [Larry] Hogan wants to take care of the rural-tier families. In rural, $40,000 is the cutoff for household income, but here $40,000 doesn't get you much. We need universal pre-K. We're told that if the locals want to do it, they can do it [fund universal pre-K].

> COUNCIL CHAIR: We prefer for the state to do it and we provide a small match. Montgomery County's revenue stream allows them to do more of a match.

In this exchange, the council showed awareness of the capacities and actions of neighboring Maryland jurisdictions. The council sought to ensure that Prince George's was exercising all of its options, not only to increase capital investment but to expand its education system, such as by offering universal pre-K. Council members learned from the state delegate that there are no magic solutions. Regarding universal pre-K, specifically, the county already struggles to serve its existing student population in its school facilities. Therefore, increasing Prince George's County's student population is not prudent, since doing so would intensify strain on an already overburdened system, regardless of how important early education is for students' learning and social and emotional outcomes. In my interview with the council chair, he expressed his vision for state aid for PGCPS:

> The state bears the first responsibility for education for every jurisdiction in the state. And the funding formula, when Thornton I [funding formula enacted in 2017–2018] came in, we talked about the disparity and poverty and all of those pieces, and the state funding formula rewarded some things. And if the state invested in universal pre-K, I just took $50 million off the table that I ain't got to put in. I ain't mad at that, right? With the state funding formula, what I need them to do is take the state's largesse because the state has all of these different jurisdictions pouring in. Montgomery County pours in a lot more than they take out of the state. Prince George's County, a little different. I need the state to take care of all of its children appropriately. It needs to take into consideration poverty. It needs to take into consideration performance. It needs to take into consideration all of the things necessary for it to say it's spending its money wisely.

The exchange between Prince George's officials and the state delegate show that in many respects Prince George's manages urban challenges similar to those of Baltimore City, while seeking to create the conditions for sustaining a school system comparable to those of Fairfax and Montgomery Counties. Ideally, Prince George's County would have the fiscal capacity to meet the needs of all of its students, irrespective of neighborhood, ethno-racial and class statuses, and learning needs.

In 2021, Maryland replaced the funding formula in effect when I did my research. The new formula, titled "Blue Print for Maryland's Future," also distributes funding to schools on a per pupil basis. Schools receive a base amount for each student and a weighted amount, given each student's characteristics, such as whether the child comes from a low-income household or is an English language learner. The primary differences between the old and new formulas are that the new formula increases funding over the next ten years and does so within five "pillars": early childhood, high-quality and diverse teachers and leaders, college and career readiness, more resources for all students to be successful, and governance and accountability.[55]

How Relative Regional Burden Undermines PGCPS Capacity

Relative regional burden, the mechanisms through which Prince George's County subsidizes Whiter, wealthier jurisdictions, is captured in table 4.1, which shows spending levels in Prince George's County Schools compared to spending in the Montgomery County and Fairfax County school systems. I disaggregate the budget in terms of the county, state, and federal contributions and include per pupil spending levels and the percentage of students from low-income families. That is, I show what each jurisdiction contributes from its own revenues and what is transferred to it from the state (Maryland or Virginia), and the US government.

The amount of state aid Prince George's receives is greater than what Montgomery County receives because the Maryland funding formula for schools is weighted to support high-needs students, such as those from low-income families and those who are English language learners, and Prince George's serves more of these children. Because Prince George's and Montgomery Counties are in the same state, it is possible to see the effects of state aid between these jurisdictions more readily. The terms of state aid are different for Fairfax County, which is subject to the funding formula of another state, Virginia. Notwithstanding this limitation, it is still clear that Prince George's County has double the number of students who come from economically distressed households. Thus, irrespective of state transfer levels, Prince George's has a significantly higher number of students requiring above-average levels of funding to meet their learning needs. Finally, although a small part of the budget, Prince George's County also receives a larger federal contribution than do Montgomery and Fairfax Counties. Most federal funding is for students from low-income families through Title I of the Elementary and Secondary Education Act, and Prince George's serves a greater share of this student population.

Table 4.1 also shows that Prince George's allocates less of its own funding to its public schools than do the other two counties. This disparity suggests that Prince George's total revenue is insufficient for funding public goods and services adequately, schools among them. In other words, counties with higher local tax revenue can afford to fund their public goods and services without making hard budget tradeoffs among them. School systems that

Table 4.1 Public School Spending in Prince George's, Montgomery, and Fairfax Counties, Fiscal Year 2018

	Prince George's	Montgomery	Fairfax
Total student enrollment	132,667	161,302	189,022
Total spending[a]	$1.9 billion	$2.5 billion	$2.8 billion
County contribution	$739 million	$1.67 billion	$1.97 billion
State contribution	$1.1 billion	$680 million	$636 million
Federal contribution	$125 million	$75 million	$42 million
Per pupil allocation	$14,322	$15,499	$14,813
Low-income students[b]	61%	34%	29%

Source: Author's calculations.

[a]Does not add; remainder is other grant contributions and rounding.

[b]Those qualifying for reduced-price meals.

receive lower local tax revenue are more dependent on state and federal transfers to reach sufficient funding levels.

In terms of per pupil spending, all three counties spend within $2,000 of each other, and at first blush, these county differences in spending may seem almost negligible. But given the PGCPS student population of over 132,000 students, were PGCPS to have the same budget as its neighbors it would have over $156 million more each year. Furthermore, absolute differences in per pupil spending do not capture all of Prince George's K-12 education system needs and challenges, particularly those resulting from serving a disproportionate share of the DC region's high-needs students, while also managing the long-term effects of failed racial desegregation efforts.

As Prince George's County educates more harder-to-serve students, it effectively subsidizes Montgomery and Fairfax Counties because these counties can use more of their school revenue to invest in operating and capital expenditures that improve their schools' performance. And as school performance increases, so does demand for homes in these jurisdictions, which expands these counties' tax bases and, in turn, increases the tax revenue they have available to invest in all public goods and services, not just public schools. Thus, Prince George's County's relative regional burden bolsters neighboring counties' budget bottom lines, which is a relative regional benefit, or subsidy. Chronic inadequate funding compels Prince George's County to manage the reality of severe budget constraints, while touting programs that are most likely to keep as many middle- and upper middle-class students in the system.

How PGCPS Manages Fiscal Constraint and Reputational Fallout

The public schools in Prince George's County offer a wide range of educational opportunities to their students, from language immersion, to vocational training, to International Baccalaureate and advanced placement coursework. Yet the school system struggles to maintain high-quality schooling throughout the county and to provide it to all students, irrespective of their ethno-racial and class statuses and geographic location. School system resource constraints reflect Prince George's County's struggle to fund all public goods and services at adequate levels. The jurisdiction makes trade-offs between public goods and services and within the school system itself. Decision-makers who shape school resource allocation—most notably, the county council and school board—often have different priorities than parents. For instance, in the 2018 budget, county officials prioritized increasing teacher compensation to retain qualified instructors, while parents petitioned to hire more teachers to expand curriculum options.

Additionally, as stakeholders—parents, teachers, administrators, and advocacy groups, among others—seek to hold the school system accountable for student outcomes, they are increasingly frustrated by the lack of improvement in school performance. This disappointment often leads to people not giving PGCPS the benefit of the doubt when staff make mistakes and to not offering sufficient time and discretion for implementing long-term improvement plans. Furthermore, because the school system faces many issues worthy of attention but is given too few resources to remedy them adequately, consensus about what to prioritize can rarely be reached. Consequently, many critical issues are left un- or under-addressed.

In this context, some people pursue external means to pressure the school system to be responsive to them. One such strategy is inviting news teams from local television stations to highlight PGCPS deficiencies, such as the need for major repairs—for instance, abatement of lead in drinking water fountains and of mold in some schools. This is a layered, ironic situation: On the one hand, a Black jurisdiction has insufficient tax revenue to meet public goods and services needs because White jurisdictions hoard material resources; on the other hand, Black people who are frustrated by the lack of adequate material resources seek to meet their needs by inviting the scrutiny of the White gaze on the Black-led system to increase the visibility of their specific concerns to force action in their favor.

When I arrived in the field in 2017, county officials were discussing the loss of a $6.4 million grant for Head Start, a federally supported pre-K program for children from low-income families.[56] That same year, an adult working for the school system was investigated for inappropriate physical contact with a student. The next year administrators and teachers at a high school were removed from their positions after an investigation into the school's grading and graduation certification procedures.[57] The grading and graduation concerns stemmed from a Prince George's official writing to the governor's office about irregularities he observed. All of these issues were reported to local news media, which covered these incidents in detail for weeks.

In his interview, the PGCPS superintendent/CEO commented on the need for effective management processes to improve accountability within the school system and to build trust in the system. He also discussed the limits of using media as a tool for garnering school system attention and resources:

> Every district has issues and things they need to improve on, and they put systems and structures, processes in place, like hotlines and audits and those kind of things, to try to keep focused on getting better, identifying issues, improving, repairing, whatever. But there are some people who just feel like their goal is to tear things down, not be supportive, not to sit around a table and say, "We have these issues. How can we work together on them?," but rather to just throw the issues out and say, "This is an issue and it's this person's fault." That is not helpful to improving districts, to improving education. It's in, some ways, about power and control, who has it, who doesn't have it. This is just trying to undermine the public belief, undermine the political support, undermine all those things is an issue in this county, and it's been that way for a long time. You may be familiar with the graduation audit that we had. A letter goes to the governor. I think that was their choice, that was their decision, but it didn't need to be that way, but the audit that resulted from that even points out that there's a tendency in this district to go to the media instead of coming to the school system to get things

fixed. . . . Instead of spending our energy working on improving the district, we're spending our time trying to explain things, and some of that explanation is wonky and hard to understand. It doesn't play well to [the] public.

The management processes that the superintendent noted are especially hard to maintain when there is rapid turnover in top leadership positions within PGCPS. Most superintendents—who are appointed by the county executive—hold their post for less than five years.[58] And whoever leads the school system faces deep challenges, the most intractable of which is improving student outcomes in the absence of the material resources the school system needs to achieve that goal.

All PGCPS superintendents, since the 1990s, have needed more revenue. These officials also need buy-in and trust from fellow administrators and teachers and parents about their vision, as well as time to implement that vision. As it stands, superintendents often come to PGCPS proposing promising paths forward but garner limited resources and stakeholder buy-in. Recall the "game change" budget that the school board chair insisted upon, even as he knew it was highly unlikely that the county council would approve that level of funding, given the county's other public goods and services needs.

When successive rounds of school system leadership fail to meet parents', teachers', and other stakeholders' expectations, they become increasingly doubtful that the system can improve. Even with severe budget constraints, stakeholders want PGCPS to maximize what it can do—and they want immediate results. But closing the gap between expectations for PGCPS and the school system's capacity to meet them will continue to be elusive until there is sufficient revenue for operating and capital expenses. And were the school system to attain adequate revenue, there are bound to be problems in a school system as large as PGCPS. Indeed, many neighboring counties' school systems probably have some of the problems that beset PGCPS, but their problems are just less likely to be reported to or covered by the media.

Black Middle-Class Agency in Pursuit of Optimal Schooling Options

To be sure, many PGCPS schools offer excellent educational opportunities. But because schools with strong reputations and student outcomes are in short supply, most of these high-performing schools must use a system to ration their seats. Some schools select students through lotteries, randomly choosing students from a list of applicants. This process is the most likely to yield a student body with representation across ethno-racial and class groups, given that everyone on the list has the same chance of admission.

Nonetheless, Black middle-class students are overrepresented in schools that require applications, including those with lottery-based admissions. African Americans from lower socioeconomic statuses and Latino students, most of whom are from working-class and low-income households, are underrepresented. Parents from economically strained households or who have limited English proficiency are less likely to be on the lottery list in the first place.

Any school with a selection process requires parents to take above-average action to secure a slot for their child. For example, parents usually must apply to selective schools well before the next school year begins, and middle-class parents are more likely than their working-class peers to know these deadlines. Affluent parents also benefit from networks of other middle-class Black people who alert them to the deadlines, and class-advantaged parents generally have more education, time, and money than working-class parents. All of these factors equip Black middle-class parents to draw down education system resources. Middle-class parents are even advantaged in getting their children into schools that do not require application. As with selective schools, affluent parents often rely on word of mouth and school reputation to select the best-performing schools for their children.

Black middle-class agency manifests not only in how some affluent Black parents pursue selective public schools but also in how some opt out of public schools and into private and parochial schools. In Prince George's County, as Black middle-class parents seek the ideal conditions for their children's education, they have two main options: work within the public system or send their children to private or religious schools. And a small minority homeschool their children.

Parents who select private and parochial schooling for their children use a strategy that is not consistent with "linked fate" solidarity. Overall, Black people, irrespective of their other social statuses, seek political and social cohesion with other Black people because all African Americans endure White domination and anti-Black racism. Political scientist Michael Dawson, in his book *Behind the Mule*, refers to Black social solidarity as a "linked fate" perspective.[59] In my study, Black people's decision not to send their children to public schools shows the limits of linked fate. Other scholars also find that a sense of linked fate among African

Americans is not universal across issues and contexts, particularly in the presence of severe material and social resource scarcity.[60]

But the limits of linked fate across issues and contexts is not evidence that Black Americans have abandoned social and political solidarity altogether as a guiding principle for how they relate to other African Americans. Indeed, Michael Dawson himself, in his book *Not in Our Lifetimes*, published about fifteen years after *Behind the Mule*, highlights how class and other social status variation among Black Americans make Black political solidarity increasingly complicated but does not erase it altogether.[61]

My findings regarding middle-class Black Americans opting out of the school system show that Black Americans, like most Americans, act strategically in discrete instances to meet their material and social needs. The stakes—equipping Black children with skills and resources for navigating a society not designed for them to thrive—could not be higher. The Black parents I spoke to who sent their children to private or parochial schools continued to believe, in principle, that public schools are the best way to educate children. In practice, however, these parents decided not to send their children to PGCPS because they did not find a school that met their expectations, or if they did, their child was not admitted. Indeed, many parents I interviewed and spoke to informally said high-performing public schools are critical for Black people's economic, political, and social advancement, in keeping with Black political perspectives and actions since post–Civil War Reconstruction, when Black people were first elected to local, state, and federal offices.[62]

Prince George's officials, while seeking to educate all children in the county well, are especially sensitized to middle-class parents' desire for more educational opportunities for their children. School system leaders, recognizing that affluent parents are willing and able to opt out of PGCPS, want to keep these parents in the system because their children, on average, do not require as many resources for academic success. Moreover, affluent Black parents often lend their educational, time, and monetary resources to bolster school performance, such as by participating in parent-teacher associations.

At the same time, most affluent Black parents advocate for more spending on specialty schools, gifted and talented programs, and tracks offering enhanced curricular opportunities. Black middle-class parents who are deeply involved in the school system bring economic, social, and cultural capital that expands schools' capacities, but their advocacy patterns can also widen the gap in educational resource attainment between children from middle-class homes and those from working-class and low-income homes. This is true even as Black middle-class parents usually attain fewer educational resources for their children than do their White middle-class peers.

As county officials seek to fulfill middle-class families' interests, they are also navigating the general budget constraints of the school system. When county leaders prioritize the programs preferred by middle-class parents, they often exacerbate the strain on the school system, given that investment in one area requires decreasing the investment in another. In a briefing regarding PGCPS transportation challenges, which reflect the additional transportation costs of sending children to non-neighborhood schools, including specialty schools, a council member described how specialty programs intensify school system funding challenges:

> Every year the same story—it's extremely frustrating—issues are systemwide. We're so busy expanding programs that we've gotten away from neighborhood schools. We haven't gotten the foundation correct, but we're busy expanding these programs—$100 million in the system can't work if we're shipping students from north county to south county. I understand challenges all the way around, but we're talking about for years. We might as well go back to the days of busing in the 1970s [the desegregation period].

Still, parents who have already opted out of PGCPS highlight for county officials that they risk losing even more middle-class parents if they do not satisfy these parents' requests. Valerie, introduced earlier, exemplifies what I heard from affluent Black parents: She preferred to send her children to public schools, but PGCPS' reputation led her to select private schooling for her children. Valerie's comments also highlight the role of word of mouth—the influence of neighbors and social networks on residents' perceptions of the county school system before they try it for themselves. Each family who has a negative experience with PGCPS, and then decides to send their children to private school, is likely to encourage others to do the same. Valerie said:

> I have two children, and they both ended up going to private school only because our local public school has had a reputation, or has a reputation, that I knew they weren't going to that school. I had three neighbors on my

block—they warned me and they told me, "Don't even waste your time sending your child to that school." Because they told me about their experiences. All three of them removed their children from the school. One ended up homeschooling her son, another one used another family member's address so he could get rezoned to a different school. And then the third one, she sent her child to private school. So, just based off of their experiences and what I was hearing from other families, I wasn't going to do that to my children. So we spend a lot of our tax dollars, they're earmarked—about 50 percent of our taxes are earmarked for educational services, and I just don't see it being reinvested back to the classroom.

Valerie recognizes that private schooling is costly—both because she pays tuition for schooling and because she is not using the public school system she supports with her taxes. She also expressed frustration that a substantial amount of tax revenue is dedicated to public schools ("about 50 percent of our taxes are earmarked for educational services"), yet she felt that the public schools' performance was not adequate for educating her own children.

In her interview, Arlene, who is a Black middle-class parent of one child and lived in a single-family home in Capital Heights, an inside-the beltway neighborhood, demonstrated the fallout from Prince George's County's efforts to stretch the county budget to cover the programs that affluent residents want, while also seeking to maintain the integrity and learning rigor of all programs. Arlene's son was in a language immersion program, but the school offered him less than what she expected:

ARLENE: But I knew that he [her son] was only be coming out of public schools because, in my opinion, they passed my kid along the last two years.

AUTHOR: Oh, really?

ARLENE: In the language immersion program. Yeah. I was really concerned about where he was, and it's an immersion school. But at the same time, the structure of that program, and it's been in existence for a number of years now, should have been revitalized, refreshed, and renewed at this point. It has not been. What you have is teenagers and faculty that is sick of the teenagers because of, for whatever reason, they're not getting what they need, or I guess the teachers, children are pissed off because they know they're not getting what they need. They're giving them the answers is my point. I found they were giving him the answers to some of the tests. I was like, dang. I can't leave you in here. You know what I mean?

AUTHOR: Right, right.

ARLENE: I was like, well, we're going to move on and we'll see how it works out. I have tutors. I've spent a lot of money on stuff like that. Tutors and counselors and stuff like that. When I said "counselors," I just mean people that will tutor him in math, reading, whatever the heck he's not scoring well in, just to make sure that he can at least get here.

Assessments of PGCPS by some parents, like Arlene, are informed by direct experience. Other parents, like Valerie, form their opinions based on their social network's evaluation of the public school system. One of the congressional representatives for Prince George's noted that the reputation of the county's public schools undermines Black middle-class parents' confidence in PGCPS:

> Prince George['s] County has probably the highest percentage of families that send their kids to private schools. And they're not Georgetown Prep. There's schools that are probably no better than the public schools. But there's this perception that I got to get out of the public schools. And when families aren't in the public schools, they're not invested in our public schools. They still pay taxes, but they don't really care about the public schools. So they certainly don't want an increase in any form of taxes to invest in that because they're already paying another tax in private tuition.

Importantly, this federal official explains that many of the private and parochial schools that Prince George's youth attend have not had better learning outcomes than PGCPS.[63] Many parents are likely, however, to continue to send their children to nonpublic schools because the county's schools have a poor reputation. In general, choice gives people a sense of agency. Yet choice is not a panacea. What matters as much, if not more, are the options people have to choose among and what it takes for them to activate and utilize the option they select.[64]

Affluent Black parents, like class-advantaged White parents, deploy class-based resources to enable their children to attain their own socioeconomic standing or higher. However, Black parents have a heavier lift in this regard than do White parents. African American parents must teach their children core life skills that all children need to thrive as adults in the United States, as well as the particular repertoires necessary for navigating a White-dominant society.[65] And Black parents do this with fewer material resources, on average, than White parents.

Middle-class Black parents are especially interested in ensuring that their children take pride in themselves as African-descendant people and that their children enjoy and appreciate Black people and culture.[66] Many Black middle-class parents are also concerned that their children not adopt behaviors they associate with Black people who are economically constrained, such as speaking Black vernacular English in mixed-race settings. Affluent African American parents want their children to "code-switch"—that is, to understand how to present themselves in Black versus White spaces and how to leverage social and material resources in Black versus White spaces.[67] Upper-middle-class Black people have the material resources to focus even more on the cultural capital associated with elite society—from private piano and tennis lessons to trips abroad.[68]

Given the range of Black middle-class parents' educational and socialization goals for their children, even if PGCPS quality improves demonstrably, there is likely to still be a contingent of parents who opt out of PGCPS for reasons other than dissatisfaction with school quality. Some Prince Georgians want more control over the school curriculum, particularly given the unique challenges encountered by Black children and teenagers. For instance, some parents want their children to be affirmed by immersion in curricula anchored in African American and African history and identity. This perspective is exemplified by a senior pastor of one of the largest Prince George's congregations. He explained the rationale for his church's K-8 school:

> I always wanted to have a school where we taught our own, as some other cultures do. . . . There wasn't any emphasis [in Prince George's County public schools] on the African American experience in Africa, our origin. So I wanted to make sure that the Black experience was captured early on in the minds of our young people. . . . Ground them in who they are, so they value who they are.

While it is likely that some parents would reinforce African American identity formation by choosing nonpublic schools for their children, even if the school system improved, opting out of PGCPS for this reason is categorically different from what is occurring now. Many middle-class parents are leaving PGCPS because they do not trust the system to provide their children with an effective education in core subjects, like reading and math.

Ameliorating challenges in PGCPS stemming from underinvestment must be undertaken in concert with addressing the county's broader fiscal constraints—most notably, the relative regional burden the jurisdiction bears for the DC region. Faced with significant budget pressures across public goods and services, Prince George's County is constantly seeking new revenue generation mechanisms. Given the county's limited choices, owing to state and local policy on what can be taxed, Prince George's officials have chosen the pursuit of private investment as their primary strategy to attain more revenue. In the next chapter, I discuss how the county seeks private development and the extent to which its efforts yield additional tax revenue.

CHAPTER 5

The Pursuit of Private Investment in a Context of White Domination and Anti-Black Racism

The plan's framework is organized around the themes of Work, Live, and Sustain, which helped guide the plan goals of capturing a greater share of the region's forecasted job growth, creating walkable urban places, meeting the needs of the County's changing population, and preserving valuable natural and historic resources.

—Elizabeth M. Hewlett, chair of Prince George's County
Planning Department, foreword to *Plan 2035* (2014)

SEEKING INCREASED PRIVATE investment is the core strategy employed by most local governments to generate new tax revenue. As the chapter epigraph suggests, Prince George's County's development opportunities are nested within the growth patterns of the DC region as a whole. Prince George's officials aim to position the county to receive its proportionate share of private investment, while keeping in mind the jurisdiction's revenue needs and other interests.

Development potentially creates opportunities for additional tax income through multiple mechanisms. Corporations pay taxes and fees during the permitting and construction phases of their projects and then commercial taxes on an ongoing basis once their businesses are established. New firms also expand a county's economy. Prince George's, like most jurisdictions, is interested in the fastest-growing and most lucrative industries, such as technology and health care. Once enough businesses in a certain sector

https://doi.org/10.7758/bwmi8829.7673

have clustered in an area, they create synergies that lead to more efficient production and collaboration processes among firms.[1] From the county government's perspective, such sector hubs are desirable because other businesses are organically drawn to the county, enabling the jurisdiction to gain more commercial tax revenue without the effort of recruiting businesses.

An example of such a hub is College Park. Prince George's is nurturing a technology corridor in this municipality in large part because it is home to Maryland's flagship state-funded university. Businesses can use university research and facilities to enhance their production. The university is also a place from which to recruit high-skilled workers. Employees, if they choose to live in Prince George's, pay local income taxes, thus increasing revenue for the county—and all the more so when these new residents earn middle- and upper-middle-class salaries.

College Park is a success story—among others that I discuss later in this chapter—but overall, Prince George's faces significant limitations as it seeks private investment. The county competes with other DC metropolitan area jurisdictions. And the region's development context is shaped by developer preferences for investing in White space and by private investors' strategy of pitting jurisdictions against one another. Developers use jurisdictions' desire for investment to leverage tax concessions. Local governments willing and able to offer the most tax and fee breaks are the most likely to "win" new projects.

Prince George's is disadvantaged in such competitions because businesses catering to upper-middle-class and elite clienteles, though they can earn a profit in Prince George's, are likely to earn even more in neighboring jurisdictions that are Whiter and wealthier. Furthermore, because these other jurisdictions have more tax revenue margin in their budgets, they can afford tax and fee concessions without compromising public goods and services quality. Historical and ongoing White domination and anti-Black policies and the exclusion-extraction 2-step create contemporary tools for neighboring jurisdictions to attract and retain a disproportionate share of the region's development benefits, bolstering their budget bottom lines.

Despite the uncertainty and possibly limited returns of private investment, Prince George's officials still focus on development. Their other options include higher levels of state and federal revenue transfers and county tax and fee increases, all of which require others' approval. Therefore, county officials have an incentive to emphasize private development because they can take direct action themselves. Additionally, if officials can recruit high-end commercial development, they can meet the desire of middle- and upper-middle-class Prince Georgians seeking more high-end retail and restaurant options within county borders. Recall from previous chapters that many affluent Prince George's residents lament having to leave the county to enjoy the entertainment and shopping options they prefer. Prince George's County's focus on development is not a new strategy. It dates back to the 1990s when Prince George's transitioned to a majority-Black and middle-class jurisdiction.

Prince George's County—The "Land of Milk and Honey" for the Black Middle Class?

Prince George's officials' vision for the county is captured in its twenty-year master plan, Plan 2035.[2] Issued in 2014, it is the most comprehensive articulation of the development trajectory sought by county officials and the strategies they will use to achieve it. This master plan is consistent with national trends in development. It centers projects oriented around "smart growth," which entails increasing population density near transit hubs and establishing mixed-use communities where people work, play, shop, and have recreation opportunities. Neighborhoods with dense populations and concentrated amenities are walkable and bikeable, reducing residents' need for cars. Mixed-use communities also help to reduce the county's environmental footprint.[3]

"Smart growth" in Prince George's County targets development near its fifteen Metro subway stops and other areas with Metro bus transit access. During a council briefing where the Washington Metropolitan Area Transit Authority (WMATA) shared an update on WMATA's sustainability, a council member, noting the centrality of the transit system to Prince George's development plan, made this statement:

> We have to work with federal, state, and other officials to move citizens to and from safely. We're the guys who squeeze tomatoes with you. The expectation is that we can do all things, but that's not the case. We want to keep economic development moving. Very consistently we have talked about transit-oriented development. We have fifteen Metro stations. The

county is involved in land use strategies. A lot of our opportunities come at the Metro stations—for jobs and housing, places people trend toward. At Union Station and Metro Center [stations in Washington, DC], you see a bustling economy. We can create that here.

Another council member discussed the importance of Metro in the county's development vision when she said during her interview:

If you go to the District of Columbia and you're at a Metro stop, you have essentially probably double the rent that you would pay if you were in Prince George's County. In my district alone, where I have five of the fifteen Metro stations—I have the most out of any council district, and the potential for economic development is just over the moon.

While county leaders almost uniformly champion Metro-focused development projects, county residents and neighborhoods have different interests, capacities, and vulnerabilities as Metro development intensifies. The inner-ring communities within the Interstate 95 Capital Beltway have the densest populations and the most "urban" feel. They also have the most Metro subway stations and bus lines, and therefore the greatest ability to attract residents who want to be proximate to the District of Columbia, but find living in DC proper too expensive.

Race and class groups are unevenly distributed across Prince George's County. Population distribution patterns influence development opportunities and constraints as well as the types of private investment residents want. Neighborhoods outside of the beltway are mostly Black and middle- and upper-middle-class. Communities within the beltway vary in their ethno-racial mix and are home to a range of middle-class, working-class, and economically distressed households. The largest share of low-income households is found along and near the Prince George's–DC border.

The 1990s Development Vision Alongside Today's Vision

Plan 2035 extends the vision the county created in the 1990s when it transitioned to majority-Black and Black people started to win most major county offices. The initial cadre of African American leadership, led by the first Black county executive, Wayne Curry, believed that the county could compete successfully for Black upper-middle-class residents and commercial enterprises catering to these elites.[4] Elected officials and senior civil servants who worked for the county during the Curry administration stated that Curry wanted Prince George's to become "the land of milk and honey" for affluent African Americans.

Curry sought to provide Black elites with what he called "executive housing." He also wanted to offer public goods and private amenities commensurate with upper-middle-class lifestyles. That is, he likened Prince George's to the Promised Land of the Israelites in the Bible. Drawing out this analogy, Curry took on the roles of Moses and Joshua. He sought to lead Prince Georgians through the development wilderness and into a place replete with resources for a high quality of life. But the Promised Land of Prince George's contains the giants of White domination and anti-Black policies and the exclusion-extraction 2-step—formidable obstacles, both then and now.

Amid their constraints, Prince George's officials have acted discerningly, working to enable investors to realize profits while not capitulating the county's ability to yield meaningful tax revenue. Indeed, county leaders have reasoned that precisely *because* Prince George's has not experienced private development on par with the county's class composition, the jurisdiction is ripe for investment. Prince George's, they wager, is the only "new frontier" for middle- and upper-middle-class-oriented development among jurisdictions contiguous with the District of Columbia.

According to a Maryland–National Capital Park and Planning Commission (MNCPPC) senior official who has served in senior posts in Prince George's since the Curry administration, Curry and other high-level county leaders recognized that Prince George's assets set the county apart from other DC region jurisdictions—and these factors are still in play:

Wayne [Curry] looked at the fact that we were the last vestige in the metropolitan area for development, which meant we also had the opportunity to get it right. He looked at where we're located. We have easy access to the BW [Baltimore-Washington] Parkway and Route 50. We're ensconced right between DC and Baltimore. He looked at our rivers—the Anacostia, Potomac, and Patuxent. He looked at the potential for development, the potential for executive housing, the potential to bring businesses here and lure them because of our location. He looked at the opportunity for Metro development.

County leaders since Curry have largely sought to reinforce and extend his vision. During his interview, the council chair during the Curry administration and the current leader of the Greater Prince George's Business Roundtable, a coalition of the county's most profitable businesses, affirmed Curry's desire to draw affluent African Americans to Prince George's: "What we didn't have, Mr. Curry thought, was sufficient high-end housing to attract the business executives and the growth that we wanted to see from an economic development standpoint. Obviously, part of my objective was to help him achieve those objectives."

As county executives, council members, agency administrators, and other Prince George's leaders have sought to realize Curry's development vision, they have achieved some of their goals. For instance, there are beautiful, palatial homes in the county's outer ring. But the "rising tide" of development lifting DC jurisdiction boats has not led to the revenue necessary for the county to consistently deliver high-quality public goods and services, nor does the county have the types and amounts of private amenities sought by upper-middle-class residents. Nevertheless, there were significant development breakthroughs from the 2010s onward, as I discuss later.

One reason Prince George's County's development vision remains elusive is that the county competes with wealthier, Whiter jurisdictions for private investment. Prince George's also has a disproportionate share of the region's moderate- and low-income residents, and the county is the primary destination for residents pushed out of DC, which has experienced especially intense gentrification since the early 2000s.[5] People displaced from DC move to Prince George's because it is the closest and most affordable jurisdiction, and the county is connected to DC through transit.[6] Thus, Prince George's has more residents who pay moderate and low levels of taxes, compared to neighboring counties, while it also shoulders responsibility for residents with a relatively greater need for public goods and services and manages the pressure those needs put on the county's already-too-thin budget.

In this context, Prince George's officials are challenged to deploy the "right" development strategies. On the one hand, officials want to attract firms in growing industries by offering few, if any, tax concessions. This scenario has the highest tax revenue generation potential. On the other hand, if Prince George's does not offer concessions, the county may lose development opportunities, given that other nearby jurisdictions are likely to provide such incentives. While there is debate about what the specific development initiatives and strategies should be, economic growth through private development is consistently a priority among top county leaders and those running for county offices.

For instance, at a town hall for county executive candidates, all of them except one named "economic development" as a primary issue when asked to state their policy platforms and priorities:

CANDIDATE #1 (*Black woman, forties, high-level county elected official*): I'm focused on schools, elders, housing, and the economy.

CANDIDATE #2 (*Black woman, fifties, former federal elected official representing Prince George's County*): I'm running on innovation, smart development—we, and not developers, decide what gets built—better schools, accountability for your tax dollars.

CANDIDATE #3 (*Black man, early thirties, former Obama administration official*): I'm running on education, economic development, restorative justice, and a culture of stewardship. The county can't be run like a club.

CANDIDATE #4 (*Black man, sixties*): My focus is education, quality of life, and economic development.

CANDIDATE #5 (*Black man, fifties*): We need to move to an area where we are fair and honest to all citizens. We need to bring prayer back to our public schools.

Schools are another nearly universal priority among current and prospective county leaders. And economic development and high-performing schools are inextricably tied. Private investment is not likely to achieve the revenue generation that county officials seek if the county's schools are not well regarded, given that middle- and upper-middle-class residents of childbearing age consider school quality when deciding where to live. Yet without private development—or another means of generating more revenue—schools, like other public goods and services, are likely to continue to fall short of leaders' and residents' expectations. The Greater Prince George's Business Roundtable chair captured the link between development and public school performance during his interview:

There are two things that impact a jurisdiction. And if those two things aren't perceived by the public to be in good shape, you're not going to get the investment. You're not going to get the residents, and you're not going to get folks that you want to have a good diverse community economically, and certainly racially and otherwise. Schools and public safety.

Beyond schools, this leader added public safety to the prerequisites for high-end commercial development. Public perception of both schools and public safety are largely based on reputation rather than on direct experience.[7] An example of direct experience is turning on the water tap in one's home to assess the water quality. Public perception of schools and police is usually shaped by news, other media, and word of mouth. Media often reinforce anti-Black stereotypes, such as the stereotype that African Americans are criminally inclined and have less intellectual aptitude than White people.[8]

As discussed in the introduction, Black Americans' supposed pre-disposition to break the law dates back to the post–Civil War period of the mid-1800s, when Jim Crow segregation regimes were taking hold across states and White elites were asserting new justifications for treating Black people differently than White people.[9] In Northern states—particularly in cities rapidly becoming denser owing to mass immigration from eastern and southern Europe and the Black Great Migration from the South— crime rates were high across racial groups. But White decision-makers framed the crime committed by White people and immigrants as stem-ming from housing, schooling, employment, and other material and social deprivations.[10] In contrast, the crimes that Black people committed were framed by White elites as resulting from Black people's inherent nature as a racial group. Crime statistics from the late nineteenth and early twentieth century are the baselines for measuring crime rates today and serve as the baseline for many Americans' assumptions about who is likely to commit crimes now.[11]

Today, Black people, including middle-class African Americans, face the evolution of the stigmatization of African-descendant people. To the extent that Prince George's County's crime rates are higher than those of nearby counties, the disparity is consistent with national crime patterns—crime tends to increase in areas experiencing economic and social distress.[12]

One of the congressional representatives for Prince George's emphasized how local media descriptions of where crime occurs in the DC region drives public perceptions of Prince George's as less safe than nearby Whiter locales:

> At points in the twenty-five years I've been here, our crime rate has been higher than surrounding jurisdictions. And the newspaper will always say a crime in Prince George's County. So everyone, oh, Prince George's County. When it happens in Montgomery, they'll say a crime in Burtonsville. Nobody knows where Burtonsville is. So it's not Montgomery County, or a crime in Olney, people don't know where Olney is. Certainly not people in the DMV. People in Montgomery County do. But people in Virginia don't know where Olney is. So they're not even thinking, oh, another crime in Montgomery County, another crime in Montgomery. But it's always reported not as a crime in District Heights, a crime in Bowie, where people went, oh, I wonder where that is. It's crime in Prince George's.

Taken together, Prince George's leaders contend with constraints connected to anti-Black policies and racial capitalism as well as limitations linked to White people's expectations of Black people. Undaunted, county leaders forge ahead. And rewriting the zoning code is one of the ways they have done that.

Expediting Development: Zoning Ordinance Overhaul

County officials, through major zoning code amendments, sought to make zoning ordinances clearer, more streamlined, and aligned with "smart growth" development. Between 2014 and the zoning code's adoption in 2018, the staff of the Maryland–National Capital Park and Planning Commission hosted over three hundred public meetings, including "listening sessions," focus groups, and workshops. MNCPPC serves as Prince George's County's planning board. The board makes initial zoning decisions and the county council determines final approval.

During the deliberation period, MNCPPC staff sought input from residents, civic groups, community-based businesses and nonprofits, and corporate entities, including developers, regarding prospective zoning code changes.[13] Residents' most common concern was increasing their influence on zoning decisions, especially the types of projects proposed for their neighborhoods. They also wanted adequate notice about hearings in the decision-making process, with a timeline sufficient for substantive community-developer negotiations that could, if residents' interests were not addressed, end in non-approval of projects. Those in attendance at resident listening sessions openly discussed the racialized and classed nature of private development and the county government's limited authority or willingness to ensure that developer interests did not undermine residents' aims for community well-being.

The fall 2017 listening sessions were among the most well attended and also reflected input from earlier rounds of public comment. These forums offer insight into leaders' and residents' core values. The following statements, made at an October 2017 meeting, in Landover, exemplify what I heard from residents at these listening sessions:

SPEAKER #1 (*Black man, seventies*): I served on the board for President Clinton. Industry in poor neighborhoods—it's cute. We notify the community: "I'm telling you what I'm going to do, but you can't do anything about it." It's a false sense of hope. If it's a permitted use and it's going to be used, you don't even consider that there are already five in the community, it's just permitted use. Johns Hopkins put out a report on the fact that the communities with the least influence get these things. Most of these things are inside the beltway. It's a waste of time to go to the planning board, to go down and complain about a permitted use.

SPEAKER #2 (*Black woman, fifties, former Maryland delegate*): In Bladensburg [neighborhood inside the beltway and along the DC border], there's a plant that wants to add concrete batching. They're going through the special exception process. I've watched the special exception process. I'll be shocked if the examiner doesn't approve it. There should be an assessment as to whether that area can stand it. There should be some kind of weight where you'd say adding something like this would tip the scale.

SPEAKER #3 (*White woman, sixties*): I'm concerned about protecting the historic nature [of Greenbelt, a planned community built during the Franklin D. Roosevelt administration]. I have language from a petition. I want to read it [an excerpt from her petition] for the record: "No increase in density, height, and mass. . . . We want to protect the Roosevelt Community center and forest reserve."

SPEAKER #4 (*Mayor of Seat Pleasant, Black man, fifties*): Grocery stores—we lost a grocery store. We're trying to bring one back. We've talked to developers. They've done their feasibility studies. They say we have adequate grocery stores. They cited PG [Prince George's] Atlas, which says there are three grocery stores. PG Atlas had identified a convenience store as a grocery store. They also identified CVS as a grocery store—it's not accurate and that hurts us. . . . They trust the data. People who look like me don't get our needs met. There are deceptive practices. This works against the people who live there. I will advance the causes of our people. This will continue until gentrification comes. When will you address certain stores coming to our communities? You don't take into consideration what our concerns are—we don't want more liquor stores, pawn shops.

SPEAKER #5 (*White woman, thirties*): You're focusing on high-end economic development only. You're not focusing on the entrepreneurs and small business owners. You're denigrating the immigrant community. The low-end retail community is vital. What I'm hearing is shocking!

The range of topics and level of detail in community members' comments demonstrate that many county residents are well informed about how development works, including the particular vulnerability of Black people. Residents also show that they are aware of the legal limitations the county faces as it pursues development and tries to stop certain kinds of private investment. Since the zoning code's adoption in 2018, it has taken effect in phases, with 2022 the year when core sections of the code became law.

Many resident concerns were ostensibly addressed, including through required pre-application meetings in neighborhoods affected by large projects. The new code also standardizes the public notification processes with time built in for community input.[14] It will take time to learn whether these provisions have their intended impact on meaningful inclusion of residents' interests. But at the outset it is clear that these measures do not prevent developers from pursuing projects to which residents object. The zoning code, like all laws, is subject to judicial review. County officials sought to increase resident input, while staying within the bounds of property right protections established by courts.

Developer Recruitment Strategies
Within Racialized Constraints

Prince George's leaders deploy many of the same strategies as their peers in White-majority jurisdictions. But unlike officials in those locales, Prince George's officials must overcome many private investors' racist presumption that majority-Black spaces do not have sufficient numbers of middle- and upper-middle-class consumers to support their businesses. At a hearing regarding the county's strategy for recruiting retailers and restaurants, an Economic Development Corporation (EDC) official revealed what the county loses when Prince Georgians shop and dine outside of the county because Prince George's does not offer the options they seek: "I had no idea this seepage is $1.4 billion. We can use those resources and those dollars to circulate within the county."

One way that county officials seek to bring that $1.4 billion back to Prince George's is by sending a contingent to the Innovating Commerce Serving Communities (ICSC) conference in Las Vegas, Nevada. It is the largest conference of retail and restaurant chains. Council members and other county leaders focus their time and energy there because it is an efficient opportunity to meet with many high-level executives about the benefits of bringing their businesses to Prince George's. The council chair, when explaining why the council goes to ICSC, said: "Why? Because I'm a bear, and the salmon are swimming upstream in Vegas. They're not swimming upstream down here. I need to go to where they are and try to grab them and bring them back."

A senior EDC administrator who is charged with developer recruitment and uses multiple tools to overcome developer resistance to investing in Prince George's described his experience at the ICSC conference in Las Vegas:

> Many people still think it's crime-ridden . . . difficult to do business with, slow permitting process, under-educated workforce. You don't really have the talent to be able to satisfy their needs. I really have to sell hard to show them [developers and other private investors] the facts on it, because I think some of that is just . . . the 65 percent African American—I think the perception is, is that you really may not have the kind of talent, but we really do.

We've got eighty-three thousand students that are going to our top three universities at any given time, we're cranking out ten thousand graduates a year.

This same official brimmed with excitement at the hearing on retailer recruitment when he explained breakthroughs in bringing new restaurants to the county: "We have two major steakhouse chains to come. A potential investor said, "This is the best presentation I've had all day." . . . We've had great success, many signed an LOI [letter of intent]. I can barely hold back from saying their names! We had the shopping center owner in the room [at ICSC]—two steakhouses!"

This official's enthusiasm reflected his satisfaction that his efforts had yielded higher levels of investment after years of tepid response from developers. But the conditions under which retailers and restaurants come to Prince George's ultimately determine the likelihood that their investment will expand the county's commercial tax base. In 2017, the Prince George's County Office of Finance reported thirty payment in lieu of taxes (PILOT) agreements and ten tax increment financing (TIF) agreements, as well as three special taxing districts in the county, for a total of forty-three non-standard tax arrangements designed to attract and retain private investment.[15] PILOTs allow companies to pay a lump sum in taxes and fees that is lower than what they would normally pay. TIFs involve issuing county-backed bonds to pay for roads, parking, stormwater management, and other infrastructure, based on the expected increased tax revenue from the development project.[16]

Despite the risk of not generating sufficient tax revenue from alternative tax and fee arrangements, most council members and other leaders I spoke to supported their use. Those in support of such arrangements believed such measures could bolster the county tax base in the long run. A senior EDC official's comments during his interview reflect what I heard from Prince George's leaders who supported tax incentives:

I'd say 80 percent of the deals we do, incentives don't even come up. They're [potential investors] focused on speed of permitting, location. . . . Prince George's County, coming out of DC, we can save you about 40 percent on your leasing costs. So that's always a big win. Where they do come up is when another municipality is offering incentives, where we've got to either meet competition or beat competition. And so that's where we want to get in there, and to be competitive. For the right kind of employer that's paying good, high-wage jobs, way above, at at least 150 percent above minimum wage. So we're focused again on those high-wage sectors, which would be IT, medical type of jobs, professional services, engineering, transportation jobs. . . . We're willing to go into the $50 million economic development incentive fund.

This official explained that Prince George's is attaining the majority of business investment without using tax and fee incentives. Furthermore, some high-end commercial investors find Prince George's to be a welcome bargain. The county offers ready access to DC and significantly lower rents. Most of these businesses are located at or near the county's Metro stations. Similarly, many federal government agencies locate their head-quarters in Prince George's because the costs of maintaining buildings and meeting worker needs are lower in the county than in DC. The federal government does not pay local taxes, but federal civil servants at these agencies who choose to live in Prince George's contribute to the county tax base. These workers also contribute to the county's economy when they dine and shop.

At the same time, for the 20 percent of cases in which the EDC official said that Prince George's needed "to get in there"—that is, compete with nearby jurisdictions—the county uses tax and fee incentives. Given that the fastest-growing enterprises and a significant number of high-paying jobs are in the information technology and health sectors, most US local juris-dictions prioritize recruiting them, Prince George's included. Knowing that local governments highly desire them gives these companies an advantage as they negotiate with local governments about tax concessions.

I asked the Prince George's representative to the Washington Metro-politan Area Transit Authority (WMATA) whether the county should be more stringent in its use of tax concessions, given that the county offers advantages that make it attractive without such incentives. He responded by explaining the stiff competition for private investment in the DC region:

AUTHOR: I'm hearing from those against tax incentives things like: "Well, look, they have nowhere else to go." Developers know there's money to be made here. Prince George's County should be in a position to say, "No." What do you think of this perspective?

WMATA Representative: That's just not true. . . . What I mean by that is this, we remain in an environment where Prince George's County is discriminated against. Folks got to understand that. I mean, it is still very, it's not easy. We are still in a place where people who are investing in Prince George's County are doing so when others are taking a pass. It is still that way. And folks, it's just the reality. We remain, as I shared with you earlier, we don't have our own pot of money or group of people [African American private investors] to go to to suggest, "Well, just give us a fair shake." Right? "Do the right thing." These are people who are here to make money. They're just like, "Look. Listen, I have this amount of money that I can invest." We're competing with Virginia, for example, which is a far more lenient state with regard to regulation and is just as a general business friendly environment that we're fighting against, where you grew up, which of course has changed dramatically in the time, I'm sure, since when you've been there.

Author: Prince William County, right.

WMATA Representative: People are willing to look at Prince William [County] and say, "Even if you do have a crazy person leading your county, we'll still go over there, because you will give us whatever we ask for." We have to compete with that. . . . That hasn't changed. They are, they're a little bit further away from DC than we are. Fair enough. But they don't have—it's a "right to work" state [referring to more union restrictions in Virginia compared to Maryland]. They got all kinds of other things that we do have to compete with. The thing about it is this, what also goes along with that is that oftentimes because of the irrational part, refusal to invest when Black people have the financial means to support the business, that I was telling you about, all they need is one piece to say no. All the other numbers can be right. But if there's one piece, in the back of their mind they don't want to do it. You know what I mean? So, you provide any kind of negative or something where you are unwilling to do what other jurisdictions have been willing to do in order to bet on themselves— remember, that's what I said, we're betting on ourselves. . . . I mean, I've bluffed on some of this stuff too, to along the lines of what you're saying and said to people, "All right, fine. You don't want to do it this way, then leave. We'll find somebody else to do it." But I've been called on that bluff too. Like, "Okay, well then, who do you have?" And I don't. There isn't a Rolodex of African American developers that I could say, "Hey, listen, this is a good deal, not a great deal, not a slam dunk. This is a good deal. You need to come and do this good deal." We're not talking about slam dunk deals. We're talking about good deals. You know what I'm saying?

AUTHOR: What's the difference between a "slam dunk" and a "good deal"?

WMATA REPRESENTATIVE: The risk profile is so far less. Take, for example, this greater DC area, median income, $94,000. The country is $45,000. That, just in and of itself, becomes slam dunk territory for people, presuming that you can get your other costs in line. Prince George's County is $74,000. I mean, that's a huge reduction from a region of $94,000 to $74,000 for Prince George's County. Still good, no matter what, because the country's $44,000, $45,000. But it ain't $95,000. Then you put on top of that, for some of what happens in Prince George's County is that we are, because we're these suburbs that you're talking about, we're somewhat married to Montgomery County on certain things. Well, we don't have Montgomery County income. You know what I'm saying? . . . The profile of what they're looking at is always going to look different than what it's going to look like in Prince George's County. But the cost structure, some of the cost structure, is the same. We have the same minimum wage, you know what I'm saying? . . . That becomes something that we have similar regulation to them, but we are a third less as far as economic power. That's what I'm saying. You'd be more than good. But you do have to take that into consideration.

As the WMATA representative stated, in the final analysis, tax concessions gamble with the future. Prince George's officials, in an effort to compete with nearby Whiter and wealthier jurisdictions, try to play the cards they are dealt deftly. If county leaders' strategies are favorable, Prince George's gains increased tax revenue directly through commercial enterprises' success and indirectly through the collateral effects that successful businesses catalyze. Additionally, in this favorable scenario, as firms' incomes and property values increase, they make higher tax payments. But if the cards are not favorable, Prince George's loses tax revenue, loses the time and effort of elected officials and civil servants, and—less tangible but no less significant—loses "face," reputation, with county residents.

Many concession packages contain "clawback" measures—terms under which the county can end tax and fee arrangements and seek reimbursement if businesses fail to abide by the agreement. Still, activating clawback measures takes time and energy, such as navigating court and arbitration proceedings. Even when PILOTs and TIFs have their maximum impact, Prince George's County needs additional revenue at a scale beyond what commercial tax revenue can generate. The more the county sets precedents for encouraging certain types of business activity through tax and fee incentives, the more it reinforces a norm that businesses do not have to pay their full tax bills in Prince George's.

Some Prince George's officials expressed concerns about tax and fee concessions. While county leaders generally supported tax incentives in principle, they often disagreed about which firms should receive them—and if so, the type, amount, and forms of accountability to include. County decision-makers who wanted to restrict tax concessions argued that Prince George's has the most land available for development near Washington, DC. Therefore, developers have no choice but to come to Prince George's if they want easy access to the nation's capital. This portion of the council often used the refrain "the county gives away too much" during discussions about business recruitment strategies. One council member went a step further, noting that making money should not be the only reason businesses come to Prince George's when she said during a hearing on county development strategies: "Businesses that want to come to Prince George's need to show themselves willing to invest in the community, not just make a profit."

Other council members were more willing to assume that businesses would invest in the county if they believed that they could earn the profit they sought. Even if anti-Black racism is a factor shaping developers' decisions, they argued, it might not be decisive in determining where they invest. This council member's comments during his interview captured this perspective:

> There are a number of factors that they [prospective businesses] consider about where they want to put their business. If you're saying for our area,

we opened up a Harris Teeter in the Bowie area. Could we have tried to get them to go down to south county or mid-county? I guess, but they made a decision that they thought this was the area. Whether it's discrimination, redlining, or just business sense, I'm not going to go into a community where I'm expecting a certain amount of return if that income level is not there. . . . They're looking at all kinds of information—demographics, income. If parts of the county don't have those things, how do we encourage them to go there? Because at the end of the day, they have to make money, right?

As Prince George's leaders deliberate the extent to which they should incentivize development, they are also evaluating the need for more or enhanced infrastructure associated with development.

Walking the Development-Infrastructure Tight Rope

Within Prince George's County's five hundred square miles are areas of urban, suburban, and rural densities. In areas of high affluence and low density, the council has considered increasing density to facilitate the kinds of high-end shopping and cultural options that upper-middle-class residents desire. But achieving such density at a rate that would allow the county to invest in the necessary infrastructure, such as roads, is a delicate balance to strike.

Prince George's needs new revenue to pay for infrastructure maintenance and creation. Without such investment, developers are less likely to consider the county a prime prospect. Also, if investment comes without appropriate infrastructure, residents' quality of life could be compromised. For instance, in the short term residents would probably have to endure more traffic if lanes are not added to two-lane roads. In out-years, intensified use of infrastructure could lead to faster decline in public works, from sewers to roads and bridges.

In an example of how officials navigate this chicken-or-egg problem of development and infrastructure growth, a proposal was made to bring a mixed-use development complex to Brandywine in southern Prince George's. Brandywine is largely rural, and many of its roads are two lanes. About fifty residents came to the hearing on this project, and all but a few were opposed to changing the zoning designation necessary for the project to move forward. The council member representing the district where this project would be located responded to his constituents concerns:

> We heard you loud and clear. It [the project] purports to accomplish many objectives, including to increase infrastructure. It's a public-private partnership. We increased the fees developers have to pay for road construction. This is an unprecedented plan. There is no magic pot of money. This area [the southern tip of Prince George's County] has long been ignored. . . . We receive flow-through traffic everyday—from Waldorf and points south. [Many people commuting from Charles County to Washington, DC, drive through this area.] There is a lack of high-end retail. Development zoning that allows a mix of uses is the trend. The reason for that is the flexibility that allows for developments to be successful. . . . It's very easy to scare people about development. One the one hand, we want more retail, but we are leery of development. I know broken promises have broken trust. Commitments from developers must be iron-clad.

In the words of the council member, there is "no magic pot of money." Prince George's County has limited options for meeting residents' needs and desires for public goods and services and private amenities. In this context of constraint, council members use various tools to accommodate and expedite development projects. Residents' core interests include a desire for more premium shopping and a desire to minimize traffic and other negative externalities of development.

The threat of negative externalities diminishing the quality of life is particularly acute in rural areas because these parts of Prince George's already have some of the greatest infrastructure needs in the jurisdiction. More densely populated portions of the county tend to be prioritized for public works maintenance and construction, given that the county often rations resources with the aim of improving quality of life for the greatest number of people with each project. Furthermore, as the council member acknowledges, Prince George's residents have lost confidence that the county government will deliver the public goods and services it promises.

For mixed-use zoning specifically, Prince George's residential construction outpaces commercial development; as a result, places designated as "mixed-use" are effectively just another all-residential development. When spaces offer a combination of residential and retail options within walking distance, residents enjoy more amenities and the county has the greatest potential to receive new tax revenue. Without new revenue or a means to guarantee that new development would be prioritized for infrastructure funding, new developments compete alongside long-established communities for infrastructure investment.

As Prince George's leaders consider development options, they account for factors unique to the county as well as regional and national development patterns. Prince George's navigates the constraints of the political economy arrangements of the DC region and the changes in how Americans shop and entertain themselves. Two key aspects of change include the rise of online shopping and the continued sprawl of the DC metropolitan area. As I discuss later, the DC region is starting to converge with other nearby metropolitan areas. With the increase in online shopping, retailers invest in fewer brick-and-mortar sites. Consequently, sprawl at the edges of the DC region and in nearby metropolitan areas often creates pockets of White affluence on the edges of metropolitan areas. Retailers sometimes view these White enclaves as "safer" bets than majority-Black spaces—even majority-middle-class Black spaces like Prince George's County.

The Mobility of Capital and Prince George's County's Pursuit of Investment

Suburban Sprawl

As Prince George's bids for development, its competition extends beyond the DC region. The Eastern Seaboard of the United States—especially between New York City and Richmond, Virginia, is so densely populated that metropolitan areas merge into each other, adding another layer of complexity to jurisdiction competition for private investment. DC-area exurban sprawl on the outer fringes of the metropolitan area touches the outermost sprawl of metropolitan areas centered in Baltimore, Maryland, and Richmond. Thus, Prince George's seeks to stand out among dozens of local jurisdictions.

For instance, people living in Stafford and Spotsylvania Counties in Virginia can drive to DC or Richmond within less than an hour by car during non-rush-hour times. Similarly, residents of Howard and Ann Arundel Counties in Maryland can drive to DC or Baltimore in less than an hour. Maryland, Virginia, and Amtrak rail systems and the DC Metro subway system offer transit options for connecting people and supply chains. Hence, businesses have ample worker and supplier pools. Additionally, congestion has been reduced in the DC region over the past fifteen years by the widening of Interstates 95 and 66 and use of E-ZPass toll roads.

The Rise of Online Retail

Prince George's is seeking to expand its premium shopping options at a time when retailers are maintaining and opening fewer physical stores.[17] As more consumers shop online, demand for stores decreases, and site selection for those stores that do open is still racialized, disadvantaging majority-Black jurisdictions, like Prince George's County. According to the Prince George's County High-End Retail Market Analysis, when new businesses open more stores, "their initial locations are most likely near established concentrations of luxury retailers, none of which are located in Prince George's County."[18] For instance, upper-middle-class residents I spoke to who lived in southern Prince George's said that they drove to Tyson's Corner in Fairfax County for high-end shopping options, and those who lived in northern Prince George's said that they went to Columbia Mall in Howard County for such options.

In addition, Black middle-class communities, like Prince George's, endure "retail redlining"—the tendency of clothing and grocery stores and restaurants to not come to majority-Black and affluent areas as quickly as they do to White affluent areas.[19] A council member at a hearing on the county retail recruitment strategy expressed her frustration with retail redlining:

> I think it's discrimination that Prince George's County doesn't see the opportunity. The staff—we go out and try to sell our county. I don't know how we tackle that particular issue. If you look at our neighbors, when their community began to change, that's when their retail changed. . . . Don't tell me my people can't afford to spend money in this county. If they can buy a $600,000 home, they can buy a $3 cup of coffee.

Because companies are concerned about stores' long-term viability, majority-White spaces offer less risk because they are more familiar and have already proven their ability to generate certain profit margins. Of course, it is also true that companies are familiar with making money in White enclaves because they have chosen to invest in them.

DC Region Development and the Uneven Playing Field: The Case of Amazon's HQ2

The competition among DC region local jurisdictions for Amazon's second headquarters (HQ2) in 2017 and 2018 shows the inherent disadvantage of Black jurisdictions created by anti-Black policies and racial capitalism. To be sure, this competition could crown only one winner. But how the competition played out illustrates the relative regional burden that Prince George's carries for the DC metropolitan area.

Amazon considered potential sites through rounds of competition. This whittling down process entailed eliminating a certain proportion of proposals at each stage. When Amazon made it clear that the DC region was in the final round, the short list retained all DC region jurisdictions that applied for consideration, except Prince George's.[20] Ultimately, Amazon named Arlington County, Virginia, a plurality-White county bordering DC, as its second headquarters site, reinforcing Arlington's strong economic position in the DC region.[21]

Prince George's, in contrast, will be the site of Amazon fulfillment and delivery centers, which store and manage the distribution of the corporation's products.[22] The headquarters will employ a greater percentage of middle- and high-income earners than will fulfillment centers, which will largely employ moderate- and low-income workers. Indeed, many employees at fulfillment centers will earn the county minimum hourly wage or close to it. Many of the moderate- and low-income workers are likely to choose to live in Prince George's because it is the most affordable place to live among the counties neighboring DC.

Arlington County, even before Amazon arrived, had a greater share of the DC region's upper-middle-class households. With Amazon's headquarters, Arlington stands to gain even more economic advantage. The computer engineers, lawyers, and finance specialists, among other upper-middle-class professionals, employed by Amazon are likely to choose to live in Arlington—and if not Arlington, then one of the other majority- or plurality-White counties in the DC region. White-collar workers will probably select these counties because they can afford to live in them and because these counties offer high-quality public goods and services, including public schools, and private amenities catering to upper-income households.

In this Amazon example, we see that both individual-level race and class differences and the places where race and class groups cluster within the DC region contribute to divergent fiscal trajectories across DC region jurisdictions. Jurisdictions already advantaged by their race and class compositions are better positioned to attract yet more high-end development. Prince George's will receive corporate tax revenue from its Amazon fulfillment and delivery locations and income taxes from workers who choose to live in the county. But that revenue will be less than what Arlington will receive in corporate taxes from the headquarters and from the incomes of the upper-middle-class workers who choose to live near HQ2.

Upper-middle-class employees are also more likely to buy homes in already high-demand neighborhoods. This will bolster home values in these communities and yield greater home equity wealth for homebuyers. And majority- and plurality-White counties in the DC region will receive more property tax revenue. Certainly, the tax incentives that Amazon negotiated with Arlington will attenuate the county's tax revenue from Amazon in the short term. But whatever potential there is for new revenue will accrue to Arlington to a far greater extent than the tax revenues Prince George's will receive from Amazon's fulfillment and delivery centers.

The Amazon headquarters site selection process was disheartening for many Prince George's leaders. Most understood that fierce competition for HQ2 gave all local jurisdictions only a small chance of being selected, even if they offered ideal conditions. Prince George's officials felt most disappointed that the county was excluded from the short list, indicating that Amazon had assessed the county as not offering a baseline quality of life comparable to neighboring jurisdictions with smaller Black populations. One of the congressional representatives for Prince George's, speaking generally about the county's challenges in attracting high-end development like Amazon's headquarters, said that Prince George's does not offer the suite of public goods and private amenities that corporate leaders seek:

> We have underperforming schools. So folks don't want to come to a community where they can't educate their kids in that community. . . . When you think about, especially, not the retail employers, but the corporate campuses, the corporate offices, the headquarters, they're thinking that CEOs making a few hundred thousand dollars a year saying, "Hey, I want to set up my headquarters in a place where I have a short commute. And in that

short commute I want to know that I can drop my kids off at good schools. I've got good hospitals for me and my employees and there's a safe neighborhood." And relative to our neighbors, we don't stack up so well. So it's just this perpetuating struggle to attract what I think certainly income level could support here in Prince George County.

Being chosen as the site for Amazon's fulfillment centers, rather than its headquarters, illustrates the political economy patterns reinforcing Prince George's County's relative regional burden and neighboring jurisdictions' relative regional benefit. Another indicator of Prince George's County's economic position in the DC metropolitan area is the disproportionate share of polluting industries it hosts.

Dirty Development Temptations

Another instance of the relative regional burden that Prince George's County shoulders for the DC region is the disproportionate share of polluting industries within the jurisdiction. The construction boom in the DC region, especially in the District itself, has intensified demand in construction-related businesses. In Prince George's, many polluting firms were "grandfathered" into the county zoning code, allowing them to remain in operation, even though they no longer meet zoning requirements. Residents living near businesses that create substantial pollution endure compromised air quality, which increases their rates of asthma and other health ailments.

From businesses' perspective, it is easier to expand an existing operation than to open a new one. And this is particularly true when the business generates pollution. To open a new site, firms first have to find a jurisdiction with a zone where they can build. If they find such a place, the business must invest time, money, and energy into the permitting, design, public hearing, and construction processes. Furthermore, construction industries seek proximity to current and likely construction sites. Given the rapid gentrification in Washington, DC, construction industries in Prince George's are close to dozens of active construction sites.

In an instance of a Prince George's business pursuing intensified production at an already established site, a concrete plant in Bladensburg, a Prince George's municipality bordering DC, sought in 2017 to add concrete blocks to its concrete batching business. Residents and leaders in Bladensburg were divided about the proposal, in part because making concrete blocks would increase pollution-generating activity. But the majority of those who testified at hearings objected to the business's proposed expansion.

People who supported intensified forms of concrete production argued that the plant had taken and would continue to take sufficient steps to mitigate harm to human and environmental health. They wanted the plant to maximize its potential because it provided employment and other opportunities to local residents. At one of the hearings on the plant's proposal, the mayor of Bladensburg characterized the plant as a "good corporate citizen" and read a letter stating that the municipality offered "conditional support" for the plant's expansion. Among the conditions for support: restricting the amount of truck traffic, limiting the streets that trucks could use, and increasing plant maintenance, such as installing a new watering system and hiring a sweeping service to minimize dust accumulation.

Others strongly objected to expansion. Those opposed argued that Black communities across the United States, and Prince George's specifically, already had a disproportionate share of polluting industries when compared to majority-White jurisdictions. The following three speakers' comments represent the range of opinions—pro and con—that I heard at hearings about the plant's proposal:

SPEAKER #1 (*Black man, sixties, pastor of a church next door to the concrete plant*): We're longtime neighbors. We've learned to coexist together. The experiences haven't been pleasant, but we've survived. I have stressed concerns to [plant owner]—just the dirt, it accumulates on the street, on the sidewalk. We're the only building not considered industrial [on that block]. During the week, it's their street—they have business to take care of, we get that—even a funeral during the week, we have it somewhere else. The dirt accumulation is a problem.

SPEAKER #2 (*White man, seventies*): I have been a resident of Bladensburg for forty-two years. Adding concrete batching will ruin this historical area. The wastewater will run into the Anacostia. It's next to our commercial area—it will cause traffic congestion. Every year pedestrians are killed near Kenilworth Avenue. This plan will make this area much more dangerous. The public library and elementary school are nearby—the trucks will be dangerous to schoolchildren. I am asking Park and Planning to refuse the special exception.

SPEAKER #3 (*Latino man, thirties, Maryland state representative*): We oppose the batch expansion because of safety and environmental concerns.

SPEAKER #4 (*White woman, fifties, apartment building owner in Bladensburg*): The plant is an eyesore—its chain-link fence doesn't hide it. It's bleak and dismal. Urban planning encourages integrating industrial areas in certain ways. This added procession of trucks is spewing pollutants. In Edmonston [a neighboring municipality] and on Kenilworth [Avenue], they use their roads at their discretion. Prince George's County already has low air quality. Their programs [the concrete plant's] do nothing to counteract emissions. They have not conducted a health study—anything they say cannot be substantiated. I understand that it's an industrial zone and it was done to make ends meet. However, this is one of the greatest burdens. . . . If they want to expand, let them do it elsewhere. If you approve this, you would cut us off from other clean, smart development. . . . If you approve this application, you will tell our residents that we cannot count on county representatives to act in our collective best interest, and I will discontinue my investment because I cannot guarantee my residents' safety.

SPEAKER #5 (*Black woman, fifties*): I'm undecided about whether to support the project. An environmental impact study would establish what is right. [The plant owner] has been a friend to our youth. He provided jobs for our youth. I believe Bladensburg will act in the highest and best interest of residents.

Given the constant construction in DC, the concrete plant's products are in constant demand, which generates significant profit for the plant and increased commercial tax revenue for Prince George's. But those benefits carry significant costs: harms to residents' health and to the environment. Furthermore, related burdens in the long run increase county budget pressures, such as higher health and social services costs as disease incidence among residents increases.

At a community meeting hosted by residents opposed to the plant's expansion, a University of Maryland public health professor, a Black man in his forties, was invited to help residents understand the broader economic, political, and other social dynamics in which the business's request was embedded. He argued that polluting industries were a net loss for communities:

> The law is letting you down. How do we require other agencies to be a part of the process, like the Department of Health? The traffic study did not have to look at diesel, but we know it has health effects—it's a stressor. . . . They didn't look at the aggregate of the current process plus the new one. There was nothing about what PM [particulate matter] would be in the air at the site-specific location. We know the site is producing dust—no data about what's already occurring. We have a problem with air quality already in the community. The question is, what you can do about it? You have to think about, how can you change the law? What types of development are you seeking? What's congruent with your eco-district vision? Another thing you can ask for—you can say to county council: "Hey, we want the best control technologies to be implemented." The EPA [Environmental Protection Agency] has a map that allows you to screen communities for environmental hazards relative to other communities. Bladensburg ranks in the ninetieth percentile for cancer risk. When I look at this, I say there are disparities between us and the US and the state. There's environmental racism and classism. That's why you have to fight for better development laws. You want equitable development.

As noted by the professor and the pastor who regularly swept dust from his church's doorsteps, particulate matter diminishes health outcomes and quality of life. According to the US Environmental Protection Agency (EPA), dust particulates, if inhaled over a long period, can lead to severe respiratory illness and premature death. Black Americans are more likely to be exposed to this sort of hazardous material, irrespective of their class status.[23] When I left the field in 2018, litigation over the concrete batching plant was still ongoing.

The professor connected the Bladensburg concrete plant proposal to other industrial activity in Prince George's, amplifying the point that the county already carries a disproportionate share of the DC region's pollution burden:

I also want to highlight Brandywine. They have five or so proposed power plants, three coal-fired and two natural gas. Why aren't people complaining? They bring jobs? Don't bring crap jobs to the county! It should be equitable development. The community is low-income and poor, so we're going to bring the factory. Many people who work there don't live there. Brandywine is unincorporated. The money is not going to go them. The benefits go to the county, not to that community. That's contamination without representation. They're suing in alternative dispute resolution. Brandywine is absorbing externalities, their bodies are sinks for pollution. There's a major public health impact to this.

To be sure, some of the polluting industries were in place before Prince George's became majority-Black. In these cases, White working-class people bore the burden for wealthier White neighboring jurisdictions. Still, that a concrete business already polluting in excess of current standards seeks to expand its business evinces disrespect for Black people's lives. The wide-ranging opinions for and against the plant's expansion reveal the factors that county officials weigh as they seek to garner sufficient tax revenue in a context of few tax-generation options and where they shoulder significant relative regional burden. Yet, in the face of these formidable challenges, Prince George's County's fight for equitable development has yielded some "wins."

Development "Wins" Within Racialized Constraints

Prince George's leaders have ushered in significant high-end development over the past fifteen years. Their achievements required considerable time, money, and energy. Neighboring counties with smaller Black populations attained premium development organically, enabling those counties to expend time, money, and energy on their residents' other needs. Prince George's is primed for investment in large part because developers systematically under-invested in the county for years. Once prospective developers assess Prince George's market, they often find significant pent-up demand among its middle- and upper-middle-class residents. Thus, the county is a "new frontier" for a broad array of amenities.

One of the most prominent and celebrated projects in the county is MGM Casino, which began operation in 2016 in Oxon Hill in southern

Prince George's County. Before MGM, Wegmans opened in 2010 in the Woodmore Towne Centre in Glenarden. This shopping center has other national chains, such as Costco and Nordstrom Rack, as well as locally owned shops. Excitement about Wegmans, specifically, was countywide and was received as both a substantive victory and a symbolic one. Wegmans is a premium grocery store, expanding county residents' access to high-end foods and household goods. And its opening signals recognition of Prince Georgians' class status and purchasing power. Another premium grocery store, Whole Foods, opened in 2017 in University Park, which borders College Park in northern Prince George's County.

In my interview with the Prince George's representative to the Washington Metropolitan Area Transit Authority, he shared the following regarding the county's development trajectory:

AUTHOR: In the fifteen years you've been here, how've you seen Prince George's County change? What comes to mind when you think of Prince George's when you got here versus Prince George's now?

WMATA REPRESENTATIVE: There are ways that it's changed and there are ways that it's the same. I would say, in the ways that it is the same, it remains a place that has such a strong middle class and upper-middle class, [a] full strata of African Americans and also those who may be struggling. It has all strata of African Americans. It still does. It had that when we first got here, and it still does. So, that's one. There was at that time a dearth of, let's say, retail establishments. Places like this were not here at that time.

AUTHOR: Wegmans grocery store?

WMATA REPRESENTATIVE: Yeah, Wegmans.

AUTHOR: And now there's a Whole Foods in College Park too—that's the newest one.

WMATA REPRESENTATIVE: That's something now in College Park and a variety of other things. That was what a lot of people talked about at the time, was the lack of those types of amenities.

AUTHOR: Which people are you talking about?

WMATA REPRESENTATIVE: People who lived in the county and people who lived outside the county, who were considering coming to the county, and some people who left the county. I mean, they left because they were just, there's—amenities and those kinds of things are not there. We spent a lot of time in Anne Arundel County because of that. Because where we live, you'd just be able to drive straight out Route 50 and you'd be able to go to the mall or the grocery, different kinds of grocery stores, especially if you had something special. I mean, we have Giant and Safeway here, but less the others.

This respondent, in saying, "There are ways that it's changed and there are ways that it's the same," indicated that the breakthroughs show an upward trajectory, but that the rate of improvement is not fast enough. This official also highlighted how Prince George's residents manage their lack of amenities by shopping in nearby counties—in his case, Anne Arundel. Some Prince George's officials, like this one, expressed cautious optimism about the county's development landscape, but other county leaders were more exuberant. When I asked the Economic Development Corporation (EDC) director about the increase in high-end development, he smiled and said, "Prince George's is the dustiest county in the country," indicating his pride in the increase in new businesses.

Prior to the Woodmore Towne Centre, National Harbor opened in 2008. It was the first large-scale major win for high-end shopping and entertainment in Prince George's. National Harbor, next door to MGM Casino, sits on 350 acres on the banks of the Potomac River, with views of DC and Alexandria, Virginia.[24] About 10 million people visit National Harbor annually. Its amenities include Gaylord National Resort and Convention Center, Tanger Outlets, luxury boutiques, upscale restaurants, a marina and pier, office and residential units, and a 180-foot Ferris wheel, the Capital Wheel.

The returns to Prince George's County from these businesses go beyond the products and services they offer. MGM signed a community benefits agreement (CBA) with Prince George's that established employment and contracting targets for MGM construction and operations. In 2017 and 2018, the casino largely exceeded CBA targets. For instance, MGM's goal for the percentage of Prince George's residents it employed was 40 percent, and 47 percent of the casino's four thousand employees lived in the county in 2017—just under two thousand people.[25]

However, during hearings concerning MGM, some union leaders questioned the quality of the jobs generated, noting that many were part-time, did not offer benefits, and paid lower wages than nearby National Harbor.[26] Regarding contracting, county leaders sought to have 40 percent of building and operating contracts go to county-based businesses, and MGM met this goal, creating $368 million worth of contracts with such businesses.[27] And most important for the county's budget, in fiscal year 2018, MGM generated about $23 million in tax revenue.[28]

When MGM opened in 2016, it became the third major casino in Maryland. All three of the state's casinos opened within fifteen years of each other. Horseshoe, in Baltimore City, opened in 2014, and Maryland Live, in Anne Arundel County, opened in 2012. Gaming in Maryland counties requires the state's approval. State legislators representing the districts where Horseshoe and Maryland Live are located negotiated for equal-revenue sharing from all proceeds from slot machines. Under this arrangement, Maryland receives the total amount of tax revenue for slot machines at all three casinos and then distributes equal amounts to the three jurisdictions, rather than each jurisdiction keeping the revenue generated at the casino within its borders. This state-level decision reflects the competition between local governments for tax revenue, and not just in metropolitan-area politics but in state politics too. With revenue scarce, local governments fight to get a share of new revenue opportunities and to keep what they already have.

Even with the requirement that revenues be shared with other jurisdictions, MGM still enabled Prince George's to attain significant additional revenue. The casino is expected to pay about $50 million in taxes each year. (The first year of revenue was lower because the casino opened midway through the year.) The county council and county executive decided to allocate half of all MGM-related revenue to education—broadly defined as K-12 public schools, Prince George's Community College, and public libraries—and to put the remainder in the county's general fund, the main account for public goods and services provision.

MGM bolsters Prince George's revenue streams beyond the direct taxes it pays. As noted, the casino employs county residents and buys from county businesses. MGM also has a community benefits agreement with the community within its "impact area," the three-mile radius surrounding the casino. The logic is that neighborhoods within this distance experience the greatest amount of inconvenience from the casino's presence, such as increased traffic. In addition, nonprofit organizations within MGM's impact area are eligible for funding grants.

Overall, residents and county officials I spoke to considered MGM a major success. The primary lingering questions regarding the casino's ability to support Prince George's County's economy in the long run pertained to two challenges that were not unique to MGM: sustaining the recruitment and retention of county employees in high-wage jobs, and the use of county-based businesses, especially those owned by racialized minorities and women. For instance, the president of one of the unions operating within MGM and National Harbor said that he worked to ensure that county officials kept the needs of his workers in mind, most of whom are working-class. During his interview, he said: "Yeah, it is definitely a different worldview, and it's based on class, and it's based on geography here in the county, in or out of [the] beltway. Inner beltway tends to be my workers [union workers] living in there." This union leader also stated that the debate about raising the minimum wage in Prince George's and in other Maryland jurisdictions crystallized low-wage workers' fight to benefit from development:

> I'll give you two examples. One from the county [Prince George's] and one statewide, on a $15 minimum wage, where you have in Montgomery County, the first African American county executive, an African American veto the $15 minimum wage. . . . And even though [the Prince George's executive] didn't say nothing, he wasn't supporting the $15 minimum wage as well too. And then Baltimore City . . . vetoed one too as well. So you have the three major jurisdictions with the largest African American populations in them, who, many of those workers who work in retail and service would benefit from a wage increase at minimum wage. They all said no. And it's because of what I'm talking about, the backside of it is the white political establishment saying no and tilting over to business. And then, for example, in Prince George's County, when they were debating the minimum wage and they lifted it to $10.75, or to whatever it is now, it's below, I think they got it up to $11, $12 an hour now. But when they were debating that, they created a carve-out for Six Flags.

As of 2024, Prince George's minimum wage is $17.10 per hour. Over about a five-year period, unions and other advocates achieved victories for low-wage workers in the county.[29]

Black-owned small businesses also struggle to participate in the development boom. Consistent with national trends, minority- and women-owned small businesses in Prince George's often do not have the capital and other capacities to scale up to meet the demands of enterprises the size of MGM. These small businesses, given their limitations, often become subcontractors to larger firms not based in Prince George's. Recall from chapter 3 that a resident business owner at one of the county executive's listening sessions made this very complaint.

Prince George's officials take steps to inform county-based small businesses about contracting opportunities, both those with private firms and those with the county government. For instance, agencies offer walk-in hours when business owners can receive help completing the paperwork necessary to become certified as a county-based, women- or minority-owned small business. During budget hearings, county council members pressed agencies to demonstrate that they were targeting contracts at county-based businesses.

When I left Prince George's in 2018, several development projects were expected to open within five years. The most significant among these forthcoming developments was a University of Maryland Regional Medical Center, which will be a Level II trauma site, making it a DC metropolitan area hospital complex hub. Other projects of note included the mid-Atlantic administrative headquarters for the health insurance company Kaiser Permanente; the federal government agency US Citizenship and Immigration Services (USCIS); and the Purple Line light rail system, which will connect Prince George's County with Montgomery County. The commercial development described earlier shows that Prince George's attracts commercial development that bolsters its tax base, despite the cumulative and ongoing effects of anti-Black policies and racial capitalism. But these development breakthroughs come with costs.

A Rising Tide That May Wash Away Some Boats

In seeking to generate new tax revenue through private investment, Prince George's officials focus on development strategies geared toward the interests of middle- and upper-middle-class residents and businesses catering to them. This strategy sometimes leads to marginalizing the needs of those with lower socioeconomic status. Though Prince George's is the most affordable county contiguous with the District of Columbia, the cost of living in the county is still higher than in most other major metropolitan areas. The DC region has one of the highest costs of living in the United States.

Recall from chapter 3 that landlords with properties along the DC–Prince George's border largely eschewed responsibility for improving quality of life in their buildings. They can take this stance because they serve people with few other affordable housing options in neighborhoods close to DC and that have transit access. As Prince George's leaders press for more high-end development, many of the jurisdiction's affordable units are likely to become less affordable. Precipitously rising costs of living, particularly rent costs, could lead to residential and commercial turnover patterns that markedly shift the ethno-racial and class composition in some Prince George's neighborhoods.

At a hearing regarding the county's retail recruitment strategy, a council member whose district has some of the county's most economically distressed neighborhoods—and thus people vulnerable to displacement if rent and other living costs increase—articulated her concerns: "Dense, but low-income shopping centers are full and low vacancy. The stores cater to those tenants. We're concerned this [recruitment of premium retail and restaurants] will lead to gentrification and displacement." But her position was not broadly shared by the council and other county leaders. A senior official who spearheaded development efforts offered the majority-opinion I heard from county leaders I spoke to, both formally and informally, when he said: "Most of our properties are affordable, meaning that we're the lowest rents in the region. So building more affordable housing is not something that the county's heavily focused on."

Prince George's neighborhoods where gentrification may occur soon include those along the route of a new light rail system, the Purple Line. The sixteen miles of the Purple Line move east to west, linking Prince George's County to Montgomery County. It will have twenty-one stops anchored in Bethesda, in Montgomery County, and in New Carrollton in Prince George's County.[30] This new transit investment brings significant value to the counties it connects and to the DC region as a whole. It will enable more efficient use of other public transit systems, including Metro subway and bus lines, Maryland Rail Commuter (MARC), Amtrak, and county-based buses. The Purple Line is also likely to relieve Capital Beltway car traffic, as car commuters shift to this more efficient transportation option.

Unlike the many Prince George's Metro subway stops in low-density areas, the Purple Line corridor cuts through neighborhoods with urban densities. The majority of the residents in these neighborhoods are Latino and low-income, and they rely on local businesses that cater to their material and social needs, including bargain foods and household goods, and that employ store clerks fluent in Spanish. From a developer perspective, buying buildings near the Purple Line route may look like an advantageous investment. They can buy low and reap higher rents in coming years. Private investors who create premium housing and amenities in neighborhoods along the Purple Line would be likely to start attracting people of higher socioeconomic status than current residents. At community meetings held by county officials to learn resident concerns about the Purple Line, socioeconomic inclusion was the most prominent topic.

A council member whose district contains a portion of the Purple Line said during her interview: "I mean, it could very well be that people are waiting to be displaced. Apartment building owners could sell these, what are for the most part affordable apartments, so that they can build more expensive housing near the Purple Line and Purple Line stops. That's concerning."

In her book *Right to Suburbia*, planner Willow Lung-Amam finds that community-based organizations along the Purple Line have found ways to ensure that moderate- and low-income residents living near the new rail system will benefit from development rather than be displaced. She notes that the community-based organization CASA, for example, has played a "critical role in launching the Fair Development Coalition and pushing the Purple Line Community Development Agreement" and that "their work leveraged longstanding connections and partnerships with other major anchor institutions, foundations, government agencies, political leaders, and grassroots organizations inside and outside the neighborhood. They also drew on the trust built over decades of working in Langley Park to mobilize residents and businesses."[31] CASA's effectiveness shows some of the promising strategies for class-inclusive development: well-coordinated, broad-based coalitions of residents and businesses that are persistent, remain focused on policy, and know how to forge relationships between elected officials and residents.

Hyattsville, in northern Prince George's, is another portion of the county experiencing intense gentrification. Some Black middle-class residents, particularly those on fixed incomes, such as retirees, noted that increased development was putting pressure on their household budgets. A Hyattsville retiree shared her concerns during her interview: "I moved into this house forty years ago—my husband and I raised our two children here. I see a lot of development lately. Some of it's good . . . it's getting more expensive, but I can't afford to move, and I don't want to move. This is my neighborhood."

Does Development Facilitate or Attenuate Racial Capitalism? Or Does It Do Both?

There are inherently winners and losers in development competitions among local jurisdictions in metropolitan areas, irrespective of their racial composition. But majority-Black counties are uniquely disadvantaged. And when Black jurisdictions do "win," they often concede tax revenue, a primary reason for courting development in the first place. While Prince George's has played the hand it was dealt well, as demonstrated by the development "wins" of the past fifteen years, it is clear that the present revenue gains and potential gains fall far short of what the county needs for adequate public goods and services investment. Development brings tens of millions of dollars to a county that needs billions.

One of the congressional representatives from Prince George's articulated this perspective during his interview:

> AUTHOR: To what extent, if at all, do you agree with the assessment that the county has a Black majority—so some Black political power— but behind the scenes Whites in many ways are in control?

> CONGRESSIONAL REPRESENTATIVE: I don't think that it's any different in any other county in Maryland. I think that your developer business interest in Baltimore City has significant sway. Baltimore County, big difference. Baltimore County, it's White developers, White politicians. So the issue is more stark and more maybe unacceptable to some because of the demographics of the two different groups. But I think if you go to most communities around this country . . . Prince George's County is no different. But where it's really obvious, and for many perceived to be unfortunate, to a greater degree, is that while we are African American officeholders, that the financial source is not African American.

The Prince George's representative to WMATA offered a similar assessment:

> I think what folks miss in that is that it is that way across the country. What I mean by that is your political, you have your political power. I mean, you always have an economic power. I mean, that's the way that it is. They're not the same. They aren't the same anywhere. It's not just here. The political power often provides a vehicle to build some on the economic side, without a doubt. But that's multigenerational. It just doesn't happen overnight. So the economic power that is in Prince George's County, and that is in Maryland more generally, is, again, it's multigenerational. It's not one. This is one of the real challenges that we always face as African Americans. . . . This is also a large part of the reason why I'm involved in this, because I'm actually second-generation [middle-class]. But for most, they're first-generation. Yeah, you went to college, you know what I mean? But you don't have any money, you know what I mean? You don't have wealth. . . . I mean, African Americans simply don't have that depth. That is part of what, I think, folks, they kind of miss that to a certain degree is that, you know, that takes a long time for it to develop. It takes many generations.

Meaningful racial and socioeconomic inclusion requires that policy-makers across DC region jurisdictions use their political authority to account for how some people are better positioned than others to benefit from new development. Take "affordable housing." Affordable housing lies on a continuum. The widely agreed upon metric is that households should spend no more than 30 percent of their income on rent or mortgage payments.[32] In some instances, affordable housing targets people at or near the poverty line. In other instances, it focuses on people at a certain percentage of area median income. In the latter scenario, lower-middle-class households are more likely to be helped than those who are at or near poverty.

Prince George's County's experience with private investment demonstrates that African Americans, even those living in majority-middle-class jurisdictions, have not overcome the exclusion-extraction 2-step. Racial residential segregation, a form of exclusion, means that most African Americans do not live with European Americans. And government and market investment patterns continue to advantage White people at Black people's expense, a form of extraction. For instance, when Prince George's residents cross into neighboring counties to shop and enjoy fancy restaurants, they bolster the economies of those counties. And the people who work in retail and service jobs in neighboring Whiter, wealthier counties are likely to live in Prince George's County, placing increased pressure on the Prince George's budget as the county seeks to meet the needs of an increasing share of the DC region's moderate- and low-income residents.

Middle- and upper-middle-class African Americans can mitigate some aspects of the exclusion-extraction 2-step by using their material resources. But this is an added expenditure that their White counterparts do not have to deploy to realize the same returns to their class status. Moreover, middle- and upper-middle-class Black Americans already endure greater financial precarity because they have less wealth and less wealth-generating potential, on average, than affluent White Americans, given that US policies and market practices have generally invested more in White people and the places where they live.

Development never promised fiscal salvation. Still, private development downsides do not reveal the full picture of what is happening in Prince George's. Private investment "wins" in the past fifteen years—from high-end grocery stores, to National Harbor and MGM Casino, to a prospective regional hospital—testify to that. Each new entity is in itself significant and supports residents' material well-being to some degree. Yet private development projects, by definition, require that people have incomes at levels that allow them to participate in markets regularly. For instance, dining at restaurants at National Harbor and MGM costs about $50 a meal. Most Prince George's residents can afford such an experience only occasionally. Given that the county has nearly one million residents and that MGM and National Harbor are regional attractions, they receive enough business to succeed. But if the focus is improving the quality of day-to-day life for Prince Georgians, new developments like MGM and National Harbor do not do that, whether the measure is daily experience or sufficient new tax revenue for maintaining high-quality public goods and services.

Beyond that, Prince George's County is a jurisdiction of about one million people and is diverse across ethno-racial and class lines. The county also covers a vast geographic area—about five hundred square miles. Given the county's population size, ethno-racial and class variation, and geographic expanse, what constitutes "good" development will vary based on location in the county and residents' needs and interests in particular places. Furthermore, neighborhoods and commercial corridors that have received less government and market actor attention for years, even decades, have pent-up need for resources. These neighborhoods are likely to have deferred maintenance of existing infrastructure, while also needing new infrastructure and amenities, both of which require significant public and private investment.

Thus far, new developments in Prince George's are concentrated in certain areas, such as National Harbor and MGM Casino in southern Prince George's along the DC border, and College Park, which hosts Maryland's flagship state university, in northern Prince George's. Notwithstanding increased private investment, the general pattern is still one of "retail redlining," which prevents the county from receiving the type and quantity of development expected, given residents' income levels. The recent upward trend in private development in Prince George's probably demonstrates that developers are at last acknowledging what Prince George's leaders, like the first Black county executive, Wayne Curry, have long seen—that Prince George's is a "last frontier" for major development among jurisdictions contiguous with DC. Investors, having saturated the markets in Fairfax and Montgomery Counties, are considering places that they once had not.

Prince George's County's experience with development shows that the exclusion-extraction 2-step is complex and shifts over time as market opportunities and constraints change. But the underlying fundamental pattern remains. And this is true even as Black jurisdictions have important development victories, such as those discussed in this chapter. The through line of Black incorporation, from slavery to the present, is Black Americans' inclusion into economic processes in ways that leverage resources for White Americans, and White-dominant institutions, at Black Americans' expense.

Metropolitan-area political economy arrangements—characterized by the converging fiscal constraints of anti-Black racism, classed and raced flows of people and capital, and federalism—concentrate economic benefits in White-majority jurisdictions and concentrate economic burdens in Black-majority jurisdictions. Therefore, the core issue remains: Black jurisdictions like Prince George's need billions of dollars in new revenue to sustain high-quality public goods and services consistently. And private development alone is not capable of generating that scale of additional income under current state and local tax regimes. Moreover, private investment does not alter Prince George's County's position within regional political economy arrangements.

Majority-Black and middle-class jurisdictions have fewer winning cards to play than locales with affluent White majorities. Even affluent majority-Black counties bear the cumulative effects of the exclusion-extraction 2-step and the burdens of embeddedness in regional economies, and thus they face this conundrum: (1) either play by the rules of racial capitalism and try to carve out niches that allow for increased commercial tax revenue, while destabilizing as few households as possible, or (2) confront how government policy and market practices create an unfair playing field for Black local jurisdictions as they seek sufficient revenue for maintaining high-quality public goods and services.

The governing coalition in Prince George's County is officially county elected officials. But functionally, the governing coalition is more expansive. It consists of Prince George's elected officials, Maryland elected officials, and developers and other businesses that currently or potentially invest significantly in the county. Therefore, not only is there a range of interests among Prince George's residents regarding investment priorities, but this expansive set of actors and institutions have interests that may or may not align with the county's strategies for raising additional tax revenue through private development and for improving quality of life through access to private amenities. Indeed, well-established lines of inquiry in political science include (1) the extent to which and how power is manifest through non-policymaking institutions and actors and (2) how topics become part of public debate and/or make it onto political party and candidate agendas.[33]

My research shows that the authority of political officials in majority-Black jurisdictions is limited by embeddedness within webs of political and economic power beyond those officials' control. Prince George's leaders do shape the kinds of development their jurisdiction receives to some extent. But their authority by itself cannot overcome structural factors that have advantaged White Americans at Black Americans' expense since our country's founding. Unless there is targeted investment accounting for Black jurisdictions' cumulative economic disadvantages at all levels of social organization—individual/household, neighborhood, and local jurisdiction—the White-Black stratification of local jurisdictions within metropolitan areas will remain unchanged.

Black jurisdictions may even fall further behind if federal and state governments reduce their revenue transfers to local jurisdictions more than they already have, or if sectors where Black workers are concentrated, like government civil service, shed jobs at faster rates than sectors where White workers are concentrated. Additionally, as the cost of living increases in jurisdictions neighboring Black jurisdictions, the gap in the cost of living and quality of life between majority-White and majority-Black jurisdictions expands even more. Those displaced from wealthier, Whiter jurisdictions move to the most affordable place nearby, which causes the already less affluent county's tax base to stagnate or shrink. This pattern highlights the contribution of private development patterns to the virtuous fiscal cycles of White jurisdictions and the vicious fiscal cycles of Black jurisdictions.

Within the realm of what local leaders and community stakeholders can influence, there is often no consensus about the public and private investments to prioritize, given the scale of unmet needs, class differences within the population and other social status variation, and differences in lifestyle and built environment preferences. For instance, some residents want increased density to support business development, while others want to maintain single-family zoning because they enjoy spacious lawns and parks. Nevertheless, even with these constraints, a starting point for accounting for as many factors and interests as possible when creating and evaluating policies related to development would include consideration of: (1) the core public goods and services needs, such as schools and transportation; (2) the core private amenities needs, such as housing for a range of income levels and grocery stores; and (3) a wide range of civil society and recreation opportunities and arts venues.

CHAPTER 6

Conclusion: Envisioning Institutions for All Americans' Flourishing

> In every human breast God has implanted a Principle, which we call Love of Freedom; it is impatient of Oppression and pants for Deliverance.
>
> —Phyllis Wheatley, African American colonial-era writer and poet
> (National Constitution Center 2025)

> Remember, we are not fighting for the freedom of the Negro alone, but for the freedom of the human spirit, a larger freedom that encompasses all of mankind.
>
> —Ella Baker, African American modern civil rights movement leader
> (quoted in Ransby 2003, 319)

THE PRECEDING CHAPTERS point in the same direction: US political economy arrangements constitute an exclusion-extraction 2-step (EE2S) systematically limiting Black Americans' economic opportunities at all scales of social organization—individual, household, neighborhood, and local jurisdiction—while enriching White Americans. Social movements, constitutional amendments, and legislative changes since the Reconstruction period have attenuated some of the most egregious forms of Black expropriation and exploitation, such as chattel slavery. But Americans still have differential access to US opportunity structures—from education, to employment, to housing, to local government-provided public goods and services—based on their racial status.

https://doi.org/10.7758/bwmi8829.8336

This book has focused on metropolitan-area political economy and the primary unit of analysis has been local jurisdictions, and more specifically, suburban counties. I examined the economic and political processes shaping counties' ability to generate sufficient tax revenue for maintaining high-quality public goods and services. My findings were based on an ethnographic study of the budget development process in Prince George's County, a local jurisdiction in the DC region that has the highest concentration of middle-class Black Americans. I paired that ethnographic data with budget data from Prince George's alongside budget data from two Whiter, wealthier neighboring jurisdictions—Montgomery County, Maryland, and Fairfax County, Virginia.

By centering African Americans who experience the best-case scenario for overcoming legacy and ongoing anti-Black policies and market practices, while comparing that county's fiscal capacity to that of Whiter, wealthier counties Prince George's is located between, I have revealed the metropolitan-area political economy processes creating unique fiscal challenges for majority-Black jurisdictions. I argue that despite being majority-middle-class, Prince George's contends with converging fiscal constraints. These distinct financial constrictions highlight that race remains the core category of social difference driving inequity in American society.

Local jurisdictions' fiscal capacity is the financial foundation from which they invest in public goods and services, which are critical components of daily life, such as clean drinking water, roads and other transportation infrastructure, and K-12 schools. Well-performing public goods and services also create premiums for the local jurisdictions that can provide them, including greater demand for housing in these areas. Such demand translates into an expanding tax base, given that most local jurisdictions assess taxes on residential and commercial properties, based on their market value. With an expanding tax base, local governments can keep tax rates low. Without such expansion, local governments must either raise taxes to maintain current levels of public goods and services provision or reduce provision.

In the Washington, DC, metropolitan area, Prince George's County is the most affordable county contiguous with the nation's capital. Prince George's tax base does not expand as fast as it does in neighboring Whiter, wealthier counties, owing to systemic underinvestment in Black people and Black spaces throughout US history and the present. As the most affordable county near the DC line, it is also responsible for a disproportionate share of the DC region's moderate- and low-income populations.

In contrast, the two Whiter, wealthier jurisdictions that border Prince George's attain disproportionate shares of the DC region's upper-middle-class households. Intense gentrification in the District of Columbia has also made Prince George's the destination for moderate- and low-income people displaced from the city, further straining the county's budget. The virtuous fiscal cycles enjoyed by majority- and plurality-White jurisdictions rest on the vicious fiscal cycles endured by majority-Black jurisdictions. This research is evidence that while the Black middle class is better positioned financially than Black people with fewer class resources, middle-class African Americans do not receive the same returns to their class status as their European American counterparts.

Theory Contributions

This book explains how racial subordination leads to the fiscal subordination of majority-Black local jurisdictions, irrespective of their class composition. My theoretical frameworks illuminate how metropolitan-area political economy dynamics shape relationships between local jurisdictions. The "exclusion extraction 2-step" encompasses national-level political economy contours, which are anchored in racial capitalism. In racial capitalism, profit and other material benefits are generated by White-dominant institutions and actors imposing racial distinctions—the ascription of social and political meaning to phenotypes, most notably skin tone. In the American racial hierarchy, White elites use the legal system and violence to render themselves "superior" to Black people. To be sure, racial capitalism benefits White elites the most, as European Americans do not benefit evenly from racial hierarchy. Yet, as this book has shown, White Americans, across the class continuum, continue to have greater access to US opportunity structures than Black Americans, and unlike Black Americans, White Americans do not experience unbridled expropriation.

Metropolitan-area political economy dynamics are nested within national dynamics. I specify the mechanisms through which EE2S functions in regions through the theory I call "converging fiscal constraints" (CFC). In comparing the fiscal fitness of Prince George's County, the majority-Black jurisdiction with the greatest concentration of middle-class Black Americans, to the fiscal fitness of two Whiter and wealthier neighboring jurisdictions, I show that converging fiscal constraints explain Prince

George's County's experience of persistent financial limitations that bear down only on Black jurisdictions.

CFC has three currents that together facilitate White Americans' hoarding of material resources because they create distinct harms for majority-Black jurisdictions that yield material gain for majority-White jurisdictions. CFC's first stream is the clustering of the effects of anti-Black policies in Black jurisdictions. These concentrated effects in Black jurisdictions are a downstream consequence of American history, starting with the slave era, then the Jim Crow period, and now the present moment of White domination and anti-Blackness through less explicit means. White individuals and White spaces—households, neighborhoods, and local jurisdictions—have benefited more from government policies and market practices, on average, and Black people and spaces have experienced more burden. In a context of persistent racial residential segregation, local political borders have bound material resource asymmetries to geographic space.

The second stream of converging fiscal constraints is the raced and classed sorting of people and capital into local jurisdictions. The proportions of racial and class groups in local jurisdictions shape those jurisdictions' tax base, and thus their revenue-generating potential, as well as the demand on the budget for public goods and services. Wealthier jurisdictions, which usually have substantial White populations, not only generate more revenue but have less responsibility for moderate- and low-income households, which tend to require more public goods and services to support their families' material resource needs.

The third and final stream of converging fiscal constraints is federalism—that is, the governance structure of the United States, which, according to the Constitution, consists of shared power between national and state governments. Local jurisdictions derive authority from their respective states. Local jurisdiction boundaries concentrate and amplify White Americans' resource advantages because courts have ruled that local jurisdictions' property tax revenue cannot be distributed outside of them. Overall, CFC explains the variation in Americans' quality of life based on the local jurisdiction in which they live.

To measure the direct and indirect effects of jurisdictions' financial interdependence due to their embeddedness within metropolitan-area political economy dynamics, I coined the term "relative regional burden" (RRB). The fiscal fitness of a jurisdiction is determined not just by its own ability to generate revenue, but also by the fiscal capacity of neighboring jurisdictions. The least wealthy counties in a region absorb the negative fallout of converging fiscal constraints (CFC) and the wealthiest counties experience benefits. Thus, I argue that Prince George's subsidizes the fiscal capacity of the Whiter, wealthier counties it borders, Montgomery and Fairfax Counties. I measure the subsidy by examining the per capita/per person and per pupil/per student spending in these three counties.

Together, CFC and RRB indicate that the relationships between counties in metropolitan areas are not just stratified. The relationship is best characterized as symbiotic, as that term captures counties' financial interdependence, where some counties benefit at other counties' expense. Counties with the greatest per capita and per pupil spending are ranked highest and experience relative regional benefit, and those ranked lowest experience relative regional burden. With Prince George's County increasingly responsible for moderate- and low-income residents in the DC region, its neighbors—Montgomery and Fairfax Counties—have more revenue to invest in the middle- and upper-middle-class interests of their residents, enabling these counties to maintain their economic advantage.

Finally, I argue that, since racial difference is at the core of US political economy arrangements (the exclusion-extraction 2-step), to not account for the distorting effects of White domination and anti-Blackness when enacting and evaluating policies amounts to "color-callous racism." This term has three meanings: (1) heinous disregard for Black people's lives, in the sense that Black life is not valued, protected, and invested in to the same extent as White people's lives; (2) deliberately erected barriers to counter social friction and pressure resulting from the unjust incorporation of Black people into American political economy systems; and (3) strategies for absorbing and rearticulating Black Americans' calls for redress in ways that enable White Americans to claim that United States society is meritocratic and otherwise just, despite evidence to the contrary.

Summary of the Chapters

Following the introduction, I provided five empirically based chapters in which I explained how CFC and RRB function in the Washington, DC, metropolitan area. Chapter 1 discussed the national, state, and metropolitan-area political and economic processes shaping Prince George's County's fiscal fortunes. It provided the historical, political, and economic context necessary for interpreting the findings of the next three chapters. I explained that county governing officials and residents have limited influence on— let alone control over—many of the factors influencing Prince George's fiscal capacity. Among those factors is that Black middle-class households are more financially precarious than their White counterparts because they have higher unemployment and under-employment levels and less wealth accumulation and accumulation potential due to structural factors, such as racism in hiring and promotion and the lower market value of homes in Black neighborhoods.

Another contributor to Prince George's County's fiscal limitations is the county's lower cost of living, compared to the two Whiter, wealthier counties it borders. This relative affordability makes Prince George's more likely to receive and retain a greater share of the DC region's moderate- and low-income residents. Consequently, pressure on the county's budget increases, given that these residents generally have more public goods and services needs than middle- and upper-middle-class residents, owing to their having fewer household resources. The introduction and chapters 1 and 2 also described federal government investment in Americans' primary wealth-generating asset, their homes. I showed that Black Americans and their neighborhoods were largely locked out of wealth-building through home-buying until the Fair Housing Act of 1968, and that African Americans still do not receive the same wealth returns to home-buying as European Americans.

One more national-level pattern with regional implications is that the United States has generally championed "small government." This posture, characterized by limited government investment in health, educational, and social services, compels households to bear greater responsibility for meet- ing their material needs. And when households cannot meet those needs, local governments are left to bear the financial fallout as residents seek more public goods and services to compensate for their financial constraints.

After addressing national-level patterns, I discussed the DC metro- politan area, describing how local jurisdictions in the DC region developed from the Civil War period forward. I paid particular attention to Black population migration into and within the DC region, including Prince George's County's transition from majority-White and working-class to majority-Black and middle-class in the 1990s. Then I laid out the impact of constituent-imposed tax generation limitations on Prince George's fiscal health. I next turned to externally imposed financial constraints that the county experiences, such as bond rating agencies' creditworthiness assessments, interest payments on debt, and county employee pension plan cost-sharing with Maryland. Finally, I used the provision of two public goods and services—water as well as parks and recreation—through a bi-county system to demonstrate that when Prince George's and Montgomery Counties jointly contribute to public goods and services provision "all boats rise." Such cooperation between counties leads to efficiencies, such as economies of scale, whereas competition undermines some counties, while enhancing others.

In chapter 2, I delved into the factors shaping my two meso-level theories—converging fiscal constraints and relative regional burden. These theories identify regional political economy arrangements in the DC metropolitan area and the influence of these dynamics on the financial capacities and propensities of the region's households, neighborhoods, and local jurisdictions. Local jurisdictions where affluent White Americans are longtime residents generally have the greatest concentrations of material resources and benefit from the highest-performing public goods and services. Whiter, wealthier jurisdictions enjoy the conditions for a growing tax base, which sets the stage for greater tax revenue for supporting public goods and services. These jurisdictions are also positioned to deflect the in-migration of moderate- and low-income households because economically constrained families cannot afford the cost of living there. These households usually live in the *relatively* more affordable jurisdiction among the counties contiguous with the District of Columbia—Prince George's County.

Examining the history of the DC region as a whole, as well as the history of DC proper and Prince George's, Montgomery, and Fairfax Counties, revealed core economic and political components embedded within converging fiscal constraints and relative regional burden and the evolution of these factors over time. This history also illuminated contingencies of the conditions leading to fiscal strength versus fiscal distress, including how government policy and market practices, both those explicitly anti-Black and those that do not mention race per se, create the contours within which people and capital flow into and between DC region jurisdictions. Racialized government and market contours lead to uneven distributions of racial and class groups and private investment across Prince George's, Montgomery, and Fairfax Counties. Finally, local jurisdictions' varying histories of public and private investment, given their racial and class compositions, show that their fiscal capacities and propensities have been largely determined by how great a responsibility they have borne for long-standing unaddressed and under-addressed material needs in Black households and neighborhoods.

In chapter 3, I examined the consequences of Prince George's County's experience of converging fiscal constraints and showed that the county carries relative regional burden for the DC region. In focusing on the development of Prince George's County's fiscal year 2018 budget, I showed that the county takes in too little revenue to maintain consistently high-quality public goods and services. Severe revenue generation challenges force county officials to make hard trade-offs as they appropriate money to the agencies responsible for public goods and services provision. By explaining the deliberation process and showing the appropriations trade-offs that policy officials made, I reveal that the majority-Black jurisdiction with the highest concentration of middle-class Black people in the United States lacks the capacity to fund consistently high-quality public goods and services.

Chapter 4 demonstrated that, faced with budget limitations, the public education system struggles to educate all children well, across ethno-racial and class statuses and neighborhoods. I devoted a chapter to this public good in particular because, as a core institution supporting young people's intellectual and emotional growth in preparation for adulthood, it is important in itself. Also, affluent residents usually move to local jurisdictions with the best school reputations, and they use school performance as a proxy for the quality of life in jurisdictions more broadly.

While about 60 percent of the county budget supports Prince George's County Public Schools (PGCPS), PGCPS still does not have sufficient revenue to meet its staffing, curricular, and infrastructure needs. Compared to Montgomery and Fairfax Counties, Prince George's is responsible for educating twice as many students coming from economically distressed households. African Americans are the largest population in PGCPS, and Latinos, across racial groups, are the fastest-growing population in the school system. Many Latino students need English-language learning support, which requires additional funding. Beyond the composition of the student body, I show that the system's funding constraints stem from scarring effects of school desegregation processes that took place from the 1970s to the 1990s.

Prince George's officials cannot invest significantly more revenue in the school system without severely harming other already underfunded public goods and services. Maryland's contribution to PGCPS, about half of the school system's nearly $2 billion budget, is significant. The state funding formula accounts for Prince George's capacity to generate local revenue and for the proportion of students from economically distressed households, those with special needs, and those who need English-language learning support. But this state transfer of funds is still inadequate to meet Prince George's school system needs.

Chapter 4 also noted that a portion of the Black middle class opts out of public schools and sends their children to private and parochial schools, further concentrating moderate- and low-income students in PGCPS. Most of the Black middle-class parents I spoke to who sent their children to nonpublic schools supported public schools in principle, even though they did not send their children to public schools. Indeed, most had sought to enroll their children in high-performing PGCPS schools, but when their children did not gain admission to those schools, they left the public school system. The cost of private and parochial schools puts even more strain on the budgets of Black middle-class families in a context where they usually earn less and have less wealth than White middle-class families. Fairfax and Montgomery Counties can invest more in their schools in part because Prince George's is responsible for a greater share of the DC region's high-needs students. These Whiter, wealthier counties also do not navigate the scarring effects of the school desegregation process.

Chapter 5 discussed Prince George's County officials' efforts to overcome the county's fiscal constraints. I explained how county leaders fought for financial footing by using the same strategies that most local governments deploy across the United States: recruitment and retention of affluent residents and pursuit of high-end retail and recreation spaces, as well as businesses in growing industrial sectors, such as technology and health care. Prince George's leaders focused on "smart growth"—increasing housing density and locating commercial, recreational, and entertainment venues in walkable, mixed-use spaces proximate to transit hubs. I showed that despite development "wins" in recent years, such as National Harbor and MGM Casino, the county still endures retail redlining. This form of racial discrimination in investment patterns, among others, makes private development a less effective tool for Prince George's than it is for majority-White counties. Furthermore, development alone—even were Prince George's to receive its proportionate share of investment—would not be sufficient to meet the county's revenue needs. Prince George's County requires hundreds of millions of dollars in new revenue to invest adequately in public goods and services, and private investment does not have the potential to yield that scale of income.

Taken together, the chapters of this book build the case that the majority-Black jurisdiction with the highest concentration of middle-class African Americans does not have the capacity to provide consistently high-quality public goods and services owing to structural limitations outside of the county's control. That is, Prince George's County's fiscal fortunes are shaped by its embeddedness in national and regional political economy arrangements. The findings discussed in these chapters show that race, independent of class, still shapes Americans' life chances, and that middle-class Black people—whether in households, neighborhoods, or local governments—cannot realize the same returns as their White counterparts when they "play by the rules" for financial well-being. My research also reveals that levels of social organization—household, neighborhood, local jurisdiction, and metropolitan area—mutually inform each other's capacity.

To create political and economic systems that meet all Americans' material and social needs, irrespective of race, class, and other social statuses, we must at last reckon with how *foundational* aspects of American political and economic systems are embedded in the exclusion-extraction 2-step, which exploits some Americans for other Americans' benefit. We must also commit to repudiating color-callous racism—the willful denial that racial difference, more than any other social distinction, distorts the social fabric of the United States. Truly just and inclusive political and economic structures must explicitly account for the accumulation of racial harm and then enact social processes expressly designed to help all Americans flourish.

Imagining a More Just and Inclusive Country

When Black people lay claim to rights and resource access commensurate with their citizenship, they are insisting on realizing "substantive citizenship," to borrow sociologist Evelyn Nakano Glenn's term.[1] Legal scholar Dorothy Roberts argues in a *Harvard Law Review* article that the "tension between recognizing the relentless antiblack violence of constitutional doctrine, on one hand, and demanding the legal recognition of black people's freedom and equal citizenship, on the other, animates . . . abolitionist debates on the US Constitution."[2] The "abolition constitutionalism" that Roberts identifies is akin to the "abolition democracy" that scholar-activist Angela Davis discusses in her book by the same name.[3]

Through the term "abolition," Roberts and Davis connect current racial justice movements to the work of antebellum slavery abolitionists who fought against the violent extraction of labor from African people and their explicit exclusion from the US body politic. Roberts and Davis contend that the Constitution, as written, could be interpreted more expansively, which would lead to more justice for Black Americans. And beyond that, Roberts and Davis note that our Constitution and laws should not constrain our understanding of what "justice" means as we pursue a society that is not built on exclusion and extraction, but rather affirms the equality of all Americans and facilitates all Americans' material and social well-being.

In other words, the Constitution is an *instrument* for achieving justice and for enabling participatory governance—and where it falls short in attaining these goals, the document should be amended. Roberts states:

> The Constitution is not the standard of justice we should faithfully uphold; equal citizenship is. We know what democracy means not by immersing ourselves in the Constitution's language but by imagining what it would mean for black people to be treated like free and equal human beings. The purpose of constitutional fidelity is to insist that constitutional interpretation abide by this higher standard of justice.[4]

Education scholar Bettina Love complements Roberts's and Davis's thinking regarding abolition through her term "abolition teaching."[5] This concept calls attention to the role of schools, which can encourage students to accept the status quo or to reimagine social systems that are fair and that enable all people to thrive. And scholar-activists, like Mariame Kaba, stress the importance of the constructive tension between practical strategizing for just uses of power, which often involves the state, but is not limited to it, while also seeking to remove the limitations we have individually and collectively internalized regarding what true justice—wholeness for all parties involved—looks like:

> None of us has all of the answers, or we would have ended oppression already. But if we keep building the world we want, trying new things, and learning from our mistakes, new possibilities emerge. Here's how to begin.

First, when we set about trying to transform society, we must remember that we ourselves will also need to transform. Our imagination of what a different world can be is limited. We are deeply entangled in the very systems we are organizing to change.[6]

Black feminist Audre Lorde also champions the theme of abolition when she argues that "the master's tools will never dismantle the master's house. They may allow us temporarily to beat him at his own game, but they will never enable us to bring about genuine change. And this fact is only threatening to those women who still define the master's house as their only source of support."[7]

Lorde provides three key insights. First, the American house we live in, with the Constitution as its foundation, was *designed* with a certain group's interests in mind, elite White men. Second, the tools used to keep American political and economic institutions functioning are for tinkering with the house, not for refurbishing it, let alone completely re-envisioning it from the foundation up with everyone's needs and interests in mind. Finally, Lorde reminds us that this reality is not surprising and induces fear only if we believe that this house is the only possible model for political and economic organization.

Writer and civil rights activist James Baldwin, in his book *The Fire Next Time*, also warns us that merely including more people in an unjust system does not make the system more just:

> The price of this transformation is the unconditional freedom of the Negro; it is not too much to say that he, who has been so long rejected, must now be embraced, and at no matter what psychic or social risk. He is *the* key figure in his country, and the American future is precisely as bright or as dark as his. And the Negro recognizes this, in a negative way. Hence the question: Do I really *want* to be integrated into a burning house?[8]

Lorde admonishes us that the tools we use, such as our routine policies, are inadequate for the depth and breadth of transformation necessary. Baldwin declares that the edifice and its foundation must be wholly re-envisioned. Together, Lorde and Baldwin argue that our values and ways of interacting with each other—particularly our competitive, zero-sum calculations—undermine our political project. Like Lorde and Baldwin, I believe that our current economic and political systems stunt our ability to realize the fullness of democratic and economic systems built of, by, and for all American people.

White elites' dominance, in fact, does not work that well for millions of White people. In 2023, about thirty-seven million Americans lived in poverty, and about 40 percent of those people were White.[9] Racial equity requires full repudiation of White domination, anti-Blackness, and racial capitalism—from the foundation, to the floors, to the load-bearing walls, to the curtains. Through the policy recommendations in the next section, I seek to seed our sociological and political imaginations with paths and possibilities for improving *all* Americans' quality of life.

Policies Designed for Equitable Access to Resources Across Race and Class Groups

Policy Recommendation #1: Raise Federal, Corporate, and Inheritance Taxes

Tax revenue is the lifeblood of government. Without money, governments cannot invest in the agencies—their staffs and material resources—that produce public goods and services. The trend since the Nixon and Reagan administrations of the 1970s and 1980s has been to reduce the national government's support of public goods and services not related to social control, including its bolstering of local government capacity, such as through programs like the Community Development Block Grant. Nixon's and Reagan's policy postures were a stark rebuttal of the Johnson administration's "War on Poverty." While their rationales for reduced federal investment in social services spending were linked to the changing global economy, which forced the United States to compete for markets across the globe, the 1970s and 1980s were also a period of backlash against civil and social rights advancements made by racialized minority groups, particularly Black Americans. After all, the national government continued its unprecedented investment in policing, prisons, the military, and space exploration.

Geographer Ruth Wilson Gilmore argues that many conservatives hold an "antistate state" stance: "The antistate state depends on ideological and rhetorical dismissal of any agency or capacity that 'government' might use to guarantee social well-being."[10] But government has the ability, she maintains, to create "social well-being." And tax dollars are the means through which government invests in the public's well-being.

Therefore, the first priority is ensuring that the federal government has adequate tax revenue. To that end, we should enact tax increases on the wealthiest Americans—those with incomes of $500,000 per year or more, with the richest 1 percent paying the highest rate. And as legal scholar Dorothy Brown argues in her book *The Whiteness of Wealth*, we should end tax code provisions that reinforce wealth inequality by privileging the assets disproportionately held by the most affluent Americans, such as stocks, the dividends of which are taxed at a lower rate than income earned through job salaries.[11]

Inheritance taxes should also increase significantly. As this book has shown, the White-Black racial wealth gap reflects policies based in the exclusion-extraction 2-step. That is, White Americans have experienced systemic investment in their wealth accumulation at Black Americans' expense. Regardless of when White Americans or their ancestors arrived in this country—whether in 1620 on the *Mayflower* or yesterday—or whether they intended to benefit from racial capitalism, they *do* benefit, full stop.

And the wealth they possess and have the potential to attain is tied, not to merit and hard work alone, but also to the fruit of ill-gotten gains that have evolved from the slave era to the present. This book has demonstrated that when Black people, whether households or local jurisdictions, play by the same rules for financial health as White people, they receive vastly fewer rewards for the same effort. One way to end the cycle of intergenerational transfers reinforcing and extending unjust White wealth attainment is to limit the amount of wealth people can transfer to their children or other beneficiaries. In my fifth policy recommendation, I also argue that the federal government should pay reparations to Black people and target investment toward Black neighborhoods and local jurisdictions.

Corporate taxes should increase too. Under the Biden administration, Secretary of the Treasury Janet Yellen pursued a corporate global minimum tax, which is essential, given the international nature of capital movement.[12] But regardless of what other countries do, the United States is a preferred place to invest, due to our concentrations of expertise in science and technology and other strategic advantages. Hence, the United States can raise corporate taxes and still expect both foreign and domestic investment.

Another way to have more money to allocate toward social and human services is to reduce spending on the military, policing, and prisons, and then to redirect that funding toward social and human services. Ultimately, however, we cannot deliberate over how much to distribute and redistribute revenue unless we have sufficient revenue in the first place. And the federal government is uniquely positioned to ensure that all Americans' material needs are met across state and local jurisdictions.

Policy Recommendation #2: Increase State Funding
for Public Goods and Services

With few (short-term) alternatives, local leaders tend to compete with each other for direct private investment and state funding transfers. In the short run, such investment and transfers may go to some jurisdictions more than to others, and thus some jurisdictions seemingly win. But in the long run all jurisdictions stand to gain more if their state garners more tax revenue and invests in public goods and services at higher levels. In the state of Maryland, the Maryland Association of Counties (MACo) coordinates county officials' state-level political priorities.[13] Hence, MACo is in a position to facilitate petitioning for county-level interests, like increased state transfers.

MACo members could also devise criteria for prioritizing public goods and services initiatives if new revenue could be realized. Additionally, MACo would need to consider how to reconcile the needs and desires of counties with smaller tax bases with those of counties with larger tax bases. Counties that generate the most revenue, such as Montgomery County, already contribute more to the state than they receive in return (if we measure the share of revenue, relative to other counties, that Montgomery County residents provide to the state through income taxes). At the same time, Montgomery County's financial advantages stem from racial capitalism and anti-Black policies, as is the case across majority- and plurality-White jurisdictions in Maryland and around the country.

MACo and other state and local political institutions could partner with civil society institutions to create an appetite for increased taxes among voters. This civic education might be led by political officials, academics, activists, religious groups, and other interested parties. Most voters already support raising taxes on wealthy Americans.[14] The key is convincing the public to enact higher federal and state taxes on the wealthy and on the upper-middle class, raising them at least to the levels in place in the 1960s. Public education on taxes should highlight that governments, unlike private entities, are focused on public well-being, not profit maximization; accountable to an electorate, rather than to shareholders; and capable of coordinating the movement of resources between other governments and across industries in ways that companies and nonprofit organizations cannot.

If state-level organizations, like MACo, across the country coordinated a movement to increase state taxes, wealthy people and businesses would find it more difficult to move between states and locales in pursuit of lower tax rates. State and federal tax increases combined would also create more capacity to invest in regional public goods and services projects, such as transit. Fragmentation in the American governance system has and continues to enable resource-hoarding by wealthy White people because they use political boundaries to cordon off their resources.

Policy Recommendation #3: Create Regional Taxes and Cost-Sharing Arrangements

Americans need more metropolitan-area-wide governance. In the DC region, Prince George's County, in coordination with other DC region jurisdictions, could work toward enacting tax levies to support the region's economically distressed populations. A regional tax, alongside a regional minimum wage, could be designed to support low-income households to ensure that their basic needs are met, regardless of where they live. At a smaller scale, we already see the success of local governments pooling resources through two bi-county agencies that serve Prince George's and Montgomery Counties: the Washington Suburban Sanitary Commission, which provides clean water and sewage treatment; and the Maryland–National Capital Park and Planning Commission, which manages outdoor and indoor recreation and supports zoning ordinance management.

The Metropolitan Washington Council of Governments (CoG), the primary DC region body coordinating regional activities, could lead metropolitan-level efforts. CoG identified "social equity" as a concern in its "Region Forward" planning priorities.[15] Pursuing a regional minimum wage and regional tax would be a concrete investment in meeting this goal.

Wealthier jurisdictions' decision-makers may be willing to participate in efforts to distribute (minimum wage) and redistribute (regional tax) resources because their middle- and upper-middle-class residents depend on the labor of low-income workers to support their lifestyles. For instance, a large share of those earning the minimum wage, or close to it, are childcare workers and people who work in the food industry, who are critical to supporting affluent families' daily routines. Given the constraints of our federal governance system, each state could enact taxes designated for funding the portions of metropolitan areas within their boundaries. Maryland and Virginia would fund their own program, alongside DC, and then an established institution, such as CoG, could coordinate funding distribution to policies and programs.

Regional coordination does not have to be government-to-government only. It can also be led by civil society groups consisting of residents, small-business owners, nonprofits, religious groups, and other community stakeholders. In her book *Right to Suburbia*, Willow Lung-Amam notes the importance of community-based organizations that span jurisdictional boundaries within regions. She highlights the effectiveness of organizations, such as the Fair Development Coalition, that have been pressing for class-inclusive development along the Purple Line, the new light rail line connecting Prince George's and Montgomery Counties.[16] Community-based organizations can be quite effective when they have sustainable institutional capacity, unify a broad range of community members around a shared agenda, and are strategic in targeting the political officials and policies shaping development persistently.

Policy Recommendation #4: Hold Financial Bad Actors
Accountable for Household- and Community-Level Harms

The Great Recession of 2009–2011 did not just hurt families; it also dashed the hopes of neighborhoods and local jurisdictions. Yet neither households nor neighborhoods were made whole by market bad actors. The federal government offered banks loans to prevent the implosion of the financial industry, but it did comparatively little to mitigate the financial fallout experienced by families, neighborhoods, and local jurisdictions. The Consumer Financial Protection Bureau (CFPB) has authority to protect consumers from "unfair, deceptive, and abusive practices," and the Dodd–Frank Wall Street Reform and Consumer Protection Act of 2010, which created CFPB, instituted new financial regulations to decrease the likelihood and severity of future financial industry crises.[17]

However, neither CFPB nor Dodd–Frank make explicit whether—and if so, how—industry actors are responsible for household- and community-level harms inflicted by firms' unscrupulous, if not illegal, actions.[18] For instance, at minimum, banks found liable for unscrupulous and/or illegal practices should contribute to local and state government social services programs, given that household financial hardships often precipitate families' economic instability, leading many households to seek aid from state and local governments.

Policy Recommendation #5: Establish Black Equity Funds (Reparations)

The Great Recession was just one of the most recent instances of the exclusion-extraction 2-step undermining African American households, neighborhoods, and local jurisdictions. To account for these harms, federal and state governments, as well as private entities, should be required to understand how their practices are contributing to White domination and anti-Black racism, and then they should create different types of reparations funds based on their findings.[19] William Darity and A. Kirsten Mullen, in their book *From Here to Equality*, propose that Black Americans who have at least one enslaved ancestor receive about $350,000.[20] This amount would largely close the White-Black wealth gap. Such a payment would also atone for the interlocking, compounding harms that Black Americans have endured from the slave era onward.

Scholars Linda Bilmes and Cornell William Brooks, in an article regarding reparations for Black Americans, create a "taxonomy" of harms, including those connected to housing, wages, employment and labor markets, education, criminal justice, health care, voting, and violence.[21] Bilmes and Brooks argue that "the US government has repeatedly compensated individuals for parallel nonracial harms that directly impaired health, earnings capacity, and the right to life, liberty, and the pursuit of happiness," and that the US government also has provided "financial redress when Americans have experienced physical harms or economic loss through no fault of their own."[22] They also note a wide range of compensation categories—from health and disability benefits to payments for veterans and those involved in coal and other mining activity.

Regarding race-related compensation specifically, in 1988 the federal government paid $20,000 to Americans of Japanese descent who were imprisoned by the federal government during World War II. During World War II, the US government claimed that Japanese Americans, despite being US citizens, were loyal to Japan, not to the United States. Japanese Americans were forced to live in government-monitored encampments until their release at the end of the war.[23]

Given the range and scale of compensation that the federal government has offered, and continues to offer, Bilmes and Brooks conclude that

> the numerosity and diversity of reparatory compensation programs makes clear that reparations for nonracial harms is regular and routine. Juxtaposing the audit of reparatory compensation programs with the taxonomy of reparation-less racial harms makes clear that America provides reparations to nearly everyone but Black Americans, even for comparably severe harms.[24]

If the federal government were to enact reparations for Black Americans, the first step the government should take is to establish a commission to study the harms African Americans endured during the slavery era and subsequently. Regarding the post-slavery period, the categories of harm named earlier could establish the primary categories to focus on. Next, the US Office of Management and Budget and other federal agencies could, as Bilmes and Brooks state, "conduct an audit of federal reparatory compensation programs detailing the budget, beneficiaries, legal authority, and harms alleviated by such programs."[25] Doing this would create baseline knowledge about what the federal government is *already* doing to compensate Americans, thus identifying principles for the types of reparations to offer Black Americans.

The contemporary reparations movement is part of a long history of African Americans petitioning for redress for race-based harms. In the final years of the Civil War and the early Reconstruction years, the United States established expectations for land redistribution that would enable recently manumitted people to attain economic mobility and autonomy outside of the control of White people and White-controlled institutions. Through William T. Sherman's Special Field Order 15, a land redistribution program was established. It allotted 5.3 million acres of land, from the sea islands of South Carolina to northern Florida, to be set aside for formerly enslaved Africans.[26] But President Andrew Johnson ended the program. He also removed federal troops from Southern states, effectively ending Civil War Reconstruction. Without federal enforcement of Black people's equal citizenship, White planters reasserted dominance over Southern political and economic institutions.

In more recent years, Congressman Johns Conyers started introducing House Resolution 40 in every Congress from 1989 until his death in

2019.[27] H.R. 40 would establish a commission to study reparations for Black Americans. The "40" in H.R. 40 has substantive meaning: it refers to the forty acres and a mule that formerly enslaved Africans were promised by the federal government under Special Field Order 15. In the words of Callie G. House, among the first generation of Black Americans to call for reparations, "If the Government had the right to free us, she had a right to make some provision for us; and since she did not make it soon after Emancipation, she ought to make it now."[28] Callie House spoke these words in 1899—and *now* is still the time to act.

To date, some state and local governments, such as the states of California and New York, and the city of Evanston, Illinois, have taken steps toward offering Black Americans reparations. California and New York have established commissions to study the need for reparations.[29] Evanston has begun paying reparations to Black Americans for the city's actions related to housing discrimination.[30] State and local reparations actions indicate the presence of some public support for reparations and bring attention to the issue, perhaps galvanizing further support. But state and local governments do not have the scale of funding needed to make meaningful reparations for all eligible Black Americans.

Reparations for Black Americans and other forms of redistribution will require that we empower our governing structures—federal, state, and local—with the revenue and authority necessary to allocate resources equitably across US social groups, with particular attention to Black Americans, who, alongside Indigenous Americans, have endured the most severe harms of any racial group.[31]

Finally, reparations should be paid at the individual, household, neighborhood, local jurisdiction, metropolitan area, and state levels. The exclusion-extraction 2-step has operated at all of these levels, and the remedy should repair damage accordingly. Therefore, in addition to individual and household-level reparations, the federal government should coordinate all levels of government to target investment in neighborhoods that experience insufficient public goods and services provision or poorly maintained infrastructure. Local government should be empowered to take steps to ensure that longtime residents are not displaced during or after such capital infusions. For instance, governments might consider setting aside land and buildings for land trusts and cooperatives for sustainable, high-quality housing and communal spaces that are not subject to market speculation.

A Final Word: Refusing Manufactured Scarcity and Fighting for All Americans' Flourishing

When someone says the word "taxes," what comes to mind? Many of us think of some form of "burden." But what if we reframed taxes as "funds for communal flourishing"? After all, we need not only to be able to allocate resources autonomously, in ways that reflect our personal and household-specific needs, but also to contribute to maintaining the physical and social infrastructure of our society. Indeed, this infrastructure is the very substrate within which we build our individual lives and those of our families. US society at all scales—nation, state, metropolitan area, county, municipality, neighborhood, block, household, and individual—cannot hold together through goodwill alone. Our intentions must manifest materially. And public goods and services are investments we make in our collective well-being.

We do not have to search hard for examples of more ample social safety nets in other countries. When compared to other Western capitalist democracies, such as Canada, the United Kingdom, France, Germany, and Sweden, the United States offers the fewest and least generous public goods and services to its citizens.[32] In the countries just named, taxes pay for universal health care, child care, and paid family and medical leave. The only Americans who experience universal health care are military servicepersons, through Tricare.

In drawing attention to the limitations of American-style "federalism," I have argued that the institutions of shared authority and resource provision across levels of government were initially designed for White dominance and have been reformed merely to maintain it. I have also called attention to the ways in which our political economy arrangements, characterized by the diffusion of power, enable those who are more economically advantaged to use political boundaries to hoard resources for themselves at other Americans' expense.

Additionally I have shown how earlier forms of racial capitalism and racist policies—from the slavery and Jim Crow periods—are laundered in the contemporary moment through tax regimes that are ostensibly race- and class-neutral but actually leverage historical and present resource asymmetries, thereby extending and amplifying inequitable resource access between

Black and White Americans. The major implication for Black Americans of these power dynamics is that they remain the depository from which White Americans withdraw as they engage in an exclusion-extraction 2-step, a dance to which Black Americans have never consented. But we the people can choose to end this cruelty and to imagine just political economy structures.

Certainly, Americans are not in ideological agreement—some want smaller government, others want a more expansive one. But we should not overstate ideological divisions either. For instance, most Americans believe that all people and corporations should pay their fair share in taxes. According to a 2022 Gallup survey, most Americans support increasing taxes on wealthy Americans.[33]

If there is such agreement, why has the general trend since the 1970s been to *lower* the effective tax rate of the wealthiest Americans? This discrepancy between the will of the people and government action subverts our belief that government is truly "of, by, and for the people," to borrow language from President Abraham Lincoln's Gettysburg Address. But cynicism toward government can become a self-fulfilling prophecy: because we believe that government does not work, we starve it of the resources it needs to be effective.

If government does not act, what alternative institutions should we use to mediate our access to the core material and social needs that underpin our quality of life? Businesses, foundations, religious organizations, and civil society groups do not have government's mandate to serve *all* of the people, irrespective of their social statuses; nor are nongovernmental institutions accountable to the American people through voting or any other mechanism (other than indirectly, such as through laws that prohibit fraud and boycotts of their goods and services). The missions and motivations of corporations and nonprofit institutions are limited in scope, and these organizations do not have the authority or capacity to bring new social systems to scale.

In her book *The Sum of Us*, lawyer and policy expert Heather McGhee argues that "we have reached the productive and moral limit of the zero-sum economic model that was crafted in the United States. We have no choice but to start aiming for a solidarity dividend."[34] That "solidarity dividend" yielded by cooperation and a commitment to the collective good leads to material and social prosperity across Americans, irrespective of social status, and is best mediated through public goods and services provision.

Similarly, political scientist and pastor Andrew Wilkes in his book *Plenty Good Room* argues that our economic system reflects a "scarcity and austerity" perspective, rather than a "sufficiency and abundance" perspective.[35] When we take this stance, we cannot see the full "continuum of optionality." Wilkes contends that capitalist structures often preclude consideration of forms of cooperative economics, such as democratic socialism, that enable broad-based thriving.

In her book *Collective Courage*, social scientist Jessica Nembhard, like Wilkes, writes about forms of "solidarity economics" in Black communities throughout US history.[36] She highlights a Black radical tradition grounded in self-help, shared risk, and democratic ownership. And some projects have been connected to broader political commitments to democratic socialism.

Nembhard finds that from the slave era to the present, organized groups of Black people have created mutual aid societies and held land and businesses in common. African Americans have enacted these practices to fill gaps resulting from market failures, as well as to avoid capitalist speculation and exploitation. These strategies are also a means for building broadly shared economic and social well-being. Nembhard notes three types of cooperatives: (1) consumer-owned, such as credit unions, natural food grocery stores, and rural energy cooperatives; (2) producer-owned, such as craft cooperatives; and (3) worker-owned businesses, which are jointly owned and managed by employees. Worker-owned ventures probably have the most transformative impact in Black communities because they "offer economic security, income and wealth generation, and democratic economic participation to employees, as well as provide communities with meaningful and decent jobs and promote environmental sustainability."[37]

Cooperative economics, or solidarity economies, have been staples of Black leaders' agendas for Black advancement throughout US history, including those put forward by W.E.B. Du Bois, A. Philip Randolph, Marcus Garvey, E. Franklin Frazier, Malcolm X, Martin Luther King Jr., Nannie Helen Burroughs, Fannie Lou Hamer, and Ella Baker.[38] For instance, Hamer's Freedom Farm Cooperative used funds raised through a national campaign, demonstrating the intersection of land acquisition, cooperative economics, and a national politics of solidarity that is centered on Black people's need for self-determination.

African Americans' participation in collectivist projects for Black advancement is often downplayed, including by some Black people. African Americans who do not support this approach often fear White backlash that could set them back even further, if not cost them their lives. And this fear is warranted, given the history of White violence when Black Americans pursue even individualized entrepreneurship enterprises, let alone economic independence from White Americans through noncapitalist means.[39] Still, today, cooperative land trusts are in rural and urban spaces across the country—from the Bronx Community Land Trust in New York City, to the Federation of Southern Cooperatives Land Assistance Fund in Georgia.[40] Collectives exemplify a strategy for Black agency and self-determination through which African Americans seek to build economic capacity and solidarity among themselves.

As African Americans pursue economic solidarity, strategies must intentionally seek to overcome class-based differences in priorities and vulnerabilities.[41] For instance, low- and moderate-income Black Americans are likely to be more interested in collective practices because they can use them to survive in a context where they have few alternatives for making ends meet. Middle-class and upper-middle-class African Americans, who are more financially advantaged, are probably more interested in "buy Black" initiatives targeted at consumers (for example, ByBlack.us, a platform for certified Black-owned businesses); market and government contract opportunities for Black entrepreneurs; Black professional organizations; and community uplift efforts led by historically Black colleges and universities, Greek letter sororities and fraternities, and civil rights and philanthropy organizations, such as the NAACP and the National Council of Negro Women. Black economic elites, such as LeBron James, Oprah Winfrey, and Robert Smith, often give millions to foundations and other nonprofit organizations and causes that resonate with them.

Another axis of difference within the Black population is immigration status. Immigrants and children of immigrants constitute about 20 percent of the US Black population.[42] Given that the US immigration system after 1965 immigration reform selects for highly educated people, immigrants from African and Caribbean countries are usually more educated than those in their home countries and more educated than the average Black American. Similar to the relationship between the Black middle class and low-income Black Americans, immigrants from African and Caribbean countries sometimes evince "selective solidarity" toward native-born Black Americans.[43]

Many people from African and Caribbean countries have transnational identities and networks that enhance their economic and social options.[44] Yet, as preeminent scholar Paul Gilroy discusses in *Black Atlantic*, people of African descent across African, European, Caribbean, and North, Central, and South American countries have, since the transatlantic slave trade, engaged in myriad forms of fruitful and solidaristic hybridity and cultural exchange. And I contend these resonances between peoples of African descent continue to be a basis for actively pursuing axes of solidarity within and between Black communities in the United States.[45]

Given the heterogeneity within the Black population, African Americans' efforts to achieve solidarity economics that truly transforms Black communities must be coordinated and allocated through shared agendas and infrastructures that span class lines, geographic space, and immigration status. Otherwise, African Americans risk losing opportunities for synergy and even risk working at cross-purposes, rather than in concert. Key questions to consider include, among others: Are wealthy people offering seed money and sustained support to Black-led economic enterprises that equip Black people to either withdraw from exploitative capitalist arrangements or operate in ways that enable them to compete with White-owned enterprises, which generally have more capital? What kinds of infrastructure would enable Black communities within and across states to work together to amplify each other's efforts? The main concern is to create mechanisms for the redistribution of resources within and between Black neighborhoods that center collective needs and interests, such as ready access to land and decent affordable housing.

It is no secret that African Americans with middle-class and higher socioeconomic status who seek deep cross-class collaboration are in a bind: They navigate and leverage White- dominant economic and other social systems that enable their socioeconomic advantages, while also seeking to mitigate the harm these same systems pose to Black people and communities, irrespective of class and other social status differences among African Americans. This is no easy feat, but the task remains the task. If we fail to account fully for this tension, we risk more of the same—African Americans pursuing upward mobility through individualized strategies and/or through policies embedded in White domination and anti-Black racism, both of which render Black Americans vulnerable.[46]

Pursuit of higher education and other on-ramps to upward mobility are not inherently problematic—they are just insufficient for overcoming the limitations inherent in White domination and anti-Black racism. As this book has shown, Black people, irrespective of class status, experience economic precarity. All African Americans are subject to the exclusion-extraction 2-step, although some are better equipped than others to manage it. Even many middle-class Black Americans are one paycheck away from downward mobility into poverty because they do not have significant wealth to bolster them. In the long run, cooperative economics has the potential to help the most Black Americans and Black communities.

African Americans have keen insight into the limitations of US governing and market institutions and the implications for shared prosperity in Black communities and the United States more broadly. In the Black prophetic tradition, African American leaders and layfolk do not view US federalist democracy and market economies as inherently salvific. Instead, Black Americans have a long-standing tradition of calling forth the potential in these systems while decrying their constraints—indeed, their inhumanity—while remaining open to trying out solutions that most White-dominant actors and institutions dismiss and demonize.[47]

This Black prophetic tradition dates back to the slave era, when enslaved Africans worshiped after sundown in hush harbors away from the gaze of White people.[48] It also includes the narratives of formerly enslaved people, such as David Walker's *Appeal* and the oratory of Maria Stewart, Sojourner Truth, and Frederick Douglass.[49] It is reflected in self-manumitting people ("runaways") who left forced labor camps ("plantations") and in organized slave revolts—from the Stono Rebellion in South Carolina in 1739, to the New York Conspiracy in 1741, to Nat Turner's Rebellion in Southampton County, Virginia, in 1831, among others.[50] In the post-emancipation period, people like Anna Julia Cooper, Marcus Garvey, W.E.B. Du Bois, Malcolm X, Angela Davis, and Cornel West have carried this mantle. And of course, the Reverend Dr. Martin Luther King Jr. is the quintessential icon of the prophetic tradition.

The mainstream American narrative about Dr. King, however, truncates and distorts his ideological and policy positions and thus the expansiveness of the legacy he left us. Regularly lauded by liberals and conservatives alike, most people quote his "I Have a Dream" speech, which he delivered during the 1963 March on Washington for Jobs and Freedom. The very title of the march, with its focus on "jobs and freedom," calls attention to the intersection of racism, capitalism, and autonomy over one's life. And too few people recall King's speeches and publications during the final years of his life, when the Vietnam War was well underway. Those speeches and publications emphasized the fundamental interconnections between imperialism, racism, and exploitative capitalist practices, pointing to both American and global exploitation processes.

In 1967, the year before he was killed, King delivered a speech, entitled "Beyond Vietnam: A Time to Break Silence," at Riverside Baptist Church in New York City. He decried the "evil triplets" of "racism, poverty, and militarism" threatening to strangle our country.[51] When King was assassinated in 1968, he was organizing the Poor People's Campaign, an intentionally interracial effort highlighting economic inequality in the United States. People from across the United States planned to camp on the National Mall in Washington, DC, as a form of protest. The last book King published, *Where Do We Go from Here: Chaos or Community?*, is a prescient meditation on the crisis facing the United States regarding a reckoning with racial capitalism once and for all. In the book, King contends that unless the United States quickly and decisively works to correct gross racial and class inequities, our country risks implosion—hence the question: "chaos or community?"[52]

In *Where Do We Go From Here: Chaos or Community?*, King also offers policy solutions for moving toward a more inclusive society along race and class lines. For instance, when discussing the need for full employment or a guaranteed income, he states: "We are likely to find that the problems of housing and education, instead of preceding the elimination of poverty, will themselves be affected if poverty is first abolished."[53] Effectively, King argues that poverty is a policy choice, and by extension, that an equitable distribution of material resources is critical for a stable, prosperous country.

The US federal government demonstrated that poverty is something policy can eliminate during the COVID-19 pandemic's pre-vaccine period. In 2020 and 2021, the federal government expanded the child tax credit, and child poverty was cut in half.[54] But in 2022, the policy was terminated and child poverty returned to pre-pandemic levels. A government guarantee of employment, a universal basic income, and other policies designed to provide consistent sources of money are vital measures when people must use market-provided goods for daily sustenance. And as this book has laid out, government investment in public goods and services, or the lack thereof, also shapes people's ability to meet their material needs and to sustain a high standard of living.

The expansive "freedom dreams" of Black Americans, to borrow the title of Robin D. G. Kelley's book, are not just for Black Americans.[55] For Black freedom would improve the life chances of all Americans, as McGhee's "solidarity dividend" argues.[56] And we already have previews of this reality. For example, it was the Black Panther Party for Self-Defense, a party founded in the late 1960s in Oakland, California, that first started serving breakfast to children before school.[57]

Dr. King's Poor People's Campaign is consistent with the stance of the Black Panther Party regarding the potential for cross-racial class solidarity. Kwame Ture (formerly Stokely Carmichael) and Charles Hamilton, two Black Panther Party leaders, write in their book *Black Power*: "It is hoped that eventually there will be a coalition of poor Blacks and poor Whites."[58] Ture and Hamilton caution, however, that because Black people have endured, and continue to experience, unique forms of exclusion and extraction, they should be sober about the terms under which they engage in coalitions with other social groups. As such, Ture and Hamilton offer "four preconditions" for Black Americans' participation in coalitions: (1) mutual recognition of each group's self-interests; (2) "mutual belief that each party stands to benefit" from the alliance; (3) acceptance that each party has its "own independent base of power"; and (4) specific shared goals.[59]

King and the Black Panther Party for Self-Defense recognized that moral suasion, or goodwill, alone is not likely to prove sufficient for sustained fundamental change in US political and economic systems. Clear shared interests are the most viable basis for a sustainable agenda. White people with low incomes share an economic position with Black people with low incomes, and therefore both groups stand to gain considerably from a more equitable distribution of material resources. But, as discussed in the introduction, since the slave era, racial hierarchy has often led economically distressed White people to eschew coalitions with Black people.

The labor movement, which was at its height in the first half of the twentieth century, is a prime example of this posture. Most unions refused to admit Black workers on equal terms with Whites, if they admitted Blacks at all. And most telling of all, when cross-racial alliances, such as the agrarian populist movement of the late 1800s and the Poor People's Campaign of the late 1960s, gain momentum and threaten racial capitalism,

White-dominant institutions and actors, including the US government, actively seek to undermine them.[60]

As we consider the history and implications of race and class antagonisms and the possibilities for solidarity, it is important to keep in mind that economic systems, which mediate material resource access, and political systems, which delineate the terms of social organization (economic and otherwise), work in tandem. This coordinated effort between government and markets, or political economy, contains many points of contingency. As Wilkes observes in *Plenty Good Room*, our "continuum of optionality" is often stultified.[61] To remove the constraints on our social and political imaginations, we need to know how past decisions led to present conditions, and we must understand the extent to which current policies and social processes reflect our values and meet our needs. When we do this work, we have the beginnings of the basis for political agendas that *do* reflect our needs and values. My hope is that this book equips us to identify the mechanisms of our political and economic systems that militate against shared prosperity.

Taking the perspective of the *longue durée* of history, nation-states, or countries, as we call them today, are governance structures that began to emerge four hundred years ago and have become the primary governing structures of the world. The form of government that first emerged out of the American and French Revolutions of the eighteenth century—one characterized by a written constitution and "self-rule in the name of a nation of equal citizens"—is now the primary form of governance worldwide.[62] Prior to nation-states, there were tribal governments, empires, city-states, and kingdoms on every continent in the world, except Antarctica.

But regardless of the form of rule people use to organize themselves, those who wield authority must be deemed *legitimate* by those they rule, whether that authority extends over a country of thousands or a country of hundreds of millions. That is, people must accept the governing authority, or consent. US governance took shape through settler colonialism, which removed Indigenous peoples from their land, and chattel slavery, which forced Africans to work without compensation to enrich elite White men. Our country has never corrected the political, economic, and other social distortions left in the wake. And in many ways, White elite men have doubled down on these distortions in the twenty-first century.

Even though we inherit political and economic systems based on exclusion and extraction processes, we do not have to accept them. As active citizens, we should make clear the degree to which we *re-consent*—and if we do not believe our political and economic systems reflect our values and interests, we should feel empowered to pursue fundamental change of those systems, including wholly re-envisioning them. After all, government's purpose is to provide a constellation of institutions and practices that humankind can use to manage the intricacies of relationships and exchanges necessary for sustaining life—as such, governments are not inherently moral or immoral. The key is that governments have the *potential* to work toward the common good. As we reimagine our governing and economic systems, we all have a role to play. For instance, civil society groups can partner with government. Churches and other grassroots organizations can foster public education. Historically grounded civics education enabling Americans to learn how the country's governance systems mediate material and social resources would equip Americans to think about what works and what needs improvement. Civil society groups could also be spaces where people consider alternative perspectives and find common ground for building political agendas, and where they strategize to realize their goals. "Grassroots" understanding of needs, and options for meeting them, can then inform "grasstops" policy-making and institutional reform.

As we "freedom dream" and build institutions and other social forms to make those dreams reality, we should hold two things in tension: a commitment to an ever-expansive sense of individual and collective well-being, and a commitment to taking discrete steps toward that well-being wherever we have influence. Our sense of well-being will enlarge as we stand shoulder to shoulder and put our hands to the plow, though we cannot yet see what is on the horizon. Nor do we yet know how we will individually and collectively be transformed as we are deconditioned from White domination and anti-Black racism and press toward a society we have never experienced, though believe is possible.

Incremental change is not inherently problematic—the key is to move in the right direction. In the words of Scripture, we are called to "fight the good fight." To do that, we must resist self-centeredness and the myopia that only people in our inner circle matter. We must embrace truly loving *all* of our neighbors as ourselves. I hope this book supports the "good fight" by identifying the "right fight"—the repudiation of White domination and anti-Blackness—in all its forms, root and branch—and the pursuit of social systems that usher in *shalom*, an active, just peace bringing wholeness to people and communities, nothing missing, nothing broken.

APPENDIX 1. DEMOGRAPHICS OF FIFTY-EIGHT PRINCE GEORGE'S COUNTY RESPONDENTS

Thirty Leaders

- All Prince George's County council members
- Majority of school board members
- Former and current congressional representatives
- Former and current representatives to Maryland legislature
- Business, civic, and religious leaders

Twenty-Eight Residents

Race:
All respondents were Black/African American.

Age (in years):
- Nine respondents were twenty-five to forty
- Ten respondents were forty-one to sixty
- Nine respondents were sixty-one or older

Gender:
- Twenty women
- Eight men

https://doi.org/10.7758/bwmi8829.1624

Education level:
- Bachelor's degree or higher: eighteen respondents
- Less than a bachelor's degree: ten respondents

Homeowner or renter:
- Twenty homeowners
- Eight renters

Household Income:
- $31,000–$40,000: Two respondents
- $41,000–$60,000: One respondent
- $61,000–$80,000: Five respondents
- $81,000–$100,000: Four respondents
- $101,000–$120,00: Two respondents
- $141,000–$160,000: Three respondents
- $161,000 or greater: Ten respondents

Demographics

Age

Race

Income (*Respondents are handed a large index card with income categories and asked to point to the income category that best approximates their family's household income on their last tax return: less than $25,000; $25,001 to $35,000 . . . increasing in $10,000 increments up to $200,000, which is followed by $200,001 or higher*)

Occupation

Education level

Length of time in Prince George's County

Have you always lived this location? (*If not, ask where else they have lived*)

Homeowner or renter

Number of people living in the household (*If there are children, ask whether the children attend public school in Prince George's*)

Questions for All Respondents

Identity

Walk me through a typical weekday in your life. How about a typical weekend day? (*Probe for where they shop, recreate, etc.*)

When you have free time, what do you enjoy doing? Paint me a picture of the sorts of people you hang out with when you [engage in this activity].

How do you identify racially? (*This question is asked twice, here and as one of the demographic questions at the end of the interview*) When you [engage in favorite activity], what's your rough estimate of the percentage of people who are [respondent's racial/ethnic category]? What about other racial and ethnic groups? Does the racial and ethnic composition matter to you?

What does it mean to you to be "Black/African American" [or other racial/ethnic category]?

How close do you feel to Black people? To White people? To Latinos? To Asians? How does race affect your life?

Describe your current class background. Is it the same or different from your class background when you were growing up? If upwardly or downwardly mobile, what it's been like for you to go from [class background growing up] to [current class background]?

Do you think there are political issues that pertain only to Black people [or other racial/ethnic group]? Can you give me some examples? What do you think drives this shared interest?

Do these issues overlap with issues that other racial and ethnic groups, class groups, or other groups of Americans face?

Potential Sites of Class Conflict

(*If respondent identifies as Black*) What do you think is the same and what do you think is different about being Black and middle-class versus Black and poor?

What do you like about living in Prince George's County?

What would you like to see improve? What do you think would need to change for this to happen?

If you were to describe Prince George's to a stranger, what would you say?

Questions for Respondent Subgroups

Elected Officials

What motivated you to run for [current position)? How long have you been in office? Have you held other elected positions? If so, in what positions and for how long did you serve?

What do you like most about your job? What do you like least?

Describe your constituents. Is it easier to meet the needs of some groups as opposed to others? What do you think accounts for that?

Tell me about a bill or issue where you had trouble deciding how to vote. What made that decision hard? What ultimately determined how you voted?

What keeps you up at night? What worries you most about being a [the office held]?

When big changes happen in Prince George's, who are the big players? Where do you fit in?

Can you walk me through the process of how a bill you sponsored became law? Start with the initial germ of the idea all the way to the bill being signed.

What are your top three goals this term? Who will likely be your allies on [current issue X, Y, and Z]? Who do you expect to oppose you on [issue X, Y, and Z]? How do you plan to overcome challenges?

What are your thoughts about [policy issues facing the council, such as "grant funds distributed from the soon-to-open MGM Casino at National Harbor"]?

Community Leaders

What do you like most about your job? What do you like least?

Describe your group members/clients/constituents. Is it easier to meet the needs of some groups as opposed to others? What do you think accounts for that?

What is your organization's mission? What challenges do you face in achieving it? What resources do you use to meet your mission?

What are the funding sources for [name of organization]?

Sometimes people say their personal goals for an organization differ from the official mission of the organization, sometimes people say there is perfect alignment, and some say it depends on the issue. What's the case for you? Do you have personal goals for the organization that differ from the organization's mission?

Can you walk me through an example of how your organization handled a recent contentious issue involving your organization and another organization and/or your organization and Prince George's County? How was the issue resolved? Were you satisfied with the outcome?

What are you most proud of your organization for? What would your organization need to reach its full potential?

Residents

What drew you to Prince George's County?

Looking back on what you expected to experience and what you've actually experienced, what has surprised you about living in Prince George's?

What do you like most about living here? What do you like least?

What do you think of the [current issues, such as the schools, police, roads]?

Tell me about your neighbors. How often do you interact with them? What do you do with them?

What streets do you consider to be part of your neighborhood?

Are there parts of Prince George's that you won't go to? What makes those places off-limits for you?

If you were meeting with your Prince George's council member right now, what would you tell him/her about your experience in Prince George's? Are there any actions you would request that they take?

Preface

1. Austermuhle 2018.

Introduction: The Suburban Black Middle Class in Sociohistorical and Geographic Context

1. For race as a "political category," see Roberts 2011. For the social mechanisms that reinforce the idea of race as a real and inherent category, see Fields and Fields 2012. For Whiteness as a set of privileges codified in law, see Harris 1993. Race is distinct from ethnicity because race is inherently hierarchical, with one race supposedly superior to others, whereas ethnicity refers to people who claim a common heritage or culture, such as language, religion, and other core social beliefs and practices, and often a common homeland. Thus, there can be multiple ethnicities of equal social standing. In the United States, Latino (referring to people from Mexico and Central and South American and some Caribbean countries) and Hispanic (referring to people who are Spanish speaking) constitute the largest ethnic group and may be of any race. People often use *Hispanic* and *Latino* interchangeably, though *Hispanic* does not refer to people from Brazil, given that Brazil is not a Spanish-speaking country (Treitler 2013).

2. For an explanation of the economic, political, legal, and other social mechanisms that have underpinned and continue to perpetuate White domination and anti-Blackness, see Christian 2025.

3. For income and wealth, see Conley 1999/2009; Darity and Mullen 2020; Oliver and Shapiro 2006. For racial residential segregation, see Bader and Warkentien 2016;

Krysan 2017; Massey and Denton 1993. For access to public schools and post-secondary education, see Reardon 2016. For qualification for and proximity to stable, high-paying jobs, see Wilson 1987/2012b. For neighborhood location and access to private and public amenities, see Pattillo 2013a; Sampson 2012. For levels of violence in communities, see Sharkey 2018.

4. Kahrl 2024.

5. Middle-class occupations are white-collar positions (nonmanual labor). Those in the upper-middle class are "professionals, managers, and executives," most of whom, in today's economy, have at least an undergraduate college degree, and many have a graduate or doctoral degree. Those in the lower-middle class hold "technical, clerical, and sales" positions (Landry and Marsh 2011, 379–80). I also consider income when examining class status. The US median income in 2023 was $80,000 (Guzman and Kollar 2024). Attaining this level of income puts one at the midpoint of the income distribution and thus is another indicator of "middle-class" status. Education, occupation, and income are closely connected, however, given that a disproportionate share of people with a median or higher income have a college degree or higher. But it is also true that some blue-collar professions, such as plumbing, yield incomes comparable to or greater than white-collar jobs. Nonetheless, since World War II white-collar jobs have consistently paid the highest salaries, and the service and information sectors, where most of these jobs are located, have expanded the fastest among US industries. This trend has led to an "hourglass" labor force of highly paid white-collar workers at the top of the income distribution, low-paid workers at the bottom, and few jobs in the middle that enable people to attain median or higher income without a college degree (Kalleberg and Dunn 2016). Overall, most people in the United States who have median or higher incomes have significant postsecondary training.

6. Landry 2018.

7. Wilson 1987/2012b.

8. For environmental exposures, see Bullard 1990/2000; Purifoy 2019. For health, see Erving and Satcher 2021; National Academies 2024; Phelan and Link 2013; Roberts 2012; and Washington 2006. For the criminal-legal system, see Alexander 2010; Eason 2017; Miller 2021; Muhammad 2010. For housing value appreciation, see Flippen 2004; Korver-Glenn 2021; Krysan 2017; Rhodes and Warkentien 2017. For employment, see Branch and Hanley 2022; Thomas and Moye 2015.

9. Federal Reserve Bank of St. Louis 2025.

10. Drake and Cayton 1945; Du Bois 1899/1995, 1935/2007; Landry 2018; Pattillo 1999/2013b.

11. Pattillo 1999/2013b, 30.

12. Johnson 2002, 211.

13. Conley 1999/2009; Oliver and Shapiro 2006.

14. O'Brien 2017; Pacewicz and Robinson 2021.

15. Semega and Kollar 2022.

16. Board of Governors of the Federal Reserve System 2023.

17. Darity and Mullen 2020; Oliver and Shapiro 2006. One of the main reasons that Black people are more likely to experience downward socioeconomic mobility than White people is that Black families have significantly less wealth (Picketty 2014).

18. Semega and Kollar 2022.

19. Semega and Kollar 2022.

20. Semega and Kollar 2022.

21. Frey 2014; Massey and Denton 1993.

22. Frey 2014. Immigration law selects for immigrants who are highly educated and privileges those seeking family reunification. Immigrants from Asian, African, and Caribbean countries usually evince hyper-selectivity—they are more educated than people in their sending country and more educated than the average native-born American. While this ethno-racial variation lends complexity to the Black-White "color line," Black people remain at the bottom of the ethno-racial hierarchy. Indeed, some immigration and race relations scholars discuss race in terms of "Black and non-Black" and "White and non-White," or in terms of "Black exceptionalism," to call attention to how immigrants' life chances are shaped by having been incorporated into US society with status nearer to that of Black Americans than White Americans, with greater life chances for those attaining White racial status, or White adjacency (Lee and Bean 2010; Kim 2023; Treitler 2013).

23. Imoagene 2017; Kasinitz et al. 2009.

24. Baradaran 2017; Connolly 2014; Korver-Glenn 2021; Rothstein 2017; Satter 2010/2021; Taylor 2019.

25. There are two notable exceptions: The "pre-clearance" provision of Section 5 of the Voting Rights Act, which was applied to new voting laws in jurisdictions with a history of discrimination, and the Equal Employment Opportunity Commission (EEOC). The EEOC requires companies to report on their hiring practices and can pursue legal remedies through litigation. But the commission has largely been ineffective in eradicating race-based discrimination in hiring and promotions, particularly in the private sector, and also since the influence of the modern civil rights movement began to wane in the 1980s (Stainback and Tomaskovic-Devey 2012). Section 5 of the Voting Rights Act was effective until 2013, when the pre-clearance provision was struck down by the US Supreme Court in *Shelby County v. Holder*.

26. Omi and Winant 2015.

27. Lens 2024.

28. Frey 2014.

29. Lens 2024.

30. In June 2022, the *Washington Post* reported that Charles County, Maryland, may have more class-advantaged African Americans than Prince George's (Van Dam 2022). Regardless, Prince George's remains one of the US counties with the highest concentration of middle-class Black Americans. Further, with the longest history in this position (about two decades), research can be conducted in Prince George's on the extent to which middle-class African Americans realize the same returns to their class status as their European American peers.

31. Lens 2024.

32. My study employs a Du Boisian research design and uses the "extended case method," as theorized by sociologist Michael Burawoy. I connect lower-level "social processes"—most notably, local government tax revenue generation—to higher-level "social forces"—White domination and anti-Black racism (Burawoy 1998). Social forces are long-standing and deeply entrenched social actions that shape core government and market institutions, whereas social processes are the current routine ways in which people meet their material and social needs, wants, and interests. Strategically selected "cases," or sites of study, reveal how social forces and social processes create interdependent inequities between levels of social organization. Additionally, my work reflects the sociological perspectives of W.E.B. Du Bois, one of the founding scholars of the social science discipline of sociology (Morris 2017; Wright 2016). His perspectives that shape my research and analysis include: (1) the importance of explaining interdependencies between levels of social organization, namely, how individuals' behaviors, attitudes, and interests are shaped by major institutions; (2) the role of racialized institutions in material resource distribution (Ray 2019); and (3) the importance of sociological research that supports social action in pursuit of the just inclusion of all people in society (Itzigsohn and Brown 2020).

33. I have replaced all residents' names with pseudonyms and identified county leaders by their title or role.

34. Small and Calarco 2022.

35. Wyndham-Douds 2023; Purifoy 2019.

36. Frey 2014.

37. Lacy 2016; Lewis-McCoy et al. 2023; Orfield 2002.

38. US Census Bureau 2021.

39. US National Archives 2008.

40. Marx 1867/2024.

41. For the forcible removal of Indigenous peoples and genocide, see Wolfe 2006. For chattel slavery, see Franklin 2000.

42. Mills 1997.

43. Jenkins and Leroy 2021, 3.

44. Go 2021.

45. Reed 1999.

46. Baptist 2014, xxi, 352.

47. Turner 2019.

48. Baptist 2014.

49. Du Bois 1935/2007.

50. Du Bois 1935/2007.

51. For slave revolts and self-manumission, see Foner 1998 and Franklin 2000. For "everyday acts of resistance," see Kelley 1994.

52. Kahrl 2024; Logan 2023.

53. Koch and Swinton 2023.

54. Omi and Winant 2015.

55. Baradaran 2017; Du Bois 1935/2007.
56. Edin, et al., 2023; Kahrl 2024.
57. Alexander 2010.
58. For the Black Great Migration, see Foner 1998; Franklin 2000; Wilkerson 2010. For racial residential segregation, see Rothstein 2017. For the segmented labor market, see Branch and Hanley 2022.
59. Equal Justice Initiative 2017.
60. Du Bois 1935/2007; Equal Justice Initiative 2017; Wells 1895/2015.
61. Du Bois 1935/2007; Rothstein 2017.
62. Williams 2023.
63. For the Double-V campaign, see Finkle 1973. For White people seeking to put Black people in "their place," see Combs 2022.
64. Kahrl 2024.
65. Wishart and Logan 2024.
66. Collins 1990/2000; Daniels 2021.
67. Branch and Hanley 2022.
68. Treitler 2013.
69. Katznelson 2005; McMillan 2024; Rothstein 2017.
70. Rothstein 2017.
71. Katznelson 2005.
72. Katznelson 2005.
73. Lieberson 1980.
74. Du Bois 1935/2007; Franklin 2000.
75. Omi and Winant 2015.
76. Du Bois 1935/2007.
77. Omi and Winant 2015.
78. Prasad 2012.
79. Omi and Winant 2015.
80. Marable 1983/2015. For another thorough explanation of how capitalism used racial difference to achieve White elite male dominance, see Oliver Cromwell Cox's (1948) book *Caste, Class, and Race*.
81. Fraser 2016, 167, emphasis in original.
82. Fraser 2016, 172.
83. Fraser 2016, 167.
84. Javidanrad et al. 2024.
85. Faber 2019; Posey 2024; Seamster 2019; SoRelle 2020.
86. Branch and Hanley 2022.
87. Jenkins 2021.
88. For Du Bois's perspective on the role of race in capitalist formations, see Williams 2023. For an account of the global history of racism, specifically anti-Blackness, see Christian 2025.
89. Du Bois 1915.
90. Césaire 1950/2000; Christian 2025; Fanon 1961/2004; Kim 2023; Said 1979; Verges 2021.

91. John et al. 2023; Moyo 2024; Odijie 2021.
92. Du Bois 1915.
93. Du Bois 1915, 55.
94. Furthermore, resource competition has and continues to lead to death at breath-taking scales. Take just the late nineteenth and twentieth centuries. Hundreds of millions of people died as the United States and other Western countries pursued resources and world domination through these, among other actions: the Berlin Conference of 1884, which carved European spheres of influence in Africa; US government territorial expansion in Hawaii and other parts of Oceania, in Puerto Rico and elsewhere in the Caribbean, and in the Philippines; two World Wars (1914–1918 and 1939–1945); and US-led "hot wars" connected to the Cold War (1940s–1990s), including those in Vietnam and Korea; and now many smaller-scale wars across the world, many of which reflect continued competition among Western countries, as well as Western competition with China for resources and spheres of influence (Burns 2013, Mastro 2024).
95. Du Bois 1903/2009.
96. Conroy 2022; Go 2021; Marable 1983/2015.
97. Branch and Hanley 2022; Cox 1948.
98. Bonilla-Silva 2003/2017; Omi and Winant 2015.
99. Feudalism was based in specific kinds of ranked relationships that people inherited, among the most important distinctions being that between the gentry who owned land and their tenants who rented the land and produced goods on behalf of landowners and received a portion of what they produced as compensation (Robinson 2019).
100. Quantitative scholars might consider measuring relative regional burden (per capita and per pupil spending) across US metropolitan areas by using census data on local jurisdictions.
101. Sampson 2012; Sharkey 2018.
102. Claytor 2020; Clerge 2020; Haynes 2006; Johnson 2002; Lacy 2007; Lens 2024; Lewis-McCoy 2014; Pattillo 1999/2013b, 2013a; Smithsimon 2023.
103. Alexander 2010.
104. For environmental exposures, see Bullard 2000; Faber 2007; Purifoy 2019). For everyday customs and behavior, see Combs 2022; Feagin 2006.
105. Roberts 2011; Treitler 2013.
106. Katznelson 2005; Rugh and Massey 2010.
107. Collins 1990/2000.
108. Crenshaw 1991.
109. Pacewicz and Robinson 2021, 997.
110. Pacewicz and Robinson 2021, 977.
111. Rucks-Ahidiana 2021, 174–75, emphasis in original.
112. Logan and Molotch 2007; Smith 1996, 1979/2010.
113. Evans 2025; Golash-Boza 2023; Howell and Korver-Glenn 2021; Hyra 2017; Summers 2023.
114. Roberts 2011.

115. Foner 1998; Fox 2012; Franklin 2000; Glenn 2004.
116. Branch and Hanley 2022; DiTomaso 2013; Roithmayr 2014.
117. For the modern civil rights movement, see Morris 1984. For Occupy Wall Street, see Levitin 2021.
118. Arendt 1964/1977; O'Neill 2024. Also see political theorist Achille Mbembe's (2019) book *Necropolitics* for a discussion of how Western democracies have increasingly unabashedly embraced their "nocturnal body," darkness and death-dealing that uses unrestrained violence, and the logics employed to colonize people outside their borders, against their own citizens and other residents within their country that they deem enemies of or threats to the state. This increasing violence and militarization, Mbembe argues, is hollowing out the very values, rights, and freedoms democracies claim to champion.
119. Bonilla-Silva 2003/2017.
120. Baker 2022; Brady et al., 2024; Cross 2025; Easley and Baker 2023.
121. Substituting "diversity" for "neutrality" is not the answer either. Diversity divorced from power is an invitation to superficial conviviality that provides social soothing for White Americans, while harming People of Color (Douds 2021; Okuwobi 2025).
122. Gerken 2010; Grumbach 2022.
123. Jackson 1985; Katznelson 2005.
124. Jackson 1985; Katznelson 2005; Taylor 2019.
125. Connolly 2014; Katznelson 2005; Satter 2010/2021.
126. Katznelson 2005.
127. US National Archives and Records Administration 2022a.
128. Fullilove 2004/2016; Golash-Boza 2023.
129. Branch and Hanley 2022; Wilson 1987/2012b.
130. Korver-Glenn 2021.
131. Hunter and Robinson 2018; Massey and Denton 1993.
132. Lung-Amam 2017b.
133. Frasure-Yokley 2015.
134. Lewis-McCoy et al. 2023.
135. Golash-Boza 2023; Hyra 2017; Summers 2023.
136. Rhodes and Warkentien 2017.

Chapter 1: Racial and Fiscal Subordination and Public Goods and Services Provision in Prince George's County

1. Pacewicz and Robinson 2021.
2. US Department of Labor 2023.
3. Glinton 2017.
4. McKinsey & Company 2021; Oliver and Shapiro 2006; Quillian and Lee 2022.
5. US Bureau of Labor Statistics 2020.

6. Korver-Glenn 2021; Oliver and Shapiro 2006.

7. Hermann 2023.

8. Perry et al. 2018, 2024.

9. Lens 2024.

10. Kamin 2022.

11. Rothwell et al. 2022.

12. Harvey 2007; Urban Institute 2020.

13. Frasure-Yokley 2015; Harvey 2007; Logan and Molotch 2007.

14. Howard 2023.

15. Prasad 2018.

16. Keynes 1936.

17. Friedman 1962/2002.

18. Picketty 2014.

19. Michener 2018, 22–23.

20. Harvey 2007.

21. Kahrl 2024, 288.

22. Prasad 2018.

23. Gilmore 2007; Kochhar and Moslimani 2023; Massey and Denton 1993; Picketty 2014.

24. Morris 1984; Omi and Winant 2015.

25. Gilmore 2011; Miller 2021.

26. Roberts 2019; Weaver 2007. Furthermore, "devolution," withdrawing federal financial support for and oversight of public goods and services provision across states, was a tool for reducing the capacity of all levels of government to distribute public goods and services equitably, especially in ways that account for histories of exclusion and extraction along racial lines (King-Meadows and Schaller 2006). Most states responded to Reagan-era and subsequent losses in federal funding by rationing resources among their residents. Such rationing is largely determined through state legislatures, which draw the legislative and federal district maps for their states. And these legislatures disproportionately reflect the interests of White and wealthy Americans. Additionally, across the country, White Americans are more evenly distributed across and within states, enabling them to elect more legislators who champion their interests (Rodden 2019).

27. Fuhrer 2024.

28. Schanzenbach et al. 2016.

29. Brown 2022.

30. Library of Congress 2023.

31. US National Archives and Records Administration 2022b.

32. Gilmore 2011; Miller 2021.

33. Fox 2012; Howard 2023.

34. Quadagno 1988.

35. Glenn 2004.

36. Lieberson 1980.

37. Johnson 2002.

38. Johnson 2002, 23.
39. Thornton and Williams Gooden 1997.
40. Johnson 2002.
41. Prince George's County Planning Department 2010.
42. Thornton and Williams Gooden 1997.
43. Prince George's County Planning Department 2010, 11.
44. Thornton and Williams Gooden 1997.
45. Branch and Hanley 2022.
46. Katznelson 2005; Wilson 1978/2012a.
47. Branch and Hanley 2022; Landry and Marsh 2011; Pattillo 2013a.
48. Branch and Hanley 2022.
49. Branch and Hanley 2022; Maciag 2022.
50. Pitts 2011.
51. Maryland Department of Budget and Management 2020; US Office of Personnel Management 2017.
52. Golash-Boza 2023; Hyra 2017; Summers 2023.
53. Johnson 2002, 31.
54. Lung-Amam 2024, 61.
55. Afzal 2021.
56. Evans 2025; Hunter et al. 2016.
57. Clerge 2020.
58. Hunter and Robinson 2018.
59. Claytor 2020; Dow 2019; Lacy 2007.
60. Lewis et al. 2011; Krysan et al. 2009.
61. Charles 2006; Lee and Bean 2010.
62. Goyette 2014; Owens and Rich 2023; Trounstine 2018.
63. Montgomery Planning 2022; Northern Virginia Health Foundation 2021.
64. Rothstein 2017.
65. Oh and Yinger 2015; US Department of Housing and Urban Development 2023.
66. Kurtz 2021.
67. Pierre 1998.
68. Swain 1993.
69. Williams 2014.
70. Williams 2014.
71. Prince George's County Blue Ribbon Commission on the Structural Deficit 2017, 10–11.
72. Neal and Perez-Rivas 1996.
73. Prince George's County Blue Ribbon Commission on the Structural Deficit 2017, 12.
74. Johnson 2002.
75. Johnson 2002, 59.
76. Kahrl 2024.
77. Kahrl 2024, 278.
78. *Brown v. Board of Education I*, 347 U.S. 483 (1954); *Brown v. Board of Education II*, 349 U.S. 294 (1955).

79. McCall 2013.
80. Prince George's County Blue Ribbon Commission on the Structural Deficit 2017, 10–11, emphasis in original.
81. Hernandez 2015.
82. Thompson 2011.
83. Perry et al. 2018, 2024.
84. Prince George's County Blue Ribbon Commission on the Structural Deficit 2017.
85. Prince George's County Blue Ribbon Commission on the Structural Deficit 2017.
86. Jenkins 2021.
87. Moody's Investors Service 2022.
88. Maryland State Archives 2022, 2025.
89. Trounstine 2018.
90. Trounstine 2018; *San Antonio Independent School District v. Rodriguez*, 411 U.S. 1 (1973).

Chapter 2: Converging Fiscal Constraints and Relative Regional Burden in the Washington, DC, Metropolitan Area

1. Lewis-McCoy 2014, 2018.
2. Mitchell et al. 2025.
3. Mitchell et al. 2025.
4. Golash-Boza 2023; Hyra 2017; Summers 2023.
5. Golash-Boza 2023; Hyra 2017; Mitchell et al. 2025; Summers 2023.
6. Brown-Saracino 2017; Dantzler 2021; Rucks-Ahidiana 2021.
7. Lung-Amam 2024.
8. Fullilove 2004/2016.
9. Pfau et al. 2024.
10. Dougherty 2020; Kacmarcik 2022.
11. Kacmarcik 2022; Smart Growth America and Transportation for America 2023.
12. *U.S. News and World Report* 2018.
13. Lung-Amam 2017a.
14. Pinto-Coelho and Zuberi 2015.
15. Per capita spending in each county was calculated as follows (Prince George's County 2017a; Montgomery County 2017; Fairfax County 2017). Prince George's County: $3,876,478,800 (total budget)/909,327 (total population) = $4,263. Montgomery County: $5,450,363,866 (total budget)/1,050,688 (total population) = $5,187. Fairfax County: $7,590,796,748 (total budget)/1,147,352 (total population) = $6,616.
16. Per pupil spending in each county was calculated as follows (Prince George's County 2017b; Montgomery County Board of Education 2017; Fairfax County Public Schools 2017). Prince George's County: $1.9 billion (total schools budget)/132,667 (student population) = $14,322. Montgomery County: $2.5 billion (total schools budget)/161,302

(student population) = \$15,499. Fairfax County: 2.8 billion (total budget)/189,022 (student population) = \$14,813.

17. O'Brien 2017; Tiebout 1956.
18. National Academy of Arts and Sciences 2023.
19. Purifoy and Seamster 2021.
20. Purifoy and Seamster 2021, 57.
21. Harvey 2007; Kahrl 2024.
22. Cardoza 2020.
23. Tilly 2003.
24. Rich 2013; Welch 2012.
25. Faber 2016; Lacy 2012; Rich 2013; US Department of Justice 2012.
26. Pettit and Hendey 2011.
27. Lacy 2012; Rugh and Massey 2010.
28. US Department of Justice 2012.
29. US Department of Housing and Urban Development 2010.
30. Board of Governors of the Federal Reserve System 2021.
31. Taylor 2019.
32. For excessive fines and fees charged in majority-Black jurisdictions, see Pacewicz and Robinson 2021; Page and Soss 2021. For higher property tax levies in Black neighborhoods, see Atuahene 2025; Kahrl 2024.
33. Atuahene 2025.
34. US Department of the Treasury 2022b.
35. McKernan et al. 2014.
36. Chetty et al. 2019; Reeves and Pullen 2019.
37. US Department of Housing and Urban Development 2010.
38. Bui 2018.
39. Semuels 2019.
40. Fletcher 2015.

Chapter 3: Fiscal Subordination Fallout: Prince George's County's Fiscal Year 2018 Budget Deliberations and Allocations

1. Golash-Boza 2023; Lung-Amam 2024; Rhodes and Warkentien 2017.
2. Prince George's County 2017a.
3. Prince George's County 2017a.
4. Prince George's County Blue Ribbon Commission on the Structural Deficit 2017.
5. Prasad 2018.
6. Logan and Molotch 2007.
7. Biernacka-Lievestro and Fall 2022.
8. Blackner 2016.
9. Montgomery County 2017.

Chapter 4: Prince George's County's Fiscal Distress and K-12 Public Schools

1. Maryland State Department of Education 2017.
2. Ernst & Young LLP 2017.
3. Ernst & Young LLP 2017.
4. Goyette 2014; Trounstine 2018.
5. Goyette 2014, Trounstine 2018.
6. Justice 2023; Lewis and Diamond 2015; Long et al. 2023; Pirtle 2019.
7. Lee and Zhou 2014.
8. Reardon et al. 2019.
9. Lewis-McCoy 2014.
10. Lewis-McCoy 2018; Owens and Rich 2023.
11. K. Brown 2025; Justice 2023.
12. Du Bois 1935/2007.
13. Kahrl 2024.
14. K. Brown 2025; De Brey et al. 2018; Urban Institute 2022.
15. K. Brown 2025.
16. K. Brown 2025; Koch and Swinton 2023.
17. *Brown v. Board of Education I*, 347 U.S. 483 (1954).
18. *Brown v. Board of Education II*, 349 U.S. 294 (1955).
19. Trounstine 2018.
20. Erickson 2016; Trounstine 2018.
21. Kahrl 2024; Trounstine 2018.
22. Trounstine 2018.
23. Hutchison 2004, 2; *Green v. County School Board of New Kent County*, 391 U.S. 430 (1968).
24. *Swann v. Charlotte-Mecklenburg Board of Education*, 402 U.S. 1(1971).
25. Erickson 2016.
26. Erickson 2016; *Milliken v. Bradley*, 418 U.S. 717 (1974); *Meredith v. Jefferson County Board of Education* 551 U.S. 701 (2007).
27. *San Antonio Independent School District v. Rodriguez*, 411 U.S. 1 (1973).
28. Urban Institute 2022.
29. Johnson 2002.
30. Johnson 2002, 109.
31. Johnson 2002.
32. Johnson 2002, 114–15.
33. Dougherty 2020; Johnson 2002.
34. Dougherty 2020.
35. Bell 1980; *Plessy v. Ferguson*, 163 U.S. 537 (1896).
36. Bell 1980, 1992.
37. Skrentny 1998.

38. Du Bois 1935/2007.
39. McDermott 2006; Roediger 1994.
40. Blumer 1958.
41. Bell 1980, 528.
42. Johnson 2002, 115.
43. *Milliken v. Bradley*, 433 U.S. 267 (1977).
44. Johnson 2002, 116.
45. Frazier 1998.
46. Rhodes and Warkentian 2017.
47. For school choice and the "parenting tax," see Simms and Talbert 2019. For discussions about the labor involved in school choice, see B. Brown 2025 and Bader et al. 2019.
48. Coleman et al. 1966.
49. Johnson 2014; Reardon 2016.
50. US Government Accountability Office 2022.
51. Prince George's County Public Schools 2025.
52. Prince George's County Public Schools 2017.
53. Hise et al. 2018.
54. Checovich 2016; Hutchison 2004.
55. Maryland State Department of Education 2024.
56. St. George 2016.
57. St. George 2018a.
58. St. George 2018b.
59. Dawson 1994.
60. Cohen 1999; Haynes 2006; Reed 1999.
61. Dawson 2011.
62. Dawson 2001; Du Bois 1935/2007; Logan 2023.
63. This is consistent with national trends; see Simms and Talbert 2019; US Department of Education 2019.
64. Simms and Talbert 2019.
65. Dow 2019; Lacy 2007.
66. Lacy 2007.
67. Carter 2005.
68. Lacy 2007.

Chapter 5: The Pursuit of Private Investment in a Context of White Domination and Anti-Black Racism

1. Donahue, Parilla, and McDearman 2018.
2. Maryland–National Capital Park and Planning Commission 2014.
3. American Planning Association 2012.
4. Johnson 2002.

5. Golash-Boza 2023; Hyra 2017; Summers 2023.

6. Golash-Boza 2023; Hyra 2017; Summers 2023.

7. Lareau 2014; Leopold and Bell 2017; Pew Charitable Trusts 2023.

8. Alexander 2010; Leopold and Bell 2017; Pew Charitable Trusts 2023.

9. Alexander 2010.

10. Fox 2012; Muhammad 2010.

11. Muhammad 2010.

12. Muhammad 2010.

13. Maryland–National Capital Park and Planning Commission 2019.

14. Prince George's County Planning Board 2023.

15. Prince George's County Blue Ribbon Commission on the Structural Deficit 2017.

16. Prince George's County 2023.

17. McKinsey & Company 2023.

18. Maryland–National Capital Park and Planning Commission 2016.

19. Badger 2013; D'Rozario and Williams 2005; Kwate et al. 2013.

20. Cameron and O'Connell 2018.

21. O'Connell and McCartney 2018.

22. Schweitzer 2020.

23. US Environmental Protection Agency 2021.

24. National Harbor 2019.

25. Lazo 2017.

26. Lazo 2017.

27. Lazo 2017.

28. Maryland Lottery and Gaming Control Agency 2018.

29. Prince George's County 2024.

30. Lung-Amam 2024; Maryland Department of Transportation 2024.

31. Lung-Amam 2024, 240.

32. US Department of Housing and Urban Development 2025.

33. Johnson 2002; Reed 1999.

Chapter 6: Conclusion: Envisioning Institutions for All Americans' Flourishing

1. Glenn 2004.

2. Roberts 2019, 10.

3. Davis 2005.

4. Roberts 2019, 109.

5. Love 2019.

6. Kaba 2021, 19.

7. Lorde 1984, 106.

8. Baldwin 1962/1993, 92, emphasis in original.

9. US Census Bureau 2025.

10. Gilmore 2007, 245.

11. D. Brown 2022.

12. US Department of the Treasury 2022a.

13. Maryland Association of Counties 2025.

14. McCall 2013.

15. Metropolitan Washington Council of Governments 2018.

16. Lung-Amam 2024.

17. Library of Congress 2010.

18. Library of Congress 2010.

19. Darity, Mullen, and Hubbard 2023; Darity and Mullen 2020.

20. Darity and Mullen 2020.

21. Bilmes and Brooks 2024, 33.

22. Bilmes and Brooks 2024, 40.

23. Bilmes and Brooks 2024.

24. Bilmes and Brooks 2024, 51.

25. Bilmes and Brooks 2004, 51.

26. Du Bois 1935/2007.

27. Darity et al. 2024.

28. Berry 2005, 50.

29. Ashford and Ferre-Sadurni 2023; California Department of Justice 2024.

30. City of Evanston 2024.

31. Estes 2019; Franklin 2000.

32. Adema et al. 2023.

33. Newport 2022.

34. McGhee 2021, 259–60.

35. Wilkes 2024.

36. Nembhard 2014.

37. Nembhard 2014, 4.

38. Kelley 2002/2022; Nembhard 2014.

39. Du Bois 1935/2007; Foner 1998; Kahrl 2024.

40. Northwest Bronx Community and Clergy Coalition 2025; Federation of Southern Cooperatives Land Assistance Fund 2025; Nembhard 2014.

41. I thank Columbia undergraduate student Jaden Ebanks for his insightful discussion of class variation among Black Americans and how to enact economic solidarity in his term paper for the spring 2025 seminar I taught, "Black Americans and Development Politics." My discussion of the goals for solidarity builds on Ebanks's paper.

42. Tamir 2022.

43. Imoagene 2017.

44. Balogun 2011.

45. Gilroy 1993.

46. Boyd 2008; Fortner 2023; Pattillo 2013a; Rucks-Ahidiana 2021.

47. Rogers 2023.

48. Gates 2022.

49. Walker 1829/2022.
50. Foner 1998; Franklin 2000.
51. King 2024.
52. King 1967.
53. King 1967, 173.
54. Trisi 2024.
55. Kelley 2002/2022.
56. McGhee 2021.
57. Omi and Winant 2015.
58. Ture and Hamilton 1992/2008, 186.
59. Ture and Hamilton 1992/2008, 186.
60. Omi and Winant 2015.
61. Wilkes 2024.
62. Wimmer and Feinstein 2010, 764.

REFERENCES

Adema, Willem, Pauline Fron, and Maxime Ladaique. 2023. "Sizing Up Welfare States: How Do OECD Countries Compare?" OECD Statistics, February 2. Accessed September 22, 2024. https://oecdstatistics.blog/2023/02/02/sizing-up-welfare-states-how-do-oecd-countries-compare/#:~:text=In%20many%20OECD%20countries%2C%20Welfare,Switzerland%20and%20the%20United%20States.

Afzal, Khalid. 2021. "The History of Land Use and Planning in Montgomery County." The Third Place: A Montgomery County Planning Department Blog. Accessed July 18, 2024. https://montgomeryplanning.org/blog-design/author/khalid-afzal.

Alexander, Michelle. 2010. *The New Jim Crow: Mass Incarceration in the Age of Colorblindness.* New York: New Press.

American Academy of Arts and Sciences. 2023. "Core Score: Measuring Wellbeing." https://corescore.us/wellbeing-2023-usa/core_score/2023/00?demographic=geography-overall.

American Planning Association. 2012. "APA Policy Guide on Smart Growth." Update ratified April 14, 2012. Accessed January 1, 2023. https://www.planning.org/policy/guides/adopted/smartgrowth.htm.

Arendt, Hannah. 1977. *Eichmann in Jerusalem: A Report on the Banality of Evil.* Penguin Press. (Originally published in 1964.)

Ashford, Grace, and Luis Ferre-Sadurni. 2023. "New York to Consider Reparations for Descendants of Enslaved People." *New York Times*, December 19. https://www.nytimes.com/2023/12/19/nyregion/reparations-new-york-slavery.html.

Atuahene, Bernadette. 2025. *Plundered: How Racist Policies Undermine Black Home Ownership in America.* Hachette Book Group.

Austermuhle, Martin. 2018. "DC Set to Invoke Eminent Domain to Shutter Controversial Trash Site, but Owner Cries Foul on Process." WAMU 88.5, November 27.

https://wamu.org/story/18/11/27/d-c-set-to-invoke-eminent-domain-to-shutter
-controversial-trash-site-but-owner-cries-foul-on-process/.

Bader, Micheal D., Annette Lareau, and Shai Evans. 2019. "Talk on the Playground: The Neighborhood Context for School Choice." *City & Community* 18(2): 483–508.

Bader, Michael D. M., and Siri Warkentien. 2016. "The Fragmented Evolution of Racial Integration Since the Civil Rights Movement." *Sociological Science* 3: 135–66.

Badger, Emily. 2013. "Retail Redlining: One of the Most Pervasive Forms of Racism Left in America?" *Bloomberg*, April 14. Accessed January 23, 2024. https://www.bloomberg.com/news/articles/2013-04-17/retail-redlining-one-of-the-most-pervasive-forms-of-racism-left-in-america.

Baker, Regina S. 2022. "Ethno-Racial Variation in Single Motherhood Prevalences and Penalties for Child Poverty in the United States, 1995–2018." *The ANNALS of the American Academy of Political and Social Science* 702(1): 20–36.

Baldwin, James. 1993. *The Fire Next Time.* Vintage International. (Originally published in 1962.)

Balogun, Oluwakemi M. 2011. "No Necessary Tradeoff: Context, Life Course, and Social Networks in the Identity Formation of Second-Generation Nigerians in the USA." *Ethnicities* 11(4): 436–66.

Baptist, Edward E. 2014. *The Half Has Never Been Told: Slavery and the Making of American Capitalism.* Basic Books.

Baradaran, Mehrsa. 2017. *The Color of Money: Black Banks and the Racial Wealth Gap.* Belknap Press of Harvard University Press.

Bell, Derrick A. 1980. "Brown v. Board of Education and the Interest-Convergence Dilemma." *Harvard Law Review* 93(3): 518–33.

Bell, Derrick. 1992. *Faces at the Bottom of the Well: The Permanence of Racism.* Basic Books.

Berry, Mary Frances. 2005. *My Face Is Black Is True: Callie House and the Struggle for Ex-Slave Reparations.* Alfred A. Knopf.

Biernacka-Lievestro, Joanna, and Alexandre Fall. 2022. "Nine States Began the Pandemic with Long-Term Deficits." Pew Charitable Trusts, December 16. Accessed February 21, 2024. https://www.pewtrusts.org/en/research-and-analysis/articles/2022/12/16/nine-states-began-the-pandemic-with-long-term-deficits.

Bilmes, Linda J., and Cornell William Brooks. 2024 "Normalizing Reparations: US Precedent, Norms, and Models for Compensating Harms and Implications for Reparations to Black Americans." *RSF: The Russell Sage Foundation Journal of the Social Sciences* 10(2): 30–36. https://doi.org/10.7758/RSF.2024.10.2.02.

Blackner, Emily. 2016. "County Waives Minimum Wage for Service Providers." *The Sentinel*, November 22. https://www.thesentinel.com/communities/prince_george/news/local/county-waives-minimum-wage-for-service-providers/article_8af95f8e-1acc-5031-b4af-def15a9a4593.html.

Blumer, Herbert. 1958. "Race Prejudice as a Sense of Group Position." *Pacific Sociological Review* 1(1): 3–7.

Board of Governors of the Federal Reserve System. 2021. "Credit and Liquidity Programs and the Balance Sheet: The Federal Reserve's Response to the Financial Crisis and

Actions to Foster Maximum Employment and Price Stability." Updated May 10, 2021. Accessed January 23, 2024. https://www.federalreserve.gov/monetarypolicy/bst _crisisresponse.htm.

Board of Governors of the Federal Reserve System. 2023. "Figure 1: White and Asian Families Had the Most Wealth." In "Greater Wealth, Greater Uncertainty: Changes in Racial Inequality in the Survey of Consumer Finances, Accessible Data." Updated October 23, 2023. Accessed July 15, 2024. https://www.federalreserve.gov/econres/notes/feds-notes /greater-wealth-greater-uncertainty-changes-in-racial-inequality-in-the-survey-of-consumer -finances-accessible-20231018.htm#fig1.

Bonilla-Silva. 2017. *Racism Without Racists: Color-Blind Racism and Racial Inequality in Contemporary America.* Rowan & Littlefield. (Originally published in 2003.)

Boyd, Michelle. 2008. *Jim Crow Nostalgia: Reconstructing Race in Bronzeville.* University of Minnesota Press.

Brady, David, Regina S. Baker, and Ryan Finnigan. 2024. "The Role of Single Motherhood in America's High Child Poverty." *Demography* 61(4): 1161–85.

Branch, Enobon Hannah, and Caroline Hanley. 2022. *Work in Black and White: Striving for the American Dream.* Russell Sage Foundation.

Brown, Bailey. 2025. *Kindergarten Panic: Parental Anxiety and School Choice Inequality.* Princeton University Press.

Brown, Dorothy. 2022. *The Whiteness of Wealth: How the Tax System Impoverishes Black Americans—and How We Can Fix It.* Penguin Random House.

Brown, Karida. 2025. *The Battle for the Black Mind.* Hachette.

Brown-Saracino, Japonica. 2017. "Explicating Divided Approaches to Gentrification and Growing Income Inequality." *Annual Review of Sociology* 43: 515–39.

Bui, Lynh. 2018. "Lawsuit: Bank of America Allows Foreclosed Homes in Minority Neigh-borhoods to Deteriorate; Takes Better Care of Properties in White Communities." *Washington Post*, June 26. https://www.washingtonpost.com/local/public-safety/lawsuit -bank-of-america-allows-foreclosed-homes-in-minority-neighborhoods-to-deteriorate -takes-better-care-of-properties-in-white-communities/2018/06/26/2196c286-7946 -11e8-93cc-6d3beccdd7a3_story.html.

Bullard, Robert. 2000. *Dumping in Dixie: Race, Class, and Environmental Quality*, 3rd ed. Routledge. (Originally published in 1990.)

Burawoy, Michael. 1998. "The Extended Case Method." *Sociological Theory* 16(1): 1–33.

Burns, Adam. 2013. *American Imperialism: The Territorial Expansion of the United States, 1783–2013.* Edinburgh University Press.

California Department of Justice. 2024. "Reparations Task Force Members." Accessed July 23, 2024. https://oag.ca.gov/ab3121/members.

Cameron, Darla, and Jonathan O'Connell. 2018. "The Amazon Finalists Are Already Building Tech Economies. Which Are Best?" *Washington Post*, March 7. https://www .washingtonpost.com/graphics/2018/business/amazon-hq2-tech-cities/?utm_term =.51580a773296.

Cardoza, Kavitha. 2020. "How Prince George' County Adapts to Having the Fourth Highest Number of Unaccompanied Minors in the US." *WAMU Local News*, NPR,

December 17. https://wamu.org/story/20/12/17/unaccompanied-minors-prince-georges
-county-schools-trauma/.

Carter, Prudence. 2005. *Keepin' It Real: School Success Beyond Black and White.* Oxford University Press.

Césaire, Aimé. 2000. *Discourse on Colonialism.* Monthly Review Press. (Originally published 1950.)

Charles, Camille Zubrinsky. 2006. *Won't You Be My Neighbor? Class, Race, and Residence in Los Angeles.* Russell Sage Foundation.

Checovich, Laura. 2016. "Funding Formulas and Revenue Streams: A Primer on Public School Finance in Maryland." University of Maryland, School of Education.

Chetty, Raj, Nathaniel Hendren, Maggie R. Jones, and Sonya R. Porter. 2019. "Race and Economic Opportunity in the United States." Harvard University, December. Accessed August 18, 2022. https://opportunityinsights.org/wp-content/uploads/2018/04/race_paper.pdf.

Christian, Michelle. 2025. *The Global Journey of Racism.* Stanford University Press.

City of Evanston. 2024. "Evanston Local Reparations." Accessed July 23, 2024. https://www.cityofevanston.org/government/city-council/reparations.

Claytor, Cassi Pittman. 2020. *Black Privilege: Modern Middle-Class Blacks with Credentials and Cash to Spend.* Stanford University Press.

Clerge, Orly. 2020. *The New Noir: Race, Identity, and Diaspora in Black Suburbia.* University of California Press.

Cohen, Cathy. 1999. *The Boundaries of Blackness: AIDS and the Breakdown of Black Politics.* University of Chicago Press.

Coleman, James, Ernest Q. Campbell, et al. 1966. *Equality of Educational Opportunity.* US Department of Health, Education, and Welfare, Office of Education. Accessed July 22, 2024. https://files.eric.ed.gov/fulltext/ED012275.pdf.

Collins, Patricia Hill. 2000. *Black Feminist Thought: Knowledge, Consciousness, and the Politics of Empowerment.* Routledge. (Originally published in 1990.)

Combs, Barbara. 2022. *Bodies Out of Place: Theorizing Anti-Blackness in US Society.* University of Georgia Press.

Conley, Dalton. 2009. *Being Black, Living in the Red: Race, Wealth, and Social Policy in America,* 10th ed. University of California Press. (Originally published in 1999.)

Connolly, Nathan. 2014. *A World More Concrete: Real Estate and the Remaking of Jim Crow South Florida.* University of Chicago Press.

Conroy, William. 2022. "Race, Capitalism, and the Necessity/Contingency Debate." *Theory, Culture & Society* 41(1): 39–58.

Cox, Oliver C. 1948. *Caste, Class & Race: A Study in Social Dynamics.* Doubleday.

Crenshaw, Kimberle. 1991. "Mapping the Margins: Intersectionality, Identity Politics, and Violence Against Women of Color." *Stanford Law Review* 43(6): 1241–99.

Cross, Christina J. 2025. *Inherited Inequality: Why Opportunity Gaps Persist Between Black and White Youth Raised in Two-Parent Families.* Harvard University Press.

Daniels, Jessie. 2021. *Nice White Ladies: The Truth about White Supremacy, Our Role in It, and How We Help Dismantle It.* Seal Press.

Dantzler, Prentiss A. 2021. "The Urban Process under Racial Capitalism: Race, Anti-Blackness, and Capital Accumulation." *Journal of Race, Ethnicity and the City* 2(2): 113–34.

Darity, William, Jr., Thomas Craemer, Daina Ramey Berry, and Dania V. Francis. 2024. "Black Reparations in the United States, 2024: An Introduction." *RSF: The Russell Sage Foundation Journal of the Social Sciences* 10(2): 1–28. https://doi.org/10.7758/RSF.2024.10.2.01.

Darity, William A., Jr., and Andrea Kirsten Mullen. 2020. *From Here to Equality: Reparations for Black Americans in the Twenty-First Century.* University of North Carolina Press.

Darity, William, Jr., A. Kirsten Mullen, and Lucas Hubbard. 2023. *The Black Reparations Project: A Handbook for Racial Justice.* University of California Press.

Davis, Angela Y. 2005. *Abolition Democracy: Beyond Empire, Prisons, and Torture.* Penguin Random House.

Dawson, Michael C. 1994. *Behind the Mule: Race and Class in African-American Politics.* Princeton University Press.

Dawson, Michael. 2001. *Black Visions: The Roots of Contemporary African American Political Ideologies.* University of Chicago Press.

Dawson, Michael. 2011. *Not in Our Lifetimes: The Future of Black Politics.* University of Chicago Press.

De Brey, Cristobal, Lauren Musu, et al. 2018. "Status and Trends in the Education of Racial and Ethnic Groups." US Department of Education, Institute of Education Sciences, National Center for Education Statistics, February. Accessed January 17, 2024. https://nces.ed.gov/pubsearch/pubsinfo.asp?pubid=2019038.

DiTomaso, Nancy. 2013. *The American Non-Dilemma: Racial Inequality Without Racism.* Russell Sage Foundation.

Donahue, Ryan, Joseph Parilla, and Brad McDearman. 2018. "Rethinking Cluster Initiatives." Brookings Institution, July 25. Accessed January 6, 2023. https://www.brookings.edu/articles/rethinking-cluster-initiatives/.

Douds, Kiara Wyndham. 2021. "The Diversity Contract: Constructing Racial Harmony in a Diverse Suburb." *American Journal of Sociology* 126(6): 1347–88.

Dougherty, Deidre. 2020. "Urban Redevelopment, School Closure, and the Abstract Space of Black Schooling in Prince George's County, Maryland, 1968–1972." *Journal of Urban History* 46(5): 1117–41.

Dow, Dawn. 2019. *Mothering While Black: Boundaries and Burdens of Middle-Class Parenthood.* University of California Press.

Drake, St. Clair, and Horace Cayton. 1945. *Black Metropolis: A Study of Negro Life in a Northern City.* University of Chicago Press.

D'Rozario, Denver, and Jerome D. Williams. 2005. "Retail Redlining: Definition, Theory, Typology, and Measurement." *Journal of Macromarketing* 25(2): 175–86.

Du Bois, W. E. B. (William Edward Burghardt). 1915. "The African Roots of the War." *The Atlantic*, May.

Du Bois, W. E. B. 1995. *The Philadelphia Negro: A Social Study.* University of Pennsylvania Press. (Originally published in 1899.)

Du Bois, W. E. B. 2007. *Black Reconstruction in America: An Essay Toward a History of the Part Which Black Folk Played in the Attempt to Reconstruct Democracy in America, 1860–1880*. Oxford University Press. (Originally published in 1935.)

Du Bois, W. E. B. 2009. *The Souls of Black Folk*. Oxford University Press. (Originally published in 1903.)

Easley, Janeria A., and Regina S. Baker. 2023. "Intergenerational Mobility and Racial Inequality: The Case for a More Holistic Approach." *Sociology Compass* 17(10): 1–12.

Eason, John. 2017. *Big House on the Prairie: Rise of the Rural Ghetto and Prison Proliferation*. University of Chicago Press.

Edin, Kathy J., H. Luke Shaefer, and Timothy J. Nelson. 2023. *The Injustice of Place: Uncovering the Legacy of Poverty in America*. Mariner Books.

Equal Justice Initiative. 2017. "Lynching in America: Confronting the Legacy of Racial Terror," 3rd ed. Lynching in America. https://lynchinginamerica.eji.org/report/.

Erickson, Ansley T. 2016. *Making the Unequal Metropolis: School Desegregation and Its Limits*. University of Chicago Press.

Ernst & Young LLP. 2017. *Prince George's School Continuous Business Process Improvement Study: Final Report*. Contracted through Prince George's County Public Schools. Ernst & Young LLP, April. Accessed January 16, 2024. https://pgccouncil.us/DocumentCenter/View/2512/Board-of-Education-PGCPS-Final-Report-.

Erving, Christy L., and Lacee A. Satcher. 2021. "African American Health." In *The Wiley Blackwell Companion to Medical Sociology*, edited by William C. Cockerham. Wiley-Blackwell.

Estes, Nick. 2019. *Our History Is the Future: Standing Rock Versus the Dakota Access Pipeline, and the Long Tradition of Indigenous Resistance*. Verso.

Evans, Shani. 2025. *We Belong Here: Gentrification, White Spacemaking, and a Black Sense of Place*. University of Chicago Press.

Faber, Daniel. 2007. "A More 'Productive' Environmental Justice Politics: Movement Alliances in Massachusetts for Clean Production and Regional Equity." Chapter 5 in *Environmental Justice and Environmentalism: The Social Justice Challenge to the Environmental Movement*, edited by Ronald Sandler and Phaedra D. Pezzullo. MIT Press.

Faber, Jacob. 2016. "The Dream Revisited: Segregation Exacerbated the Great Recession and Hindered Our Policy Response." New York University Furman Center, February. Accessed April 18, 2025. https://furmancenter.org/research/iri/essay/segregation-exacerbated-the-great-recession-and-hindered-our-policy-respons.

Faber, Jacob William. 2019. "Segregation and the Cost of Money: Race, Poverty, and the Prevalence of Alternative Financial Institutions." *Social Forces* 98 (2): 817–48.

Fairfax County. 2017. "Fairfax County, Virginia Adopted Budget Plan: Overview." Department of Management and Budget. https://www.fairfaxcounty.gov/budget/sites/budget/files/assets/documents/fy2018/adopted/overview.pdf.

Fairfax County Public Schools. 2017. *Fairfax County Public Schools: Fiscal Year 2018 Approved Budget*. https://www.fcps.edu/sites/default/files/media/pdf/FY18Approved%20Budget.pdf.

Fanon, Frantz. 2004. *The Wretched of the Earth*. Grove Press. (Originally published in 1961.)

Feagin, Joe R. 2006. *Racism: A Theory of Oppression.* Yale University Press.

Federal Reserve Bank of St. Louis. 2025. "Gross Domestic Product (GDP)." Updated May 29. Accessed March 10, 2025. https://fred.stlouisfed.org/series/GDP.

Federation of Southern Cooperatives Land Assistance Fund. 2025. "What We Do." Accessed April 9, 2025. https://www.federation.coop/what-we-do.

Fields, Karen E., and Barbara J. Fields. 2012: *Racecraft: The Soul of Inequality in American Life.* Verso.

Finkle, Lee. 1973. "The Conservative Aims of Militant Rhetoric: Black Protest During World War II." *Journal of American History* 60(3): 692–713.

Fletcher, Michael. 2015. "A Shattered Foundation: African Americans Who Bought Homes in Prince George's Have Watched Their Wealth Vanish." *Washington Post,* January 24. Accessed January 11, 2018. https://www.washingtonpost.com.

Flippen, Chenoa. 2004. "Unequal Returns to Housing Investments? A Study of Real Housing Appreciation Among Black, White, and Hispanic Households." *Social Forces* 82(4): 1523–51.

Foner, Eric. 1998. *The Story of American Freedom.* W. W. Norton & Co.

Fortner, Michael. 2023. "Racial Capitalism and City Politics: Toward a Theoretical Synthesis." *Urban Affairs Review* 59(2): 630–53.

Fox, Cybelle. 2012. *Three Worlds of Relief: Race, Immigration, and the American Welfare State from the Progressive Era to the Present.* Princeton University Press.

Franklin, John Hope. 2000. *From Slavery to Freedom: A History of African Americans.* Alfred A. Knopf.

Fraser, Nancy. 2016. "Expropriation and Exploitation in Racialized Capitalism: A Reply to Michael Dawson." *Critical Historical Studies* 3(1): 163–78.

Frasure-Yokley, Lorrie. 2015. *Racial and Ethnic Politics in American Suburbs.* Cambridge University Press.

Frazier, Lisa. 1998. "Judge Ends Busing in Prince George's: Settlement to Be Scrutinized Until 2002." *Washington Post,* September 2. Accessed August 4, 2025. https://www .washingtonpost.com/archive/politics/1998/09/02/judge-ends-busing-in-prince-georges /639cefe1-6135-4719-9db1-69bf344a3d9d/.

Frey, William. 2014. *The Diversity Explosion: How New Racial Demographics Are Remaking America.* Brookings Institution Press.

Friedman, Milton. 2002. *Capitalism and Freedom.* University of Chicago Press. (Originally published in 1962.)

Fuhrer, Jeffrey C. 2024. "The Cost of Being Poor Is Rising. And It's Worse for Poor Families of Color." Brookings Institution, July 29. https://www.brookings.edu/articles /the-cost-of-being-poor-is-rising-and-its-worse-for-poor-families-of-color/.

Fullilove, Mindy Thompson. 2016. *Root Shock: How Tearing Up City Neighborhoods Hurts America, and What We Can Do About It.* New Village Press. (Originally published in 2004.)

Gates, Henry Louis, Jr. 2022. *The Black Church: This Is Our Story, This Is Our Song.* Penguin Random House.

Gerken, Heather. 2010. "Federalism All the Way Down." *Harvard Law Review* 124(4): 6–74.

Gilmore, Ruth Wilson. 2007. *Golden Gulag: Prisons, Surplus, Crisis, and Opposition in Globalizing California.* University of California Press.

Gilmore, Ruth Wilson. 2011. "What Is to Be Done?" *American Quarterly* 63(2): 245–65.

Gilroy, Paul. 1993. *The Black Atlantic: Modernity and Double Consciousness.* Harvard University Press.

Glenn, Evelyn Nakano. 2004. *Unequal Freedom: How Race and Gender Shaped American Citizenship and Labor.* Harvard University Press.

Glinton, Sonari. 2017. "Some Black Americans Turn to Informal Economy in Face of Discrimination." *All Things Considered*, NPR, October 27. Accessed January 23, 2024. https://www.npr.org/2017/10/27/560239264/some-black-americans-turn-to-informal-economy-in-the-face-of-discrimination.

Go, Julian. 2021. "Three Tensions in the Theory of Racial Capitalism." *Sociological Theory* 39(1): 38–47.

Golash-Boza, Tanya Maria. 2023. *Before Gentrification: The Creation of DC's Racial Wealth Gap.* University of California Press.

Goyette, Kimberly. 2014. "Setting the Context." In *Choosing Homes, Choosing Schools*, edited by Annette Lareau and Kimberly Goyette. Russell Sage Foundation.

Grumbach, Jacob M. 2022. *Laboratories Against Democracy: How National Parties Transformed State Politics.* Princeton University Press.

Guzman, Gloria, and Melissa Kollar. 2024. "Income in the United States: 2024." Report P60-282. US Census Bureau, September 10. Accessed March 5, 2025. https://www.census.gov/library/publications/2024/demo/p60-282.html#:~:text=Highlights,median%20household%20income%20since%202019.

Harris, Cheryl I. 1993. "Whiteness at Property." *Harvard Law Review* 106(8):1710–91.

Harvey, David. 2007. *A Brief History of Neoliberalism.* Oxford University Press.

Haynes, Bruce D. 2006. *Red Lines, Black Spaces: The Politics of Race and Space in Black Middle-class Suburbia.* Yale University Press.

Hermann, Alexander. 2023. "In Nearly Every State, People of Color Are Less Likely to Own Homes Compared to White Households." Harvard University, Joint Center for Housing Studies, February 8. Accessed January 23, 2024. https://www.jchs.harvard.edu/blog/nearly-every-state-people-color-are-less-likely-own-homes-compared-white-households.

Hernandez, Arelis. 2015. "10 Things to Know About TRIM." *Washington Post*, April 8. https://www.washingtonpost.com/news/local/wp/2015/04/08/ten-things-to-know-about-trim.

Hise, Rachel, Michael Rubenstein, Kyle Siefering, and Dana Tagalicod. 2018. "21st Century School Facilities Commission: Final Report." Library and Information Services, Office of Policy Analysis, Department of Legislative Services, January. https://iac.mdschoolconstruction.org/wp-content/uploads/2020/12/Knott-Commission-Final-Report.pdf.

Howard, Christopher. 2023. *Who Cares: The Social Safety Net in America.* Oxford University Press.

Howell, Junia, and Elizabeth Korver-Glenn. 2021. "The Increasing Effect of Neighborhood Racial Composition on Housing Values, 1980–2015." *Social Problems* 68(4): 1051–71.

Hunter, Marcus, Mary Pattillo, Zandria Robinson, and Keanga-Yahmatta Taylor. 2016. "Black Placemaking: Celebration, Play, and Poetry." *Theory, Culture & Society* 33(7/8): 31–56.

Hunter, Marcus Anthony, and Zandria F. Robinson. 2018. *Chocolate Cities: The Black Map of American Life.* University of California Press.

Hutchison, Frederick. 2004. "From Thurgood to Thornton: The Thornton Commission's Contribution and the 50 Year Quest to Find Constitutional Wholeness for Maryland African American Children." Paper presented at the "Education Issues and the African American Community 50 Years After Brown" conference, Clark Atlanta University, Southern Center for Studies in Public Policy.

Hyra, Derek. 2017. *Race, Class, and Politics in the Cappuccino City.* University of Chicago Press.

Imoagene, Onoso. 2017. *Beyond Expectations: Second-Generation Nigerians in the United States and Britain.* University of California Press.

Itzigsohn, José, and Karida Brown. 2020. *The Sociology of W.E.B. Du Bois: Racialized Modernity and the Global Color Line.* New York University Press.

Jackson, Kenneth. 1985. *Crabgrass Frontier: The Suburbanization of the United States.* Oxford University Press.

Javidanrad, Farzad, Robert Ackrill, Dimitrios Bakas, and Dean Garratt. 2024. "Theorizing the Process of Financialization Through the Paradox of Profit: The Credit-Debt Reproduction Mechanism." *Journal of Post Keynesian Economics* 47(3): 566–88.

Jenkins, Destin. 2021. *The Bonds of Inequality: Debt and the Making of the American City.* University of Chicago Press.

Jenkins, Destin, and Justin Leroy. 2021. "Introduction: The Old History of Capitalism." In *Histories of Racial Capitalism*, edited by Destin Jenkins and Justin Leroy. Columbia University Press.

John, Obikwelu Ifeanyi, Gerard-Marie Messina, and Andy Chukwuemeka Odumegwu. 2023. "The Effects of Neocolonialism on Africa's Development." *PanAfrican Journal of Governance and Development* 4(2): 3–25.

Johnson, Odis Jr. 2014. "Still Separate, Still Unequal: The Relation of Segregation in Neighborhoods and Schools to Education Inequality." *Journal of Negro Education* 83(3): 199–215.

Johnson, Valerie. 2002. *Black Power in the Suburbs: The Myth or Reality of African-American Suburban Political Incorporation.* State University of New York Press.

Justice, Benjamin. 2023. "Schooling as a White Good." *History of Education Quarterly* 63(2): 154–78.

Kaba, Mariame. 2021. *We Do This 'Til We Free Us.* Haymarket Books.

Kacmarcik, Meaghan. 2022. "The Cost of Urban Renewal in Southwest DC." *Boundary Stones*, WETA, July 21. https://boundarystones.weta.org/2022/07/21/cost-urban-renewal-southwest-dc.

Kahrl, Andrew. 2024. *The Black Tax: 150 Years of Theft, Exploitation, and Dispossession.* University of Chicago Press.

Kalleberg, Arne L., and Michael Dunn. 2016. "Good Jobs, Bad Jobs in the Gig Economy." *Perspectives on Work.* Accessed January 20, 2020. http://michael-dunn.org/wp-content /uploads/2017/05/ALK-MD.-JQ-in-Gig-Economy.pdf.

Kamin, Debra. 2022. "Home Appraised with a Black Owner: $472,000. With a White Owner: $750,000." *New York Times,* June 21. https://www.nytimes.com/2022/08/18 /realestate/housing-discrimination-maryland.html.

Kasinitz, Philip, Mary C. Waters, John H. Mollenkopf, and Jennifer Holdaway. 2009. *Inheriting the City: The Children of Immigrants Come of Age.* Russell Sage Foundation.

Katznelson, Ira. 2005. *When Affirmative Action Was White: The Untold History of Inequality in the Twentieth Century.* W. W. Norton.

Kelley, Robin D. G. 1994. *Race Rebels: Politics, Culture, and the Black Working Class.* The Free Press.

Kelley, Robin D. G. 2022. *Freedom Dreams: The Black Radical Imagination.* Beacon Press. (Originally published in 2002.)

Keynes, John Maynard. 1936. *The General Theory of Employment, Interest, and Money.* Palgrave Macmillan.

Kim, Claire Jean. 2023. *Asian Americans in an Anti-Black World.* Cambridge University Press.

King, Martin Luther, Jr. 1967. *Where Do We Go from Here: Chaos or Community?* Harper & Row.

King, Martin Luther, Jr. 2024. *Beyond Vietnam: The Essential Speeches of Dr. MLK Jr.* HarperCollins.

King-Meadows, Tyson, and Thomas A. Schaller. 2006. *Devolution and Black State Legislators: Challenges and the Choices in the Twenty-First Century.* State University of New York Press.

Koch, James, and Omari Swinton. 2023. *Vital and Valuable: The Relevance of HBCUs to American Life and Education.* Columbia University Press.

Kochhar, Rakesh, and Mohamad Moslimani. 2023. "Wealth Gaps Across Racial and Ethnic Groups." Pew Research Center, December 4. Accessed January 18, 2024. https:// www.pewresearch.org/2023/12/04/wealth-gaps-across-racial-and-ethnic-groups/.

Korver-Glenn, Elizabeth. 2021. *Race Brokers: Housing Markets and Segregation in 21st Century Urban America.* Oxford University Press.

Krysan, Maria. 2017. *Cycle of Segregation: Social Processes and Residential Stratification.* Russell Sage Foundation.

Krysan, Maria, Mick P. Cooper, Reynolds Farley, and Tyrone A. Forman. 2009. "Does Race Matter for Residential Preferences? Results from a Video Experiment." *American Journal of Sociology* 115(2): 527–59.

Kurtz, Josh. 2021. "Thomas V. Mike Miller Jr., 1942–2021." Maryland Matters, January 15. https://marylandmatters.org/2021/01/15/thomas-v-mike-miller-jr-1942-2021/#:~:text =Miller%20described%20his%20mother%20as,Maryland%20Manual%20photo.

Kwate, Naa Oyo A., Ji Meng Loh, Kellee White, and Nelson Saldana. 2013. "Retail Redlining in New York City: Racialized Access to Day-to-Day Retail Resources." *Journal of Urban Health* 90(4): 632–52.

Lacy, Karyn. 2007. *Blue-Chip Black: Race, Class, and Status in the New Black Middle Class.* University of California Press.

Lacy, Karyn. 2012. "All's Fair? The Foreclosure Crisis and Middle-Class Black Instability." *American Behavioral Scientist* 56(11): 1565–80.

Lacy, Karyn. 2016. "The New Sociology of the Suburbs: A Research Agenda for Analysis of Emerging Trends." *Annual Review of Sociology* 42: 369–84.

Landry, Bart. 2018. *The New Black Middle Class in the Twenty-First Century.* Rutgers University Press.

Landry, Bart, and Kris Marsh. 2011. "The Evolution of the New Black Middle Class." *Annual Review of Sociology* 37: 373–94.

Lareau, Annette. 2014. "Chapter 6: Schools, Housing, and the Reproduction of Inequality." In *Choosing Homes, Choosing Schools*, edited by Annette Lareau and Kimberly Goyette. Russell Sage Foundation.

Lazo, Luz. 2017. "A Year After Opening MGM Casino Resort Mostly Lives Up to Expectations." *Washington Post*, December 16. https://www.washingtonpost.com/local/trafficand commuting/a-year-after-opening-mgm-casino-resort-mostly-lives-up-to-expectations /2017/12/16/58a9956c-d6c3-11e7-95bf-df7c19270879_story.html.

Lee, Jennifer, and Frank Bean. 2010. *The Diversity Paradox: Immigration and the Color Line in Twenty-First Century America.* Russell Sage Foundation.

Lee, Jennifer, and Min Zhou. 2014. "From Unassimilable to Exceptional: The Rise of Asian Americans and 'Stereotype Promise.'" *New Diversities* 16(1): 7–22.

Lens, Michael C. 2024. *Where the Hood At? Fifty Years of Change in Black Neighborhoods.* Russell Sage Foundation Press.

Leopold, Joy, and Myrtle P. Bell. 2017. "News Media and the Racialization of Protest: An Analysis of Black Lives Matter Articles." *Equality, Diversity, and Inclusion* 36(8): 720–35.

Levitin, Michael. 2021. *Generation Occupy: Reawakening American Democracy.* Counterpoint.

Lewis, Amanda, and John Diamond. 2015. *Despite the Best Intentions: How Racial Inequality Thrives in Good Schools.* Oxford University Press.

Lewis, Valerie, Michael O. Emerson, and Stephen L. Klineberg. 2011. "Who We'll Live With: Neighborhood Racial Composition Preferences of Whites, Blacks, and Latinos." *Social Forces* 89(4): 1385–1407.

Lewis-McCoy, R. L'Heureux. 2014. *Inequality in the Promised Land: Race, Resources, and Suburban Schooling.* Stanford University Press.

Lewis-McCoy, R. L'Heureux. 2018. "Suburban Black Lives Matter." *Urban Education* 53(2): 145–61.

Lewis-McCoy, R. L'Heureux, Natasha Warikoo, Stephen A. Matthews, and Nadirah Farah Foley. 2023. "Resisting Amnesia: Renewing and Expanding the Study of Suburban Inequality." *RSF: The Russell Sage Foundation Journal of the Social Sciences* 9(2): 1–24. https://doi.org/10.7758/RSF.2023.9.2.01.

Library of Congress. 2010. "Summary of H.R.4173-111th Congress (2009–2010)." Accessed August 4, 2025. https://www.congress.gov/bill/111th-congress/house-bill/4173.

Library of Congress. 2023. "Federalist Papers: Primary Documents in American History." Accessed January 9, 2023. https://guides.loc.gov/federalist-papers/full-text.

Lieberson, Stanley. 1980. *A Piece of the Pie: Blacks and White Immigrants Since 1880.* University of California Press.

Logan, John R., and Harvey Molotch. 2007. *Urban Fortunes: The Political Economy of Place.* University of California Press.

Logan, Trevon. 2023. "Whitelashing: Black Politicians, Taxes, and Violence." *Journal of Economic History* 83(2): 538–71.

Long, Daniel A., D. Betsy McCoach, Del Siegle, Carolyn M. Callahan, and E. Jean Gubbins. 2023. "Inequality at the Starting Line: Underrepresentation in Gifted Identification and Disparities in Early Achievement." *American Educational Research Association*, May 19. https://doi.org/10.1177/23328584231171535.

Lorde, Audre. 1984. *Sister Outsider: Essays and Speeches by Audre Lorde.* Crossing Press.

Love, Bettina. 2019. *We Want to Do More than Survive: Abolitionist Teaching and the Pursuit of Educational Freedom.* Beacon Press.

Lung-Amam, Willow. 2017a. "An Equitable Future for the Washington, DC Region? A 'Regionalism Light' Approach to Building Inclusive Neighborhoods." Presented at the symposium "A Shared Future: Fostering Communities of Inclusion in an Era of Inequality." Harvard Joint Center for Housing Studies, April. Accessed April 3, 2019. https://www.jchs.harvard.edu/sites/default/files/media/imp/a_shared_future_equitable _future_washington_dc.pdf.

Lung-Amam, Willow. 2017b. *Trespassers? Asian Americans and the Battle for Suburbia.* University of California Press.

Lung-Amam, Willow. 2024. *Right to Suburbia: Combatting Gentrification on the Urban Edge.* University of California Press.

Maciag, Mike. 2022. "Government Wage Growth Lags Private Sector by Largest Margin on Record." Pew Charitable Trusts, February 7. Accessed January 23, 2024. https://www .pewtrusts.org/en/research-and-analysis/articles/2022/02/07/government-wage-growth -lags-private-sector-by-largest-margin-on-record.

Marable, Manning. 2015. *How Capitalism Underdeveloped Black America: Problems in Race, Political Economy, and Society.* Haymarket Books. (Originally published in 1983.)

Marx, Karl. 2024. *Capital: Critique of Political Economy*, vol. 1. Princeton University Press. (Originally published in 1867.)

Maryland Association of Counties. 2025. "About MACo." https://www.mdcounties.org /27/ABOUT-MACo.

Maryland Department of Budget and Management. 2020. "Annual Statewide Equal Employment Opportunity Report, Fiscal Year 2020." Accessed January 23, 2024. https://dbm .maryland.gov/eeo/Documents/Publications/AnnualEEO-ReportFY2020.pdf.

Maryland Department of Transportation. 2024. "Purple Line: Project Overview." https:// www.purplelinemd.com/overview/.

Maryland Lottery and Gaming Control Agency. 2018. "Comprehensive Annual Financial Report." https://www.mdgaming.com/wp-content/uploads/2017/11/CAFR-2018.pdf.

Maryland–National Capital Park and Planning Commission. 2014. *Plan 2035: Prince George's Approved General Plan.* Prince George's County Planning Department, May 6.

Maryland–National Capital Park and Planning Commission (M-NCPPC). 2016. "Prince George's County High-End Retail Market Analysis." Prince George's County Planning Department, May 1.

Maryland–National Capital Park and Planning Commission (M-NCPPC). 2019. "Prince George's County Zoning Ordinance and Subdivision Regulation Rewrite, Presented to the Prince George's County Council." Prince George's County Planning Department, January 8. Accessed March 23, 2019. https://pgccouncil.us/DocumentCenter/View/3885/Zoning-Ordinance-Presentation-Council-Retreat-2019.

Maryland State Archives. 2022. "Maryland-National Capital Park and Planning Commission: Origin & Functions." Maryland Manual On-line: A Guide to Maryland and Its Government." https://www.msa.maryland.gov/msa/mdmanual/35interc/03mnparkf.html.

Maryland State Archives. 2025. "Washington Suburban Sanitation Commission: Origin & Functions." Maryland Manual On-line: A Guide to Maryland and Its Government." https://msa.maryland.gov/msa/mdmanual/35interc/09wsanf.html.

Maryland State Department of Education. 2017. "Maryland Public School Enrollment by Race/Ethnicity and Gender and Number of Schools, September 30, 2017." Baltimore, MD: Division of Curriculum, Research, Assessment, and Accountability. Accessed September 22, 2022. https://www.marylandpublicschools.org/about/Documents/DCAA/SSP/20172018Student/2018EnrollbyRace.pdf.

Maryland State Department of Education. 2024. "What Is the Blueprint for Maryland's Future?" Blueprint for Maryland's Future. Accessed July 17, 2024. https://blueprint.marylandpublicschools.org/about/.

Massey, Douglas, and Nancy Denton. 1993. *American Apartheid: Segregation and the Making of the Underclass.* Harvard University Press.

Mastro, Oriana Skylar. 2024. *Upstart: How China Became a Great Power.* Oxford University Press.

Mbembe, Achille. 2019. *Necropolitics.* Duke University Press.

McCall, Leslie. 2013. *The Undeserving Rich: American Beliefs About Inequality, Opportunity, and Redistribution.* Cambridge University Press.

McDermott, Monica. 2006. *Working-Class White: The Making and Unmaking of Race Relations.* University of California Press.

McGhee, Heather. 2021. *The Sum of Us: What Racism Costs Everyone and How We Can Prosper Together.* Penguin Random House.

McKernan, Signe-Mary, Carline Ratcliffe, Eugene Steuerle, and Sisi Zhang. 2014. "Impact of the Great Recession and Beyond: Disparities in Wealth Building by Generation and Race." Urban Institute, April. Accessed February 16, 2024. https://www.urban.org/sites/default/files/alfresco/publication-pdfs/413102-Impact-of-the-Great-Recession-and-Beyond.PDF.

McKinsey & Company. 2021. "Race in the Workplace: The Black Experience in the US Private Sector." February 21. Accessed January 18, 2024. mckinsey.com/featured-insights/diversity-and-inclusion/race-in-the-workplace-the-black-experience-in-the-us-private-sector.

McKinsey & Company. 2023. "What Is E-Commerce?" January 24. Accessed January 23, 2024. https://www.mckinsey.com/featured-insights/mckinsey-explainers/what-is-e-commerce.

McMillan, Tracie. 2024. *The White Bonus: Five Families and the Cash Value of Racism in America*. Macmillan.

Metropolitan Washington Council of Governments. 2018. "Leaders Elevate Social Equity as a Planning Priority." Region Forward Blog. https://www.mwcog.org/newsroom/2018 /12/19/leaders-elevate-social-equity-as-a-planning-priority/.

Michener, Jamila. 2018. *Fragmented Democracy: Medicaid, Federalism, and Unequal Politics*. Cambridge University Press.

Miller, Lisa. 2021. "Racialized Anti-Statism and the Failure of the American State." *Journal of Race, Ethnicity, and Politics* 6: 120–43.

Miller, Reuben Jonathan. 2021. *Halfway Home: Race, Punishment, and the Afterlife of Mass Incarceration*. Hachette.

Mills, Charles. 1997. *The Racial Contract*. University of North Carolina Press.

Mitchell, Bruce, Jad Edlebi, Helen Meier, Jason Richardson, Joseph Dean, and Liang Chen. 2025. "Displaced by Design: Years of Gentrification and Black Cultural Displacement in US Cities." National Community Reinvestment Coalition, May. https://ncrc.org /displaced-by-design/.

Montgomery County. 2017. "FY18 Approved Operating Budget and FY18-23 Public Services Program." https://www.montgomerycountymd.gov/OMB/Resources/Files/omb /pdfs/fy18/psp_pdf/FY18_Approved_Operating_Budget.pdf.

Montgomery County Board of Education. 2017. "MCPS FY 2018 Operating Budget." https://www.montgomeryschoolsmd.org/siteassets/district/departments/budget/fy2018 /FY2018_OperatingBudgetSummary_FINALforWeb.pdf.

Montgomery Planning. 2022. "Working Draft of Mapping Segregation Report: Racial Restrictive Covenants, Black Homeownership, and HOLC Loans in the Downcounty Planning Area." December 1. Accessed December 30, 2023. https://montgomeryplanning.org/ wp-content/uploads/2022/12/Mapping-Segregation-Staff-Report-Attachment-A.pdf.

Moody's Investors Service. 2022. "US Cities and Counties Methodology." November 2. Accessed January 6, 2024. https://ratings.moodys.com/api/rmc-documents/386953.

Morris, Aldon. 1984. *The Origins of the Civil Rights Movement: Black Communities Organizing for Change*. Free Press.

Morris, Aldon. 2017. *The Scholar Denied: W.E.B. Du Bois and the Birth of Modern Sociology*. University of California Press.

Moyo, Gorden. 2024. *Africa in the Global Economy: Capital Flight, Enablers, and Decolonial Responses*. Springer.

Muhammad, Khalil. 2010. *The Condemnation of Blackness: Race, Crime, and the Making of Urban America*. Harvard University Press.

National Academies: Sciences, Engineering, Medicine. 2024. "Ending Unequal Treatment: Strategies to Achieve Equitable Healthcare and Optimal Health for All." Accessed July 28, 2025. https://nap.nationalacademies.org/read/27820/chapter/1.

National Academy of Arts and Sciences. 2023. "Core Score: Measuring Wellbeing." https:// corescore.us/wellbeing-2023-usa/core_score/2023/00?demographic=geography-overall.

National Constitution Center. 2025. "12.3 Primary Source: Phyllis Wheatley, Letter to Reverend Samuel Occum." https://constitutioncenter.org/education/classroom-resource -library/classroom/12.3-primary-source-phillis-wheatley-letter-to-reverend-samuel -occum-1774.

National Harbor. 2019. "About National Harbor." Accessed March 5, 2019. https://www .nationalharbor.com/about/.

Neal, Terry M., and Manuel Perez-Rivas. 1996. "Prince George's Taxes Even Tighter." *Washington Post*, November 6. https://www.washingtonpost.com/wp-srv/local/reglelex /results/stories/mdballot.htm.

Nembhard, Jessica. 2014. *Collective Courage: A History of African American Cooperative Economic Thought and Practice.* Pennsylvania State University Press.

Newport, Frank. 2022. "Average American Remains OK with Higher Taxes on Rich." Gallup, August 12. https://news.gallup.com/opinion/polling-matters/396737/average -american-remains-higher-taxes-rich.aspx.

Northern Virginia Health Foundation. 2021. "Deeply Rooted: History's Lessons for Equity in Northern Virginia." Virginia Commonwealth University, Center on Society and Health. Accessed December 30, 2023. https://drive.google.com/file/d/1dhdP _BKFCtSKAL1VAwXfNX05sjVBZ5ME/view.

Northwest Bronx Community and Clergy Coalition. 2025. "Mission & Values." Accessed April 9, 2025. https://www.northwestbronx.org/mission.

O'Brien, Rourke. 2017. "Redistribution and the New Fiscal Sociology: Race and the Progressivity of State and Local Taxes." *American Journal of Sociology* 122(4): 1015–49.

O'Connell, Jonathan, and Robert McCartney. 2018. "It's Official: Amazon Splits Prize Between Crystal City and New York." *Washington Post*, November 13. https://www .washingtonpost.com/local/amazon-hq2-decision-amazon-splits-prize-between-crystal -city-and-new-york/2018/11/13/d01ec4de-e76e-11e8-b8dc-66cca409c180_story.html.

Odijie, Michael E. 2021. "Unintentional Neo-Colonialism? Three Generation of Trade and Development Relationship between EU and West Africa." *Journal of European Integration* 44(3): 347–63.

Oh, Sun Jung, and John Yinger. 2015. "What Have We Learned from Paired Testing in Housing Markets?" *Cityscape* 17(3): 15–60.

Okuwobi, Oneya Fennell. 2025. *Who Pays for Diversity? Why Programs Fail at Racial Equity and What to Do About It.* University of California Press.

Oliver, Melvin L., and Thomas M. Shapiro. 2006. *Black Wealth, White Wealth: A New Perspective on Racial Inequality.* Routledge.

Omi, Michael, and Howard Winant. 2015. *Racial Formation in the United States*, 3rd ed. Routledge.

O'Neill, Aaron. 2024. "Number of Victims of the Holocaust and Nazi Persecution 1933–1945, by Background." Statista, August 9. Accessed April 9, 2025. https://www .statista.com/statistics/1071011/holocaust-nazi-persecution-victims-wwii/.

Orfield, Myron. 2002. *American Metropolitics: The New Suburban Reality.* Brookings Institution Press.

Owens, Ann, and Peter Rich. 2023. "Little Boxes All the Same? Racial-Ethnic Segregation and Educational Inequality Across the Urban-Suburban Divide." *The Russell Sage*

Foundation Journal of the Social Sciences 9(2): 26–54. https://doi.org/10.7758/RSF.2023.9.2.02.

Pacewicz, Josh, and John N. Robinson III. 2021. "Pocketbook Policing: How Race Shapes Municipal Reliance on Punitive Fines and Fees in the Chicago Suburbs." *Socio-Economic Review* 19(3): 975–1003.

Page, Josh, and Joe Soss. 2021. "The Predatory Dimensions of Criminal Justice." *Science* 374(6565): 291–94.

Pattillo, Mary. 2013a. *Black on the Block: The Politics of Race and Class in the City.* University of Chicago Press.

Pattillo, Mary. 2013b. *Black Picket Fences: Privilege and Peril Among the Black Middle Class*, 2nd ed. University of Chicago Press. (Originally published in 1999.)

Perry, Andre, Jonathan Rothwell, and David Harshbarger. 2018. "The Devaluation of Assets in Black Neighborhoods: The Case of Residential Property." Brookings Institution. https://www.brookings.edu/wp-content/uploads/2018/11/2018.11_Brookings-Metro_Devaluation-Assets-Black-Neighborhoods_final.pdf.

Perry, Andre M., Hannah Stephens, and Manann Donoghoe. 2024. "Black Wealth Is Increasing, but So Is the Racial Wealth Gap." Brookings Institution, January 9. Accessed July 15, 2024. https://www.brookings.edu/articles/black-wealth-is-increasing-but-so-is-the-racial-wealth-gap/.

Pettit, Kathryn L. S., and Leah Hendey. 2011. "Washington, DC Metropolitan Area Foreclosure Monitor: Technical Appendix, August 2011." Urban Institute, August 25. Accessed April 26, 2023. https://www.urban.org/research/publication/washington-dc-metropolitan-area-foreclosure-monitor-technical-appendix-august-2011.

Pew Charitable Trusts. 2023. "Black Americans' Experiences with News." September 26. Accessed February 21, 2024. https://www.pewresearch.org/journalism/2023/09/26/black-americans-experiences-with-news/.

Pfau, Ann, Kathleen Lawlor, David Hochfelder, and Stacy Kinlock Sewell. 2024. "Using Urban Renewal Records to Advance Reparative Justice." *RSF: The Russell Sage Foundation Journal of the Social Sciences* 10(2): 113–31. https://doi.org/10.7758/RSF.2024.10.2.05.

Phelan, Joe C., and Bruce G. Link. 2013. "Is Racism a Fundamental Cause of Inequalities in Health?" *Annual Review of Sociology* 41: 311–30.

Piketty, Thomas. 2014. *Capital in the Twenty-First Century*. Belknap Press of Harvard University Press.

Pierre, Robert E. 1998. "Glendening Foes Look into the Past." *Washington Post*, July 15. https://www.washingtonpost.com/wp-srv/local/longterm/library/mdelect/statewide/glendening0715.htm.

Pinto-Coelho, Joanna Marie, and Tukufu Zuberi. 2015. "Segregated Diversity." *Sociology of Race and Ethnicity* 1(4): 475–89.

Pirtle, Whitney. 2019. "The Other Segregation." *The Atlantic*, April 23. https://www.theatlantic.com/education/archive/2019/04/gifted-and-talented-programs-separate-students-race/587614/.

Pitt, Steven C. 2011. "Research Brief: Black Workers and the Public Sector." University of California, Berkeley, Center for Labor Research and Education. Accessed January 23, 2024. https://laborcenter.berkeley.edu/pdf/2011/blacks_public_sector11.pdf.

Posey, Patricia D. 2024. "Information Inequality: How Race and Financial Access Reflect the Information Needs of Lower-Income Individuals." *The ANNALS of the American Academy of Political and Social Science* 707(1): 125–41. (Originally published 2023.)

Prasad, Monica. 2012. *The Land of Too Much: American Abundance and the Paradox of Poverty.* Harvard University Press.

Prasad, Monica. 2018. *Starving the Beast: Ronald Reagan and the Tax Cut Revolution.* Russell Sage Foundation.

Prince George's County. 2017a. "Budget at a Glance." Office of Management and Budget, Office of the County Executive. Accessed January 10, 2018. https://www.princegeorges countymd.gov/sites/default/files/media-document/dcv17965_budget-overviewpdf.pdf.

Prince George's County. 2017b. "Board of Education—177." Prince George's County School Board. https://www.princegeorgescountymd.gov/sites/default/files/media-document /dcv18010_board-of-educationpdf.pdf.

Prince George's County. 2023. "Tax Increment Financing (TIF) Districts." Office of the County Executive. Accessed January 15, 2023. https://www.princegeorgescountymd .gov/departments-offices/how-do-i/sign/geographic-development-incentives/county -incentives/tax-increment-financing-tif-districts.

Prince George's County. 2024. "Wage Determination Board: Wage Requirements for Service Contracts." Accessed July 19, 2024. https://www.princegeorgescountymd.gov /boards-commissions/wage-determination-board.

Prince George's County Blue Ribbon Commission on the Structural Deficit. 2017. "Prince George's County Council Blue Ribbon Commission on Addressing the Structural Deficit." https://pgccouncil.us/DocumentCenter/View/1943/Blue-Ribbon-Commission -Final-Report?bidId=.

Prince George's County Planning Board. 2023. "Zoning Ordinance and Use Tables: Current Ordinance." Maryland–National Capital Park and Planning Commission. https://pgplanning.org/development-process/zoning-applications/guide-to-zoning -categories/zoning-ordinance-use-tables/.

Prince George's County Planning Department. 2010. "Chapter 6: The African American Experience." In *Postbellum Archeological Resources in Prince George's County, Maryland: A Historic Context and Resource Guide.* Maryland National Capital Park and Planning Commission. https://pgplanning.org/resource_library/postbellum-archeological-resources -in-prince-georges-county-maryland-a-historic-context-and-research-guide/.

Prince George's County Public Schools (PGCPS). 2017. "Educational Facilities Masterplan." https://drive.google.com/file/d/1OGcICDIJJdDGqWnL7hcq-iZG0Xz_s5f6/view.

Prince George's County Public Schools (PGCPS). 2025. "Facts and Figures." https://www .pgcps.org/about-pgcps/facts-and-figures.

Purifoy, Danielle. 2019. "North Carolina [Un]incorporated: Place, Race, and Local Environmental Inequity." *American Behavioral Scientist* 65(8): 1–32.

Purifoy, Danielle, and Louise Seamster. 2021. "Creative Extraction: Black Towns in White Space." *Society and Space* 39(1): 47–66.

Quadagno, Jill. 1988. *The Transformation of the Old Age Security: Class and Politics in the American Welfare State.* University of Chicago Press.

Quillian, Lincoln, and John J. Lee. 2022. "Trends in Racial and Ethnic Discrimination in Hiring in Six Western Countries." *Proceedings of the National Academy of Sciences: Social Sciences* 120(6): 1–10. Accessed January 23, 2024. https://www.pnas.org/doi/epdf/10.1073/pnas.2212875120.

Ransby, Barbara. 2003. *Ella Baker and the Black Freedom Movement: A Radical Democratic Vision.* University of North Carolina Press.

Ray, Victor. 2019. "Theory of Racialized Organization." *American Sociological Review* 84(1): 26–53.

Reardon, Sean F. 2016. "School Segregation and Racial Academic Achievement Gaps." *The Russell Sage Foundation Journal of the Social Sciences* 2(5): 34–57. https://doi.org/10.7758/RSF.2016.2.5.03.

Reardon, Sean F., Demetra Kalogrides, and Kenneth Shores. 2019. "The Geography of Racial/Ethnic Test Score Gaps." *American Journal of Sociology* 124(4): 1164–221.

Reed, Adolph. 1999. *Stirrings in the Jug: Black Politics in the Post-Segregation Era.* University of Minnesota Press.

Reeves, Richard V., and Christopher Pullen. 2019. "No Room at the Top: The Stark Divide in Black and White Economic Mobility." Brookings Institution, February 14. Accessed February 16, 2024. https://www.brookings.edu/articles/no-room-at-the-top-the-stark-divide-in-black-and-white-economic-mobility/.

Rhodes, Anna, and Siri Warkentien. 2017. "Unwrapping the Suburban 'Package Deal': Race, Class, and School Access." *American Educational Research Journal* 54(1): 168S–189S.

Rich, Robert. 2013. "The Great Recession." Federal Reserve History, November 22. Accessed April 5, 2023. https://www.federalreservehistory.org/essays/great-recession-of-200709.

Roberts, Dorothy. 2011. *Fatal Invention: How Science, Politics, and Big Business Re-Create Race in the Twenty-First Century.* New Press.

Roberts, Dorothy. 2019. "Foreword: Abolition Constitutionalism." *Harvard Law Review* 133(1): 3–122.

Roberts, Samuel Kelton, Jr. 2012. *Infectious Fear: Politics, Disease, and the Health Effects of Segregation.* University of North Carolina Press.

Robinson, Cedric. 2019. *On Racial Capitalism, Black Internationalism, and Cultures of Resistance.* Pluto Press.

Rodden, Jonathan A. 2019. *Why Cities Lose: The Deep Roots of the Urban-Rural Divide.* Hachette Books.

Roediger, David R. 1994. *The Wages of Whiteness: Race and the Making of the American Working Class.* Verso.

Rogers, Melvin L. 2023. *The Darkened Light of Faith: Race, Democracy, and Freedom in African American Political Thought.* Princeton University Press.

Roithmayr, Daria. 2014. *Reproducing Racism: How Everyday Choices Lock in White Advantage.* New York University Press.

Rothstein, Richard. 2017. *The Color of Law: A Forgotten History of How Government Segregated America.* Liveright Publishing Corporation.

Rothwell, Jonathan, Tracy Hadden Lo, and Andre Perry. 2022. "How Racial Bias in Appraisal Affects Devaluation of Homes in Majority-Black Neighborhoods." Brookings

Institution, December 5. Accessed January 23, 2024. https://www.brookings.edu/articles/how-racial-bias-in-appraisals-affects-the-devaluation-of-homes-in-majority-black-neighborhoods/.

Rucks-Ahidiana, Zawadi. 2021. "Theorizing Gentrification as a Process of Racial Capitalism." *City & Community* 21(3): 173–92.

Rugh, Jacob S., and Douglas S. Massey. 2010. "Racial Segregation and the American Foreclosure Crisis." *American Sociological Review* 75(5): 629–51.

Said, Edward W. 1979. *Orientalism*. Penguin Random House.

Sampson, Robert. 2012. *Great American City: Chicago and the Enduring Neighborhood Effect*. University of Chicago Press.

Satter, Beryl. 2021. *Family Properties: Race, Real Estate, and the Exploitation of Black America*, 10th anniversary ed. Macmillan. (Originally published in 2010.)

S.C. Sea Grant Consortium. 2006. "African Roots, Carolina Gold." *Coastal Heritage Magazine*. https://www.scseagrant.org/african-roots-carolina-gold/.

Schanzenbach, Diane Whitmore, Ryan Nunn, Lauren Bauer, and Megan Mumford. 2016. "Where Does All the Money Go: Shifts in Household Spending over the Past 30 Years." The Hamilton Project. Brookings Institution, June 2. Accessed January 18, 2024. https://www.hamiltonproject.org/publication/post/where-does-all-the-money-go-shifts-in-household-spending-over-the-past-30-years/.

Schweitzer, Ally. 2020. "Amazon Plans Two Facilities in Prince George's County, Continuing Its DC-Area Takeover." *dcist*, WAMU, NPR, July 2. https://dcist.com/story/20/07/02/amazon-plans-two-facilities-in-prince-georges-county-continuing-its-d-c-area-takeover/.

Seamster, Louise. 2019. "Black Debt, White Debt." *Contexts* 18(1): 30–35.

Semega, Jessica, and Melissa Kollar. 2022. "Income in the United States: 2021." *Current Population Reports*. US Census Bureau, September. https://www.census.gov/content/dam/Census/library/publications/2022/demo/p60-276.pdf?ftag=YHF4eb9d17.

Semuels, Alana. 2019. "When Wall Street Is Your Landlord." *The Atlantic*, February 13. https://www.theatlantic.com/technology/archive/2019/02/single-family-landlords-wall-street/582394/.

Sharkey, Patrick. 2018. *Uneasy Peace: The Great Crime Decline, the Renewal of City Life, and the Next War on Violence*. W. W. Norton & Co.

Simms, Angela. 2023. "Fiscal Fragility in Black Middle-Class Suburbia and Consequences for K-12 Schools and Other Public Goods and Services." *RSF: The Russell Sage Foundation Journal of the Social Sciences* 9(2): 204–25. https://doi.org/10.7758/RSF.2023.9.2.09.

Simms, Angela, and Elizabeth Talbert. 2019. "Racial Segregation and School Choice: How a Market-Based Policy for K-12 Education Creates a 'Parenting Tax' for Black Parents." *Phylon* 56(1): 33–57.

Skrentny, John David. 1998. "The Effect of the Cold War on African-American Civil Rights: America and the World Audience, 1945–1968." *Theory and Society* 27(2): 237–85.

Small, Mario, and Jessica McCrory Calarco. 2022. *Qualitative Literacy: A Guide to Evaluating Ethnographic and Interview Research*. University of California Press.

Smart Growth America and Transportation for America. 2023. "Divided by Design: Examining the Damage in Washington, DC." July. https://wordpress.smartgrowthamerica.org/wp-content/uploads/2024/08/Divided-by-Design-2023.pdf.

Smith, Neil. 1996. *The New Urban Frontier: Gentrification and the Revanchist City.* Routledge.

Smith, Neil. 1979. "Toward a Theory of Gentrification: A Back to the City Movement by Capital, Not People." *Journal of the American Planning Association* 45(4, 1979): 538–48. Reprinted in *The Gentrification Reader,* edited by Loretta Lees, Tom Slater, and Elvin Wyly. Routledge (2010).

Smithsimon, Gregory. 2023. *Liberty Road: Black Middle-Class Suburbs and the Battle Between Civil Rights and Neoliberalism.* New York University Press.

SoRelle, Mallory. 2020. *Democracy Declined: The Failed Politics of Consumer Financial Protection.* University of Chicago Press.

Stainback, Kevin, and Donald Tomaskovic-Devey. 2012. *Documenting Desegregation: Racial and Gender Segregation in Private Sector Employment Since the Civil Rights Act.* Russell Sage Foundation.

St. George, Donna. 2016. "After Feds Cancel Head Start Grant over Abuse, Md. County to Have 'Early Start' Instead." *Washington Post,* September 30. https://www.washingtonpost.com/local/education/after-feds-cancel-head-start-grant-over-abuse-county-to-have-early-start-instead/2016/09/30/b606ae0e-8640-11e6-a3ef-f35afb41797f_story.html.

St. George, Donna. 2018a. "Prince George's County Removes Five Staffers at DuVal amid Grading Scandal." *Washington Post,* January 22. https://www.washingtonpost.com/local/education/shake-up-at-maryland-high-school-after-grading-scandal/2018/01/22/497f247a-ffb9-11e7-8acf-ad2991367d9d_story.html?_pml=1.

St. George, Donna. 2018b. "Maryland Schools CEO Handed Six-figure Severance Payout." *Washington Post,* July 12. Accessed July 11, 2024. https://www.washingtonpost.com/local/education/maryland-schools-ceo-handed-six-figure-severance-payout/2018/07/12/91b91558-8555-11e8-8f6c-46cb43e3f306_story.html.

Summers, Brandi Thompson. 2023. *Black in Place: The Spatial Aesthetics of Place in a Post-Chocolate City.* University of North Carolina Press.

Swain, Johnnie Dee, Jr. 1993. "Black Mayors: Urban Decline and the Underclass." *Journal of Black Studies* 24(1): 16–28.

Tamir, Christine. 2022. "Key Findings About Black Immigrants in the US." Pew Research Center, January 27. https://www.pewresearch.org/short-reads/2022/01/27/key-findings-about-black-immigrants-in-the-u-s/.

Taylor, Keeanga-Yamahtta. 2019. *Race for Profit: How Banks and the Real Estate Industry Undermined Black Home Ownership.* University of North Carolina Press.

Thomas, Melvin, and Richard Moye. 2015. "Race, Class, and Gender and the Impact of Racial Segregation on Black-White Income Inequality." *Sociology of Race and Ethnicity* 1(4): 490–502.

Thompson, Cheryl W. 2011. "Jack Johnson, Former Prince George's Exec, Sentenced to 7 Years in Corruption Case." *Washington Post,* December 6. https://www.washingtonpost.com/ilocal/crime/former-pr-georges-exec-jack-b-johnson-is-sentenced-to-7-years/2011/12/01/gIQAKa7iZO_story.html

Thornton, Alvin, and Karen Williams Gooden. 1997. *Like a Phoenix I'll Rise: An Illustrated History of African Americans in Prince George's County, Maryland, 1696–1996.* Donning Company.

Tiebout, Charles. 1956. "A Pure Theory of Local Expenditures." *Journal of Political Economy* 64(5): 416–24.

Tilly, Charles. 2003. "Changing Forms of Inequality." *Sociological Theory* 21(1): 31–36.

Treitler, Vilna Bashi. 2013. *The Ethnic Project: Transforming Racial Fiction into Ethnic Faction.* Stanford University Press.

Trisi, Danilo. 2024. "Expiration of Pandemic Relief Led to Record Increases in Poverty and Child Poverty in 2022." Center on Budget and Policy Priorities, June 10. Accessed March 10, 2025. https://www.cbpp.org/research/poverty-and-inequality/expiration-of -pandemic-relief-led-to-record-increases-in-poverty#:~:text=In%202020%20and%20 2021%2C%20in,in%20data%20back%20to%201967.

Trounstine, Jessica. 2018. *Segregation by Design: Local Politics and Inequality in American Cities.* Cambridge University Press.

Ture, Kwame, and Charles V. Hamilton. 2008. "The Myths of Coalition" from Ture and Hamilton, *Black Power: The Politics of Liberation in America* (Vintage, 1992). *Race/ Ethnicity: Multidisciplinary Global Contexts* 1(2): 171–88.

Turner, Matti. 2019. "Baskets of Rice: Creolization and Material Culture from West Africa to South Carolina's Lowcountry." *African and Black Diaspora* 12(3): 320–36.

Urban Institute. 2020. "State and Local Backgrounders: State and Local Expenditures." Accessed January 18, 2024. https://www.urban.org/policy-centers/cross-center -initiatives/state-and-local-finance-initiative/state-and-local-backgrounders/state-and -local-expenditures#:~:text=From%201977%20to%202020%2C%20in,increase%2C %20over%20the%20same%20period.

Urban Institute. 2022. "Which Students Receive a Greater Share of School Funding?" April 25. Accessed January 17, 2024. https://apps.urban.org/features/school-funding-trends/.

US Bureau of Labor Statistics. 2020. "BLS Reports: Labor Force Characteristics by Race and Ethnicity, 2019." BLS Report 1088, December. Accessed January 23, 2024. https:// www.bls.gov/opub/reports/race-and-ethnicity/2019/home.htm.

US Census Bureau. 2021. "Substantial Changes to Counties and County Equivalent Entities: 1970–Present." Updated October 8, 2021. Accessed January 22, 2024. https:// www.census.gov/programs-surveys/geography/technical-documentation/county-changes .2020.html#list-tab-957819518.

US Census Bureau. 2025. "National Poverty in America Awareness Month: January 2025." January. https://www.census.gov/newsroom/stories/poverty-awareness-month.html?os =icXa75GDUbbewZKe8C&ref=app.

US Department of Education. 2019. "School Choice in the United States: 2019." National Center for Education Statistics, September. Accessed September 16, 2024. https://files .eric.ed.gov/fulltext/ED598472.pdf.

US Department of Housing and Urban Development. 2010. "Report to Congress on the Root Causes of the Foreclosure Crisis." Office of Policy Development and Research, January. Accessed February 16, 2024. https://www.huduser.gov/portal/publications /foreclosure_09.pdf.

US Department of Housing and Urban Development. 2023. "Housing Discrimination Under the Fair Housing Act." Accessed January 22, 2024. https://www.hud.gov/program _offices/fair_housing_equal_opp/fair_housing_act_overview.

US Department of Housing and Urban Development. 2025. "HUDUser Glossary." Accessed August 4, 2025. https://archives.huduser.gov/portal/glossary/glossary_a.html.

US Department of Justice. 2012. "Justice Department Reaches Settlement with Wells Fargo, Resulting in More than $175 Million in Relief for Homeowners to Resolve Fair Lending Claims." Office of Public Affairs, July 12. Accessed December 18, 2023. https://www.justice.gov/opa/pr/justice-department-reaches-settlement-wells-fargo -resulting-more-175-million-relief.

US Department of Labor. 2023. "How Do I File for Unemployment Insurance?" Accessed January 18, 2024. https://www.dol.gov/general/topic/unemployment-insurance.

US Department of the Treasury. 2022a. "Statement from Secretary of the Treasury Janet L. Yellen on the European Union Directive Implementing a Global Minimum Tax." December 16. Accessed January 23, 2024. https://home.treasury.gov/news/press -releases/jy1170.

US Department of the Treasury. 2022b. "Racial Differences in Economic Security: Housing." November 4. Accessed February 16, 2024. https://home.treasury.gov/news/featured -stories/racial-differences-in-economic-security-housing#:~:text=From%20peak%20to %20trough%20prior,70%20percent%20for%20Hispanic%20households.

US Environmental Protection Agency. 2021. "Study Finds Exposure to Air Pollution Higher for People of Color Regardless of Region or Income." Accessed January 23, 2024. https:// www.epa.gov/sciencematters/study-finds-exposure-air-pollution-higher-people-color -regardless-region-or-income.

US Government Accountability Office. 2022. "K-12 Education: Student Population Has Significantly Diversified, but Many Schools Remain Divided Along Racial, Ethnic, and Economic Lines." GAO-22-104737, June. Accessed July 22, 2024. https://www.gao.gov /assets/gao-22-104737.pdf.

US National Archives and Records Administration. 2008. "Slaves Built the White House and Capitol—See the Records." December 10. https://www.archives.gov/press/press -releases/2009/nr09-28-images.

US National Archives and Records Administration. 2022a. "National Interstate and Defense Highways Act (1956)." Accessed August 4, 2025. https://www.archives.gov /milestone-documents/national-interstate-and-defense-highways-act.

US National Archives and Records Administration. 2022b. "16th Amendment to the U.S. Constitution: Federal Income Tax." Milestone Documents. Washington, DC. Accessed April 5, 2023. https://www.archives.gov/milestone-documents/16th-amendment.

U.S. News and World Report. 2018. "Economic Opportunity Rankings: Determining Which States Have the Least Poverty." U.S. News and World Report. https://www.usnews.com /news/best-states/maryland.

US Office of Personnel Management. 2017. "Executive Branch Employment by Gender and Race/National Origin." Accessed January 23, 2024. https://www.opm.gov/policy -data-oversight/data-analysis-documentation/federal-employment-reports/reports -publications/executive-branch-employment-by-gender-and-racenational-origin/.

Van Dam, Andrew. 2022. "Is Prince George's Still the Richest Majority-Black County in America?" Washington Post, June 29. https://www.washingtonpost.com/business/2022 /06/29/dept-of-data-prince-georges-richest-black-county/.

Verges, Francoise. 2021. *A Decolonial Feminism*. Pluto Press.

Walker, David. 2022. *Appeal to the Coloured Peoples of the World*. Martino Fine Books. (Originally published in 1829.)

Washington, Harriet. 2006. *Medical Apartheid: The Dark History of Medical Experimentation on Black Americans from Colonial Times to the Present*. Doubleday.

Weaver, Vesla. 2007. "Frontlash: Race and the Development of Punitive Crime Policy." *Studies in American Political Development* 21(Fall): 230–65.

Welch, Levin. 2012. "Neoliberalism, Economic Crisis, and the 2008 Financial Meltdown in the United States." *International Review of Modern Sociology* 38(2): 221–57.

Wells, Ida B. 2015. "The Red Record." Trade Open Road Integrated Media. (Originally published in 1895.)

Wilkerson, Isabel. 2010. *The Warmth of Other Suns: The Epic Story of America's Great Migration*. Vintage.

Wilkes, Andrew. 2024. *Plenty Good Room: Co-Creating an Economy of Enough for All*. Broadleaf Books.

Williams, Chad L. 2023. *The Wounded World: W. E. B. Du Bois and the First World War*. Macmillan.

Williams, Ovetta. 2014. "Wayne K. Curry Dies at 63; Former Prince George's County Executive." *Washington Post*, July 2. https://www.washingtonpost.com/local/md-politics/wayne-k-curry-dies-at-63-former-prince-georges-county-executive/2014/07/02/3b5660d0-d7b7-11e3-aae8-c2d44bd79778_story.html.

Wilson, William Julius. 2012a. *The Declining Significance of Race: Blacks and Changing American Institutions*. University of Chicago Press. (Originally published in 1978.)

Wilson, William Julius. 2012b. *The Truly Disadvantaged: The Inner City, the Underclass, and Public Policy*. University of Chicago Press. (Originally published in 1987.)

Wimmer, Andreas, and Yuval Feinstein. 2010. "The Rise of the Nation-State across the World, 1816 to 2001." *American Sociological Review* 75(5): 764–90.

Wishart, Benton, and Trevon Logan. 2024. "Her Property Transactions: White Women and the Frequency of Female Ownership in the Antebellum Era." Working Paper 32529. National Bureau of Economic Research, May. https://www.nber.org/system/files/working_papers/w32529/w32529.pdf.

Wolfe, Patrick. 2006. "Settler Colonialism and the Elimination of the Native." *Journal of Genocide Research* 8(4): 387–409.

Wright, Earl, II. 2016. *The First American School of Sociology: W.E.B. Du Bois and the Atlanta Sociological Laboratory*. Routledge.

Wyndham-Douds, Kiara. 2023. "Suburbs, Inc.: Exploring Municipal Incorporation as a Mechanism of Racial and Economic Exclusion in Suburban Communities." *RSF: The Russell Sage Foundation Journal of the Social Sciences* 9(2): 226–48. https://doi.org/10.7758/RSF.2023.9.2.10.

INDEX

Tables and figures are listed in **boldface**.